I08104I8

IMAGES
of Modern America

Dutch Wonderland

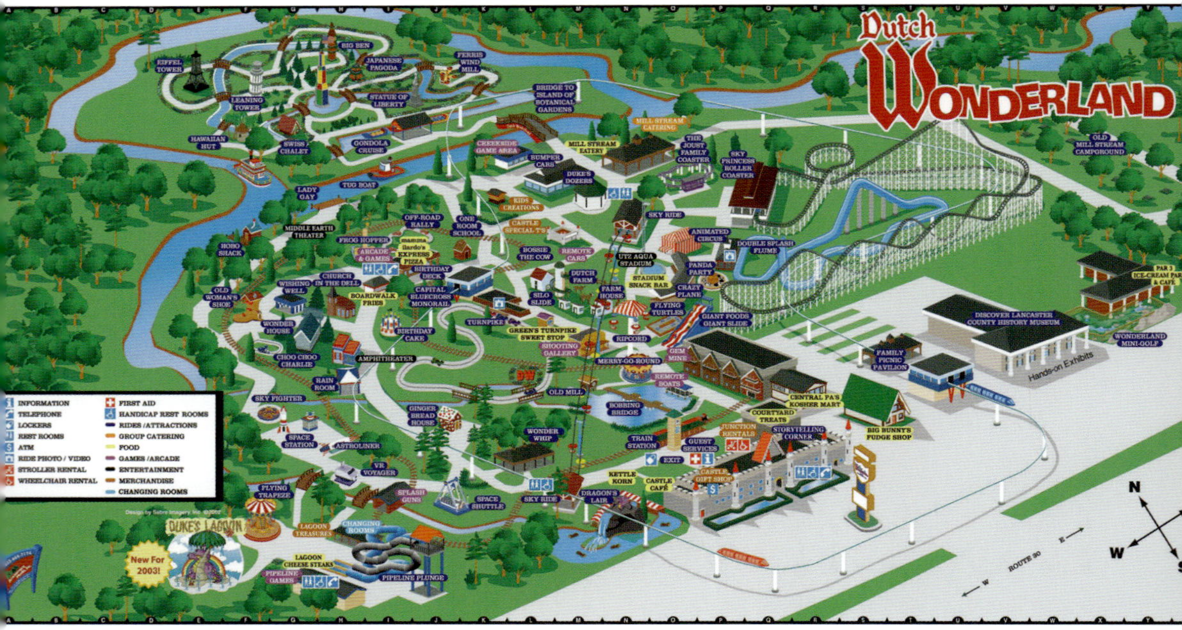

Shown here is a map of Dutch Wonderland from 2003, when Hershey Entertainment became more involved with the park. Duke's Lagoon, the Wonder Whip, and Duke's Dozers were added in this year. (Dutch Wonderland.)

On the Front Cover: Clockwise from top left:
The lit-up castle entrance (Dutch Wonderland); Exploration Island, opened in 2014 (Author's collection); Dutch Wonderland's second train, No. 123, added in 1974 (Dutch Wonderland); the Gingerbread House, a park favorite since opening day (Author's collection); the park's first roller coaster, opened in 1992 (Dutch Wonderland)

On the Back Cover: From left to right:
Dutch Wonderland's beautiful carousel, manufactured by Chance Rides (Author's collection); Duke the Dragon, the park's mascot (Author's collection); Old 99 ride, operated from 1974 to 2002 (Author's collection)

IMAGES
of Modern America

Dutch Wonderland

Austen Dennison

ARCADIA
PUBLISHING

ISBN 978-1-4671-2285-6

Published by Arcadia Publishing
Charleston, South Carolina

Printed in the United States of America

Library of Congress Control Number: 2014945554

For all general information, please contact Arcadia Publishing:
Telephone 843-853-2070
Fax 843-853-0044
E-mail sales@arcadiapublishing.com
For customer service and orders:
Toll-Free 1-888-313-2665

Visit us on the Internet at www.arcadiapublishing.com

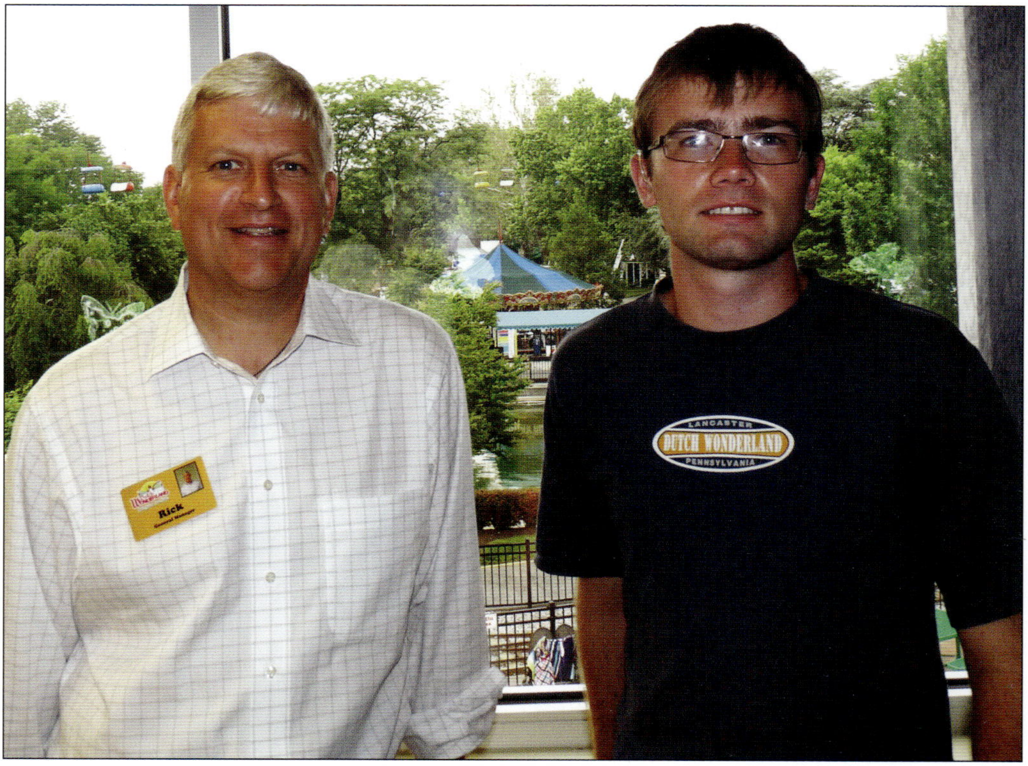

Rick Stammel (left), the park's current general manager, is pictured here in his office on the second floor of the castle with author Austen Dennison (right). (AD.)

Contents

ACKNOWLEDGMENTS

My love for amusement parks, including Dutch Wonderland, would not exist if my parents had not introduced me to them as a child. I have always been interested in the history of any amusement park, but Dutch Wonderland's history feels extra special to me because I grew up going to the park with my two younger brothers. I have also collected memorabilia from the park. With such an attachment to Dutch Wonderland, I have thought about writing a book about it for many years, but it did not become a reality until I spoke to the park's general manager, Rick Stammel, who was interested in the idea.

Researching and writing this book was a fun experience. Between writing this book, attending amusement parks, taking care of my many pets, and working, 2014 was a busy year. Even after I thought the hard part was done, I realized that I had more information than the book could hold. Because of Dutch Wonderland's expansive history, paring down the number of pictures was an exacting process.

I want to thank Rick for taking the time to talk to me about Dutch Wonderland and allowing me to look through the park's photograph archives. I also would like to thank Murl Clark, former owner, for meeting with me and sharing interesting facts and pictures, as well as Gary Chubb, former general manager, for sharing information about his years at the park. Finally, I would like to thank my family, including my brothers, Logan and Luke; my father, Roger; and especially my mother, Jacqueline, who encouraged me every step of the way.

The images in this book appear courtesy of Dutch Wonderland (DW), Murl Clark (MC), Catherine Bitner (CB), and the author's collection (AD).

INTRODUCTION

Dutch Wonderland's founder, Earl Clark, was a well-known and successful potato broker from Lancaster County, Pennsylvania. He traveled up and down the East Coast buying potatoes for Pennsylvania potato chip factories. Since the job required long hours, he often thought about getting out of the potato business and starting his own company. Because Lancaster County, Pennsylvania, had been getting a steady increase in visitors each year, Clark purchased land along the Lincoln Highway, east of the city of Lancaster, to build a motel that he called the Congress Inn. At the time, it was the largest motel in the area and the first of its size on Route 30. The timing was perfect, as Lancaster County soon became one of Pennsylvania's largest tourist regions.

The 1955 Broadway play *Plain and Fancy*, about the Amish, is credited for bringing tourists to the area. The Amish Farm & House is known for being the first tourist attraction to open in Lancaster County. By 1960, the rural area of Lancaster County had become one of Pennsylvania's largest tourist destinations, bringing in about two million visitors per year. Due to the influx of tourism, Earl Clark added 23 rooms to the Congress Inn in 1959, although he soon realized that the Lancaster area did not provide enough activities for children.

In 1962, he sold his motel and purchased 14 acres of land less than a mile away. The newly purchased land would become the home of Dutch Wonderland. The original theme of the small amusement park combined characteristics of Pennsylvania Dutch culture with elements of fantasy. Earl Clark had envisioned the entire park, with every detail carefully thought out. In order to build the park, however, Clark had to move the historic Running Pump Inn to the opposite side of the street.

After months of construction during the winter of 1962–1963, Dutch Wonderland officially opened on May 20, 1963, with only four rides: Wally the Whale Boats, Lady Gay River Boat, Turnpike, and Wonderland Special Iron Horse Train. In addition to these rides were two unique slides: the Silo Slide and the Old Woman Who Lived in a Shoe Slide.

The park eventually expanded to 75 acres, making the Dutch Wonderland Entertainment Complex one of the top attractions in Lancaster County. In 1965, newly acquired land would become home to the International Botanical Gardens, as well as the Old Mill Stream Camping Manor a year later. In 1967, Earl Clark had another dream—to build a wax museum about the history of Lancaster County. To look more realistic, Clark decided to use human hair, glass eyes, and even real false teeth for some of the figures. Trees from nearby woods were cut down and placed in the scenes, along with antiques from around the country. The new attraction officially opened to the public in 1969. The Wonderland Cinema was also added next to the museum.

In 1970, Earl Clark purchased the Weavertown One-Room Schoolhouse, located in Bird-in-Hand, Pennsylvania. The schoolhouse held classes from 1877 to May 1969. Clark turned the building into an attraction where visitors could see 30 lifelike animatronic figures acting out a school day. It also included its original bell, blackboard, and desks.

The Castle Gift Shop was expanded in 1972, and beginning in 1974, tram service was offered in the parking lot for a couple of years. Starting in 1979, the park's new amphitheater hosted everything from magic shows to musical acts. In 1985, Earl Clark bought the Amish Farm & House, which is located about a mile away from Dutch Wonderland.

The Clarks bought many first-of-its-kind rides, also called prototypes. Since the Crazy Plane was the first of its type, the success of this ride led Zamperla to make similar models for parks all over the world.

On June 24, 1993, Earl Clark passed away at age 63. Murl Clark continued his father's legacy by overseeing the park. The Clark family continued to keep Earl's dreams alive with the family-fun atmosphere of Dutch Wonderland.

Gary Chubb was chosen to manage the park after Earl Clark's death. Chubb had worked in various positions at Hersheypark from 1967 to early 1994. He remarked that working for a family-owned park was very different from working for a large corporate park like Hersheypark. As general manager, he did just about anything that needed to be done. Chubb recalls his time at Dutch Wonderland: "I thoroughly enjoyed my years at Dutch Wonderland. The park was small enough that you knew everyone that worked there, and I truly felt like it was part of being one big family. The Clark family treated me very well during my time there."

Each member of the Clark family had different ideas for the park's future. Eventually, running the park became too time consuming for some members of the family who wanted to move on to other things. Shortly after Dutch Wonderland opened for its 39th season in 2001, the Clark family decided to sell the park. Although Murl Clark still loved the park, he approached Hershey Entertainment about buying it. After the sale in November 2001, Gary Chubb was rehired at Hersheypark as the senior director of maintenance.

Once the sale was complete, Hershey Entertainment gave the general manager position to Rick Stammel, who had worked at Hersheypark for 25 years. Before moving to Dutch Wonderland, he was Hersheypark's assistant general manager, with direct responsibilities for the rides, food and beverage, retail, and games departments. Stammel admitted immediately falling in love with Dutch Wonderland the first time he saw it. After Dutch Wonderland was sold, Murl Clark continued to operate the Weavertown One-Room Schoolhouse until 2002 and the Amish Farm until 2005.

In November 2010, Dutch Wonderland would be sold once again, this time to Palace Entertainment, an American amusement park company owned by Parques Reunidos of Spain. Palace Entertainment kept the same management in place to ensure a smooth transition. Other Palace Entertainment theme parks in Pennsylvania include Kennywood in West Mifflin and Idlewild in Ligonier, as well as the Sandcastle water park in Pittsburgh. In 2012, half of the Castle Gift Shop and part of the Castle Café were renovated to create Merlin's, a full-service restaurant. The park celebrated its 50th anniversary in 2013. The following year, the former International Botanical Gardens were transformed into Exploration Island.

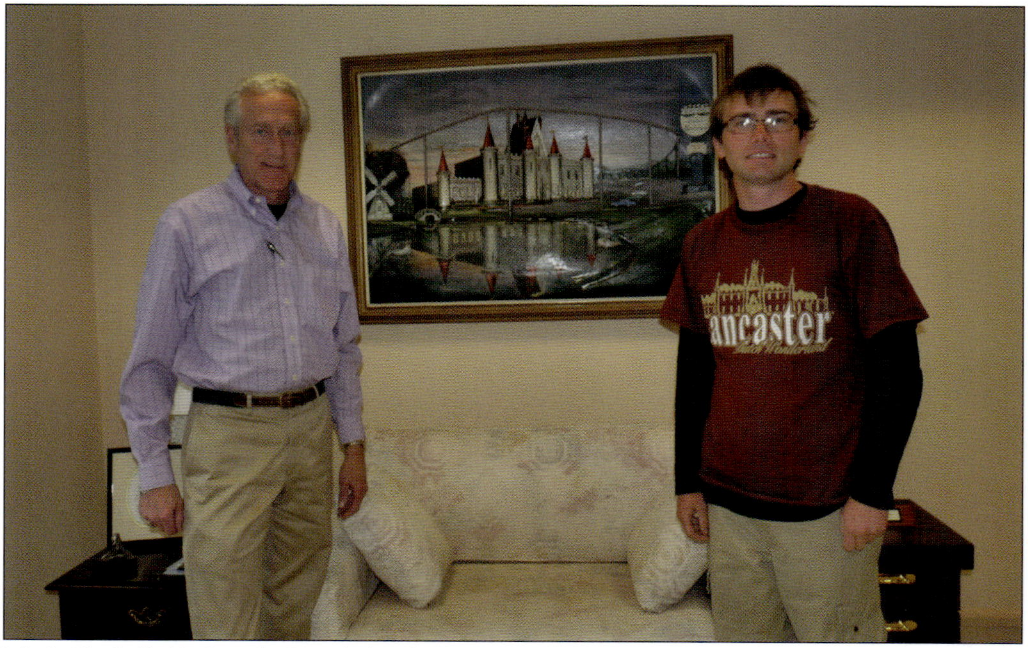

Murl Clark (left), Dutch Wonderland's former owner, and author Austen Dennison stand in front of a 3-D photograph of the park's castle that hung in Clark's office during his time at the park. (AD.)

One

Building a Dream
1959–1969

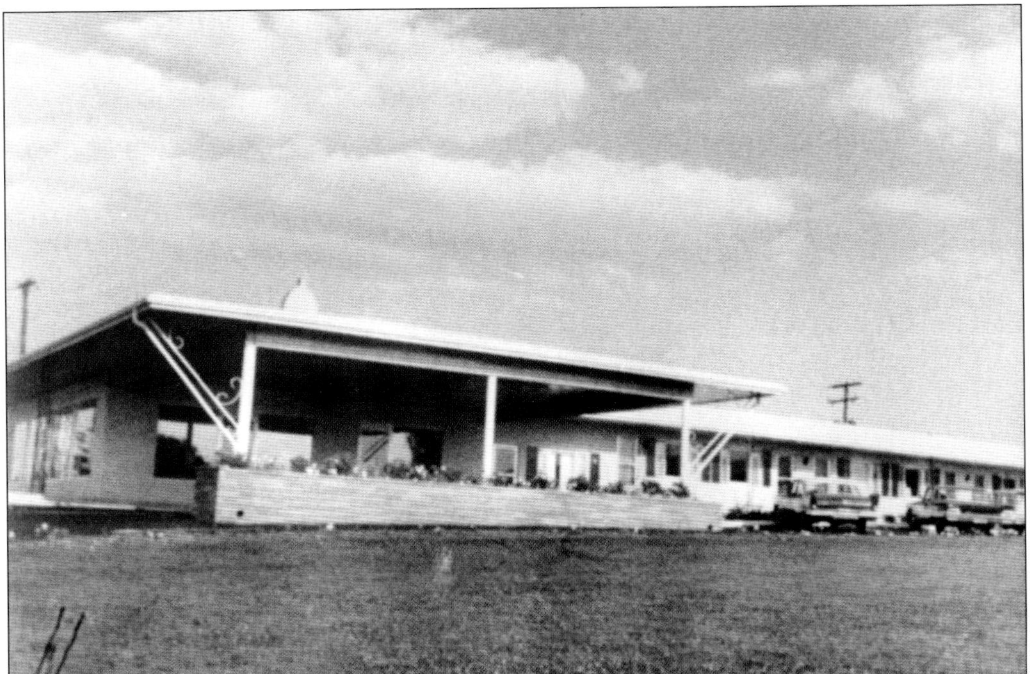

In 1959, Dutch Wonderland founder Earl Clark opened the Congress Inn. The motel opened with 52 rooms, then was expanded to 72 rooms two years later. It was the largest motel in the Lancaster area. Four years later, in October 1962, Clark sold the Congress Inn and began construction on Dutch Wonderland. (MC.)

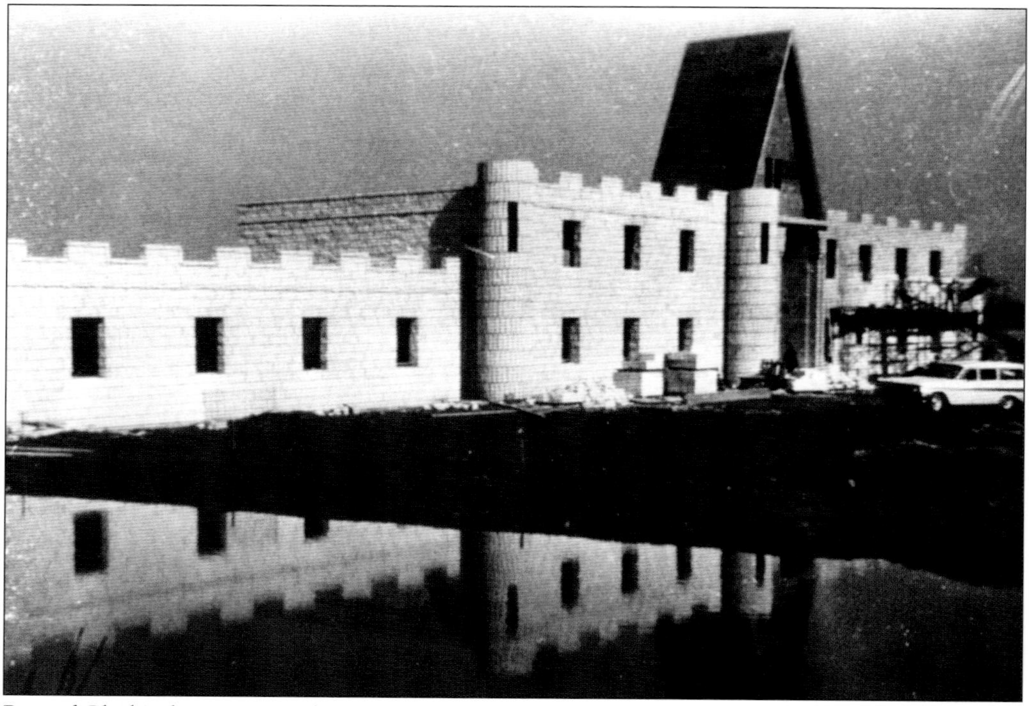

Part of Clark's dream was to have guests enter the amusement park through a giant castle. The castle entranceway is under construction in this image, taken during the winter of 1962–1963. The castle would have many purposes, including housing a café and the park's gift shop. (MC.)

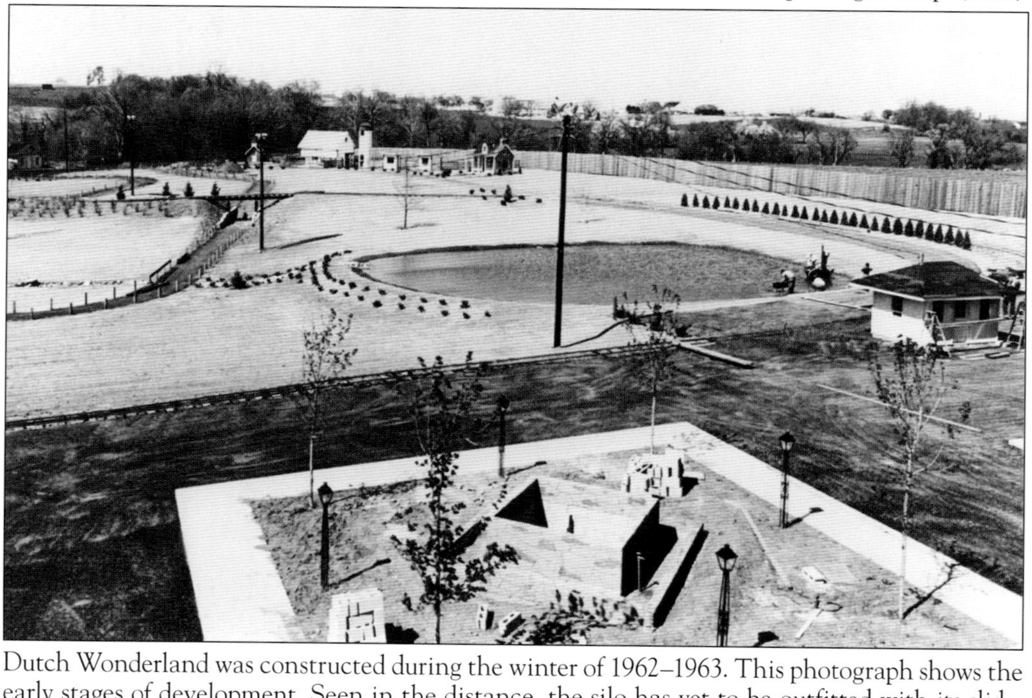

Dutch Wonderland was constructed during the winter of 1962–1963. This photograph shows the early stages of development. Seen in the distance, the silo has yet to be outfitted with its slide. Workers are constructing the man-made pond, where the bobbing bridge and mill scene would be installed. (MC.)

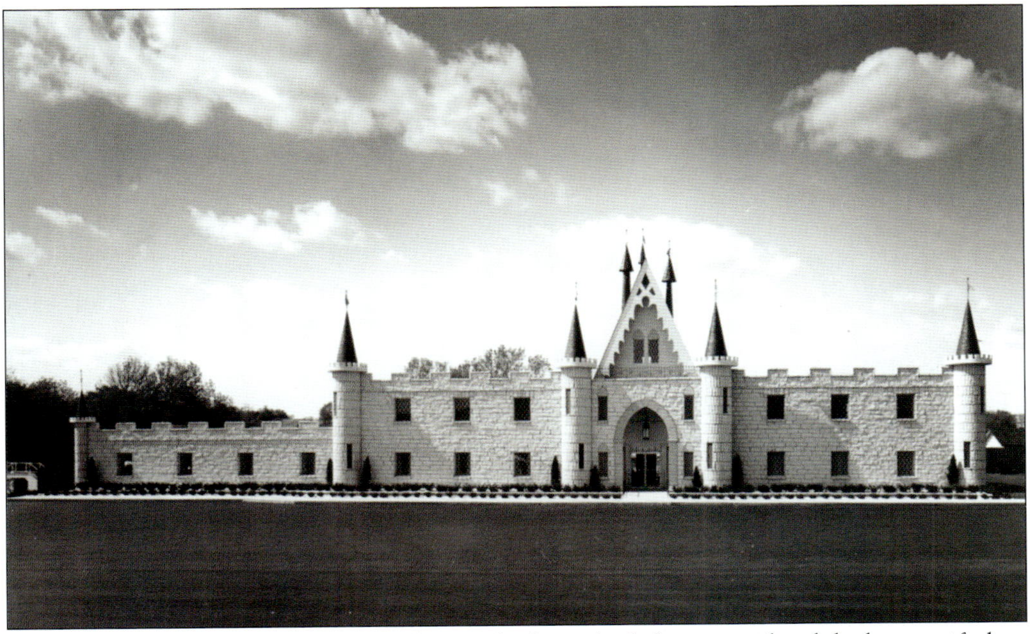

The park's entrance is a 12,000-square-foot castle-themed gift shop, considered the largest gift shop in the country. By spring, workers were putting the finishing touches on the new amusement park to ensure that everything would be ready for opening day. Dutch Wonderland officially opened on Monday, May 20, 1963. (MC.)

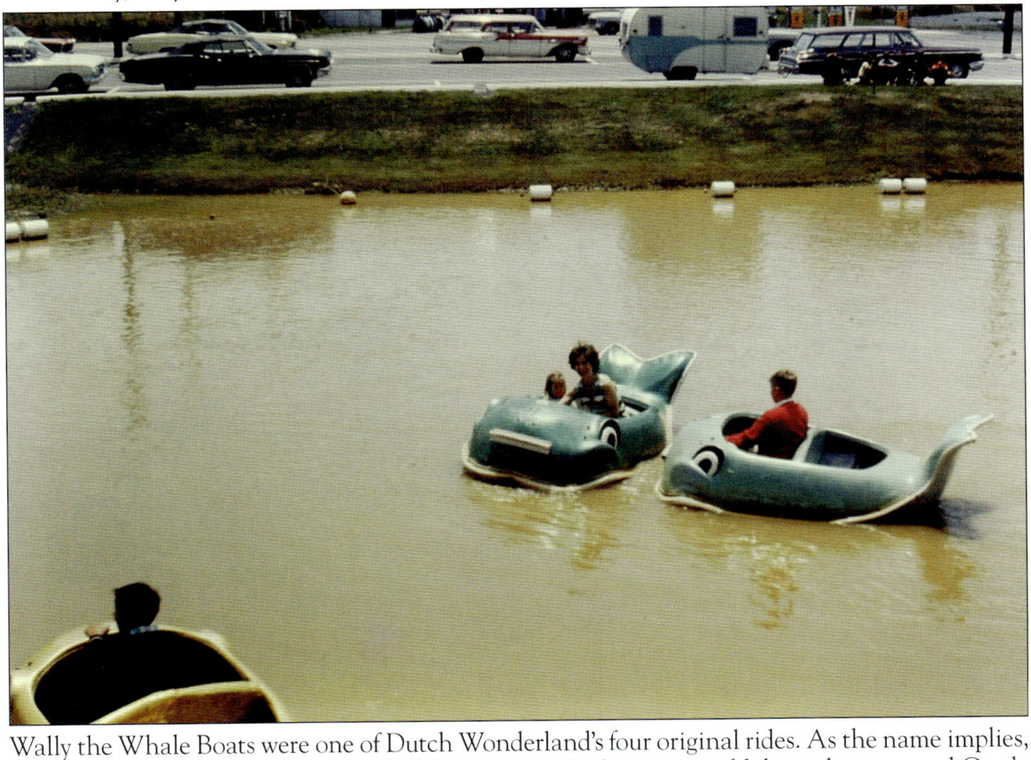

Wally the Whale Boats were one of Dutch Wonderland's four original rides. As the name implies, these small boats were designed to look like whales. Park guests could drive them around Castle Lake, a small man-made pond beside the park's castle entrance. (CB.)

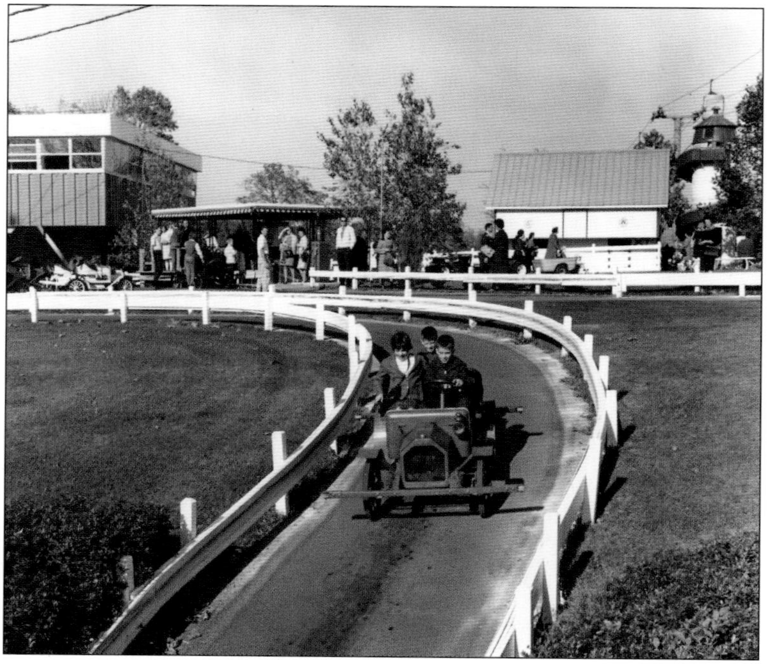

The Turnpike ride was located in the center of the park. The cars were modeled after 1910 Buicks. Unlike today, the cars did not have a center guide rail; the only thing that kept them from going off the road was a small fence on each side. (MC.)

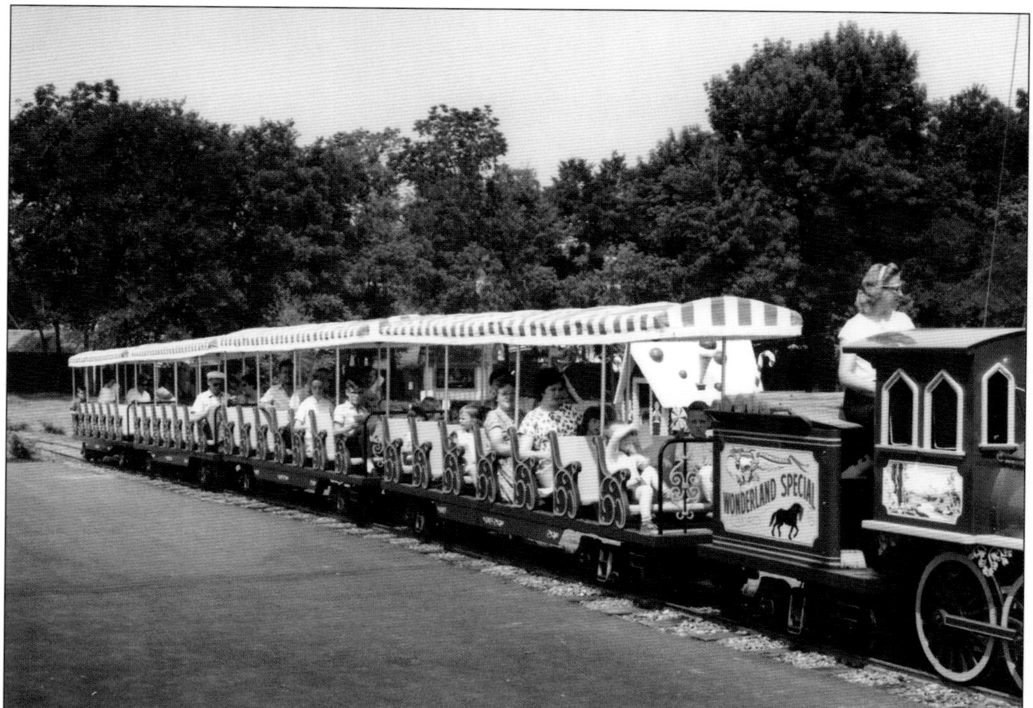

The Wonderland Special Railroad was another of Dutch Wonderland's four original rides. The Allan Herschell Iron Horse Train was modeled after locomotives from the late 1800s. These trains were manufactured in the Herschell plant in Buffalo, New York, from 1963 to 1970. The Wonderland Special took passengers on a half-mile journey around the park's perimeter. Not long after the train left the loading area, it would pass through the Four Season's Tunnel, where there were scenes with figures depicting life through each season of the year. (MC.)

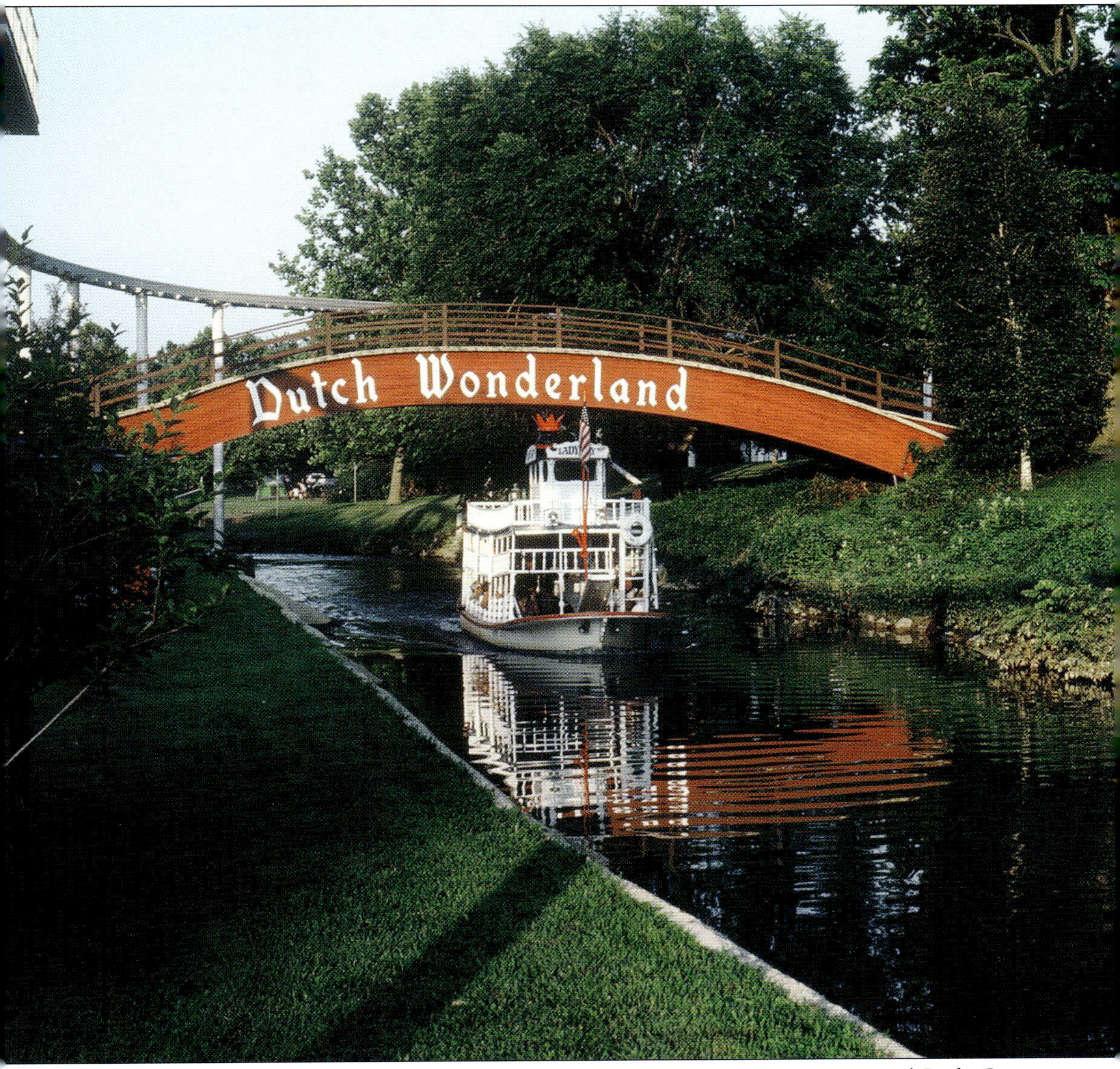

Dutch Wonderland's Lady Gay River Boat ride pays homage to Lancaster's original *Lady Gay* riverboats from the late 1800s and early 1900s. The first *Lady Gay* was a side-wheeled steamboat that sailed on the Lancaster County Conestoga Creek, carrying riders to Demuth's Park, also known as Rocky Springs Park. John B. Peoples owned the second *Lady Gay* steamboat, which also plied the Conestoga Creek, transporting passengers on a mile-long ride between his Conestoga Park and the Rocky Springs Park. Dutch Wonderland's version of the *Lady Gay* is a smaller steam-powered paddle wheeler manufactured by Sanford Company in 1963. The riverboat takes riders on a four- to five-minute trip on the Mill Stream in the back of the park. The bridge in the background was added in 1966. (DW.)

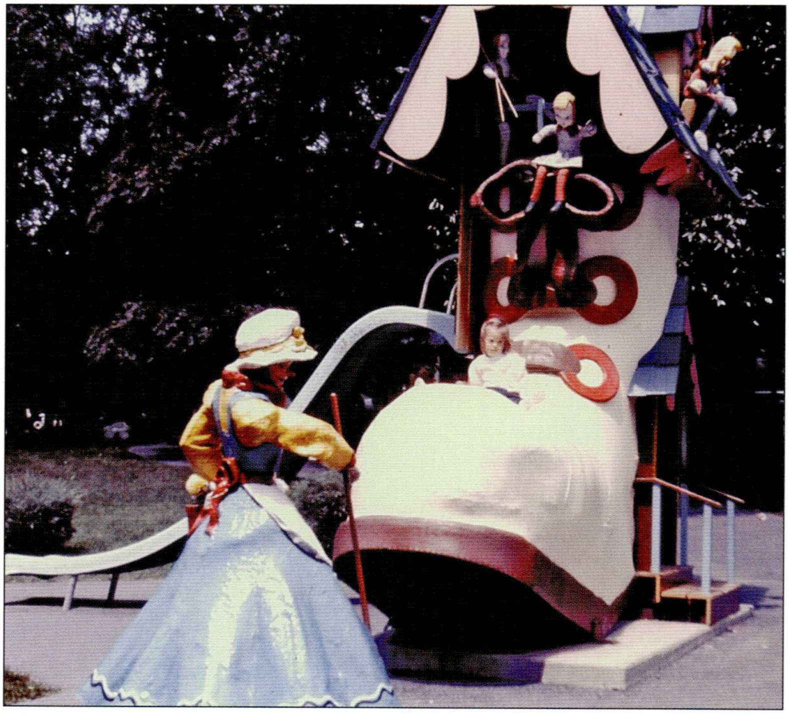

The Old Woman Who Lived in a Shoe Slide was one of two slides that opened in 1963. The fiberglass slide was based on the well-known nursery rhyme. Children would climb up steps inside the giant shoe, then slide down the other side. (CB.)

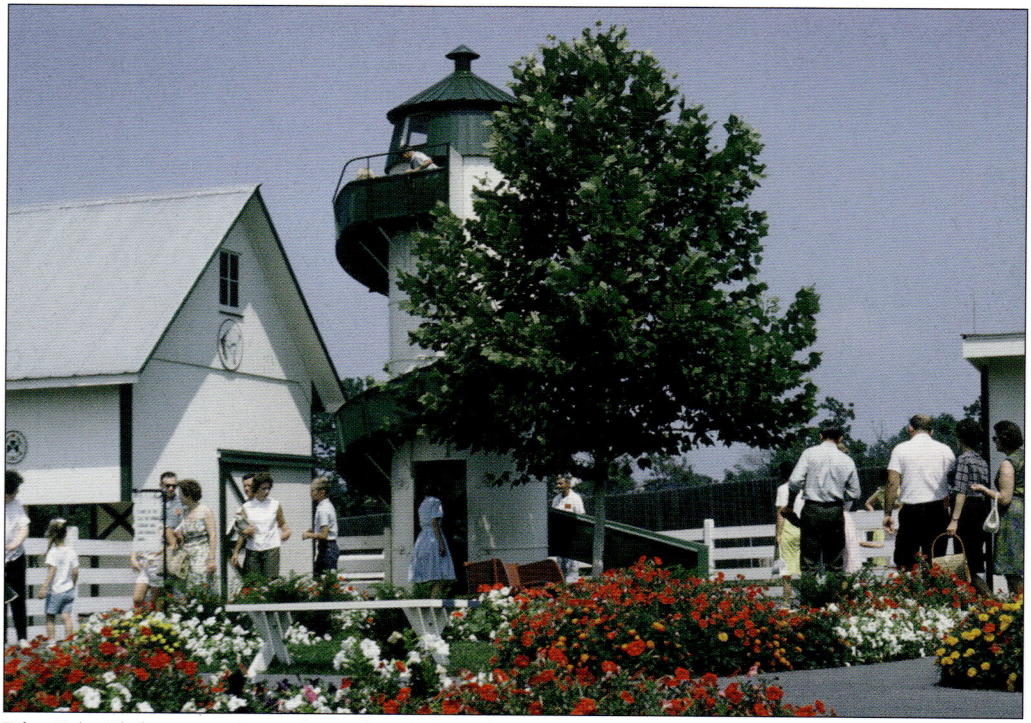

The Silo Slide is a replica silo with a slide wrapped around its exterior. Children climb 23 steps inside the silo, then slide down the spiraling shoot. The Silo Slide is located in the Little Dutch Farm section of the park. This area includes a barn, various live animals, and a replica Amish farmhouse. (DW.)

What child does not wish that every day were his or her birthday? The Birthday Cake House is one of the many unique features found in the magical wonderland. (CB.)

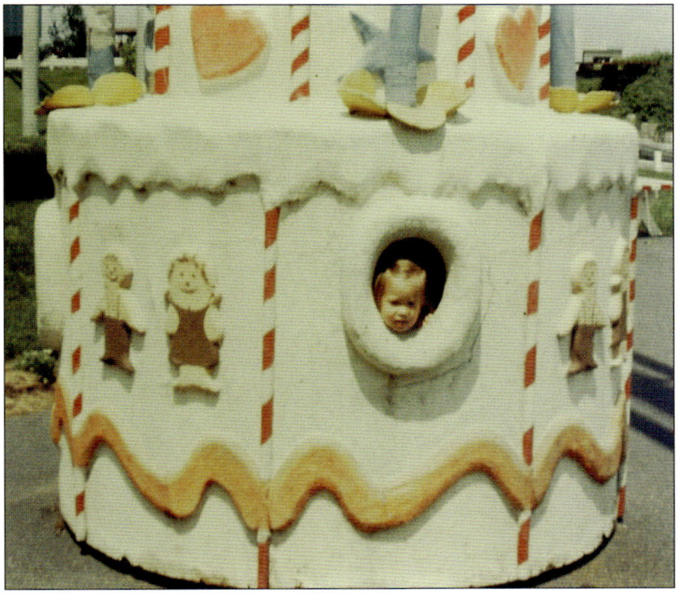

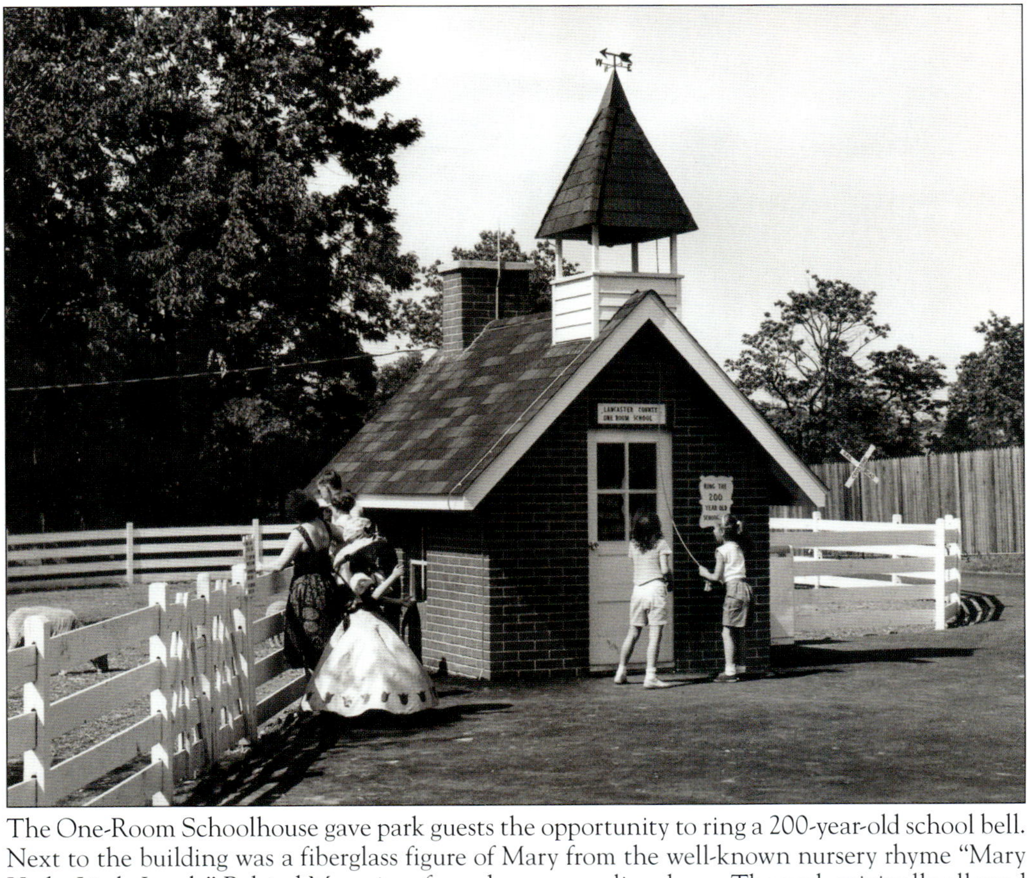

The One-Room Schoolhouse gave park guests the opportunity to ring a 200-year-old school bell. Next to the building was a fiberglass figure of Mary from the well-known nursery rhyme "Mary Had a Little Lamb." Behind Mary, in a fenced area, were live sheep. The park originally allowed guests to give milk to the sheep; however, they soon learned that the sheep were getting sick from too much milk. (DW.)

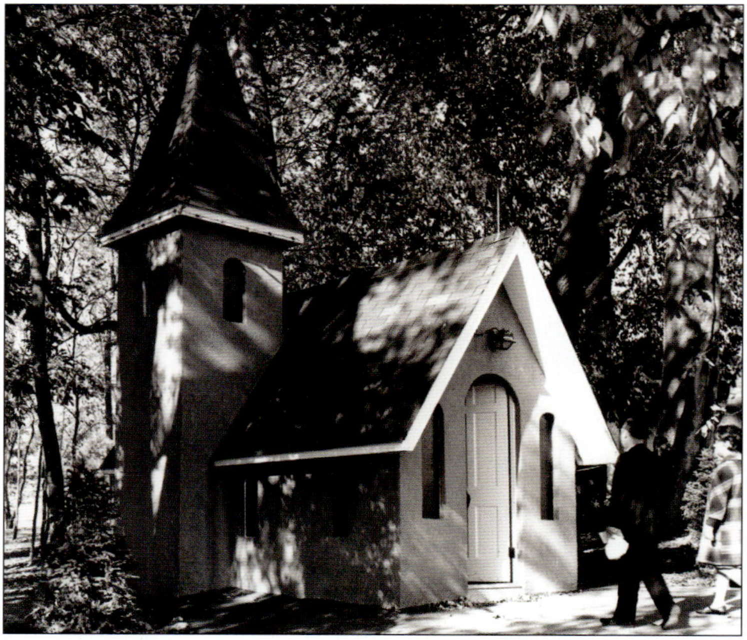

Nestled among some of Dutch Wonderland's tallest trees is the Little Brown Church in the Dell. The air-conditioned building has a bible in the front and two benches along the side for parishioners to sit on. (DW.)

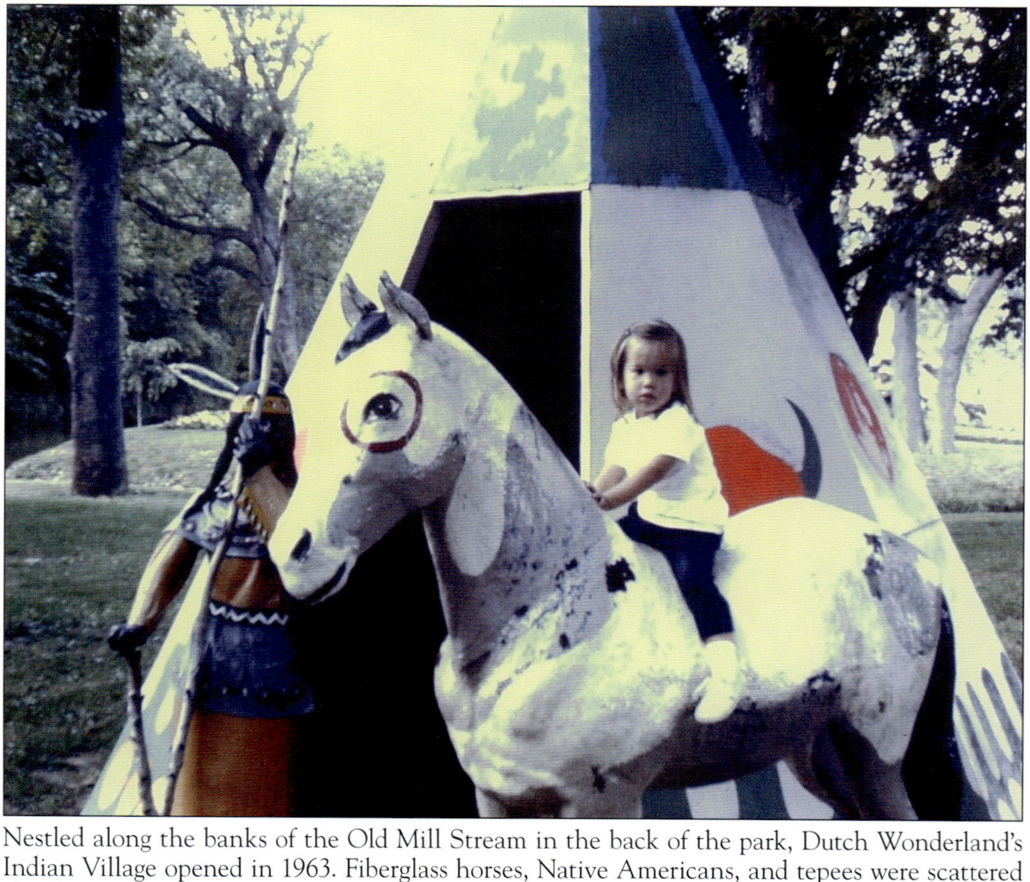

Nestled along the banks of the Old Mill Stream in the back of the park, Dutch Wonderland's Indian Village opened in 1963. Fiberglass horses, Native Americans, and tepees were scattered throughout this section. (CB.)

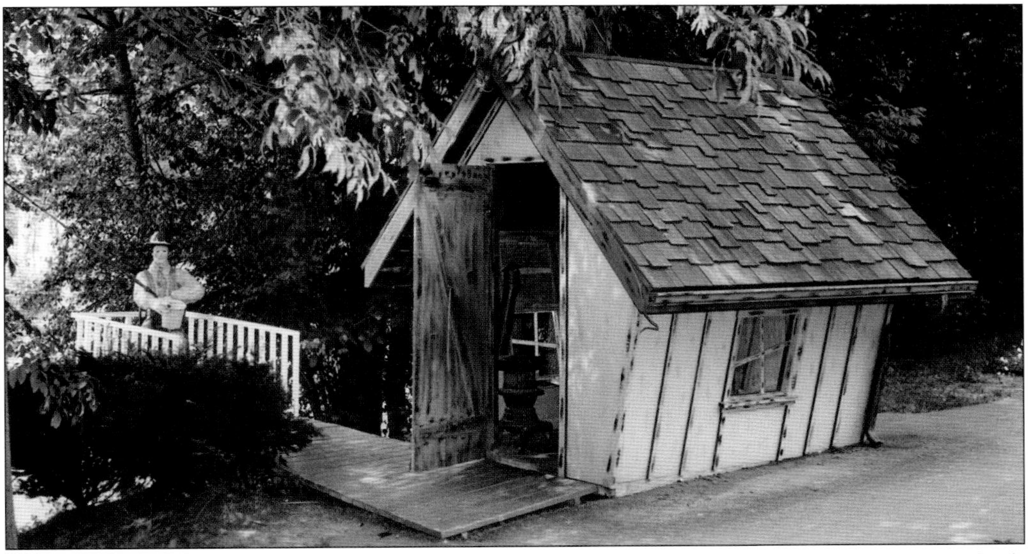

Along the Mill Stream sits the Hobo Shack. A big fan of *The Red Skelton Show*, Earl Clark built the Hobo Shack as a tribute to the character "Freddie the Freeloader." Clark's wish to meet the character came true when Red Skelton visited the park in 1975. (DW.)

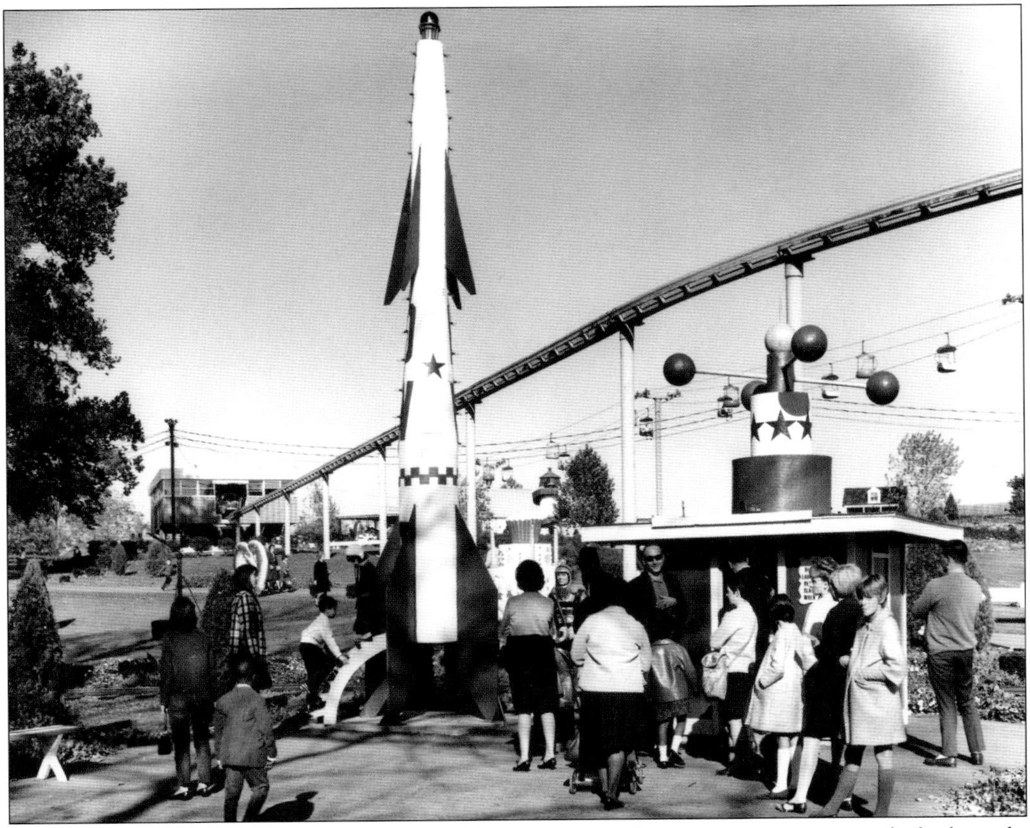

At the interactive space station, guests could pretend that they were astronauts ready for launch. This area included a radar station where guests could communicate with those inside the rocket ship. (MC.)

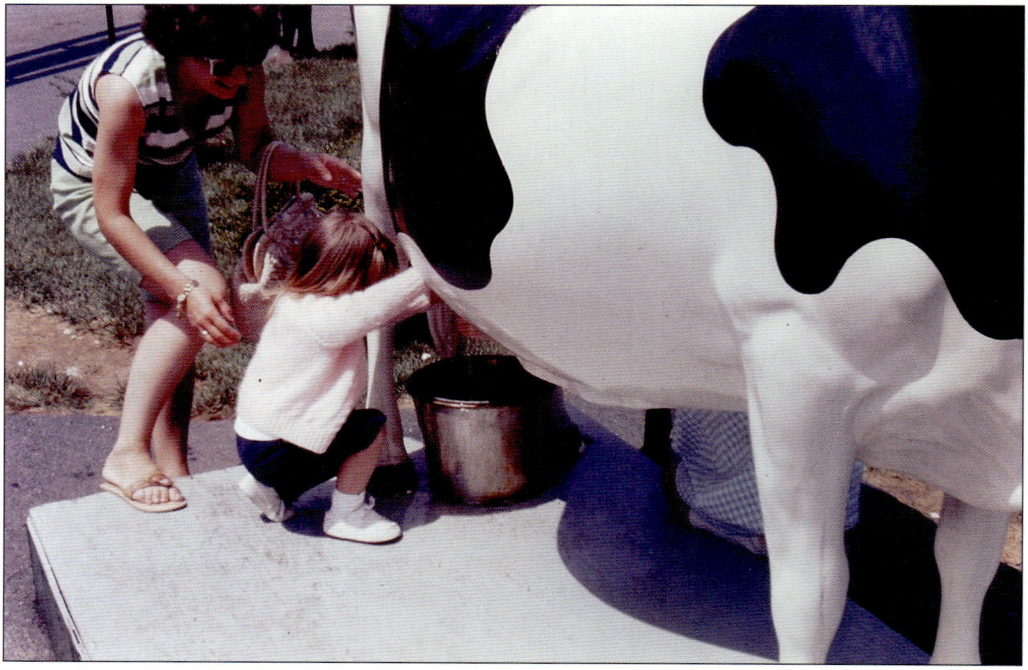

Bossy the Holstein Cow is one of the friendliest cows that guests could ever hope to meet. Park guests love to milk Bossy. As she is "milked," water comes out of her utters and goes into a bucket below. Bossy has been a park fixture for over 50 years. (CB.)

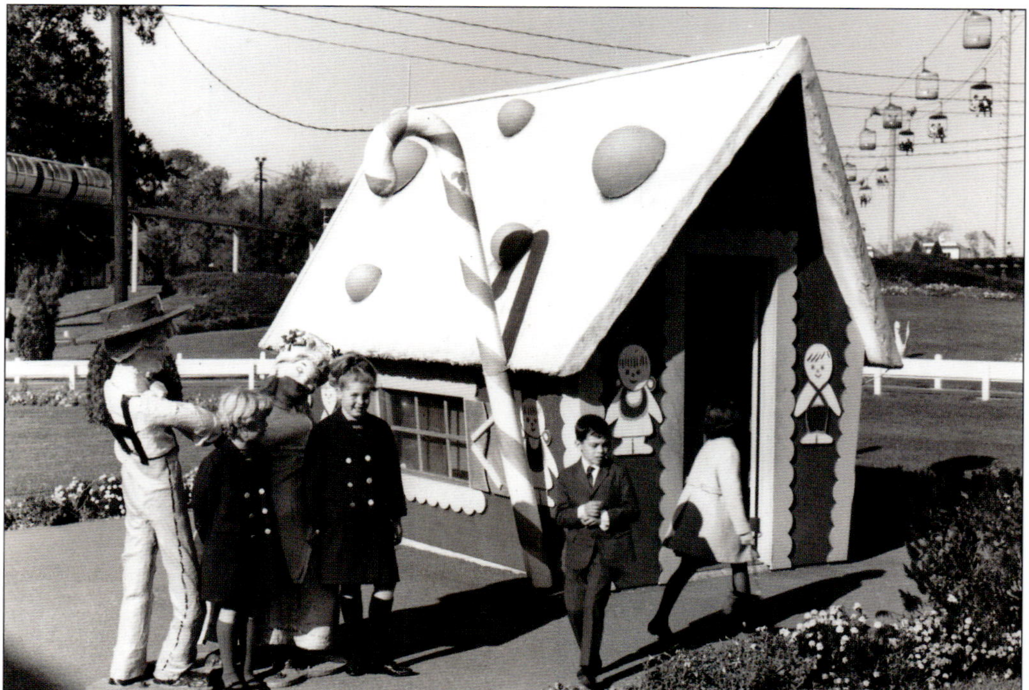

While traveling through Dutch Wonderland's magic land of make-believe, guests will come across Hansel and Gretel and their Gingerbread House. The building is designed to look like it is made of candy, just like the one from the famous fairy tale. (MC.)

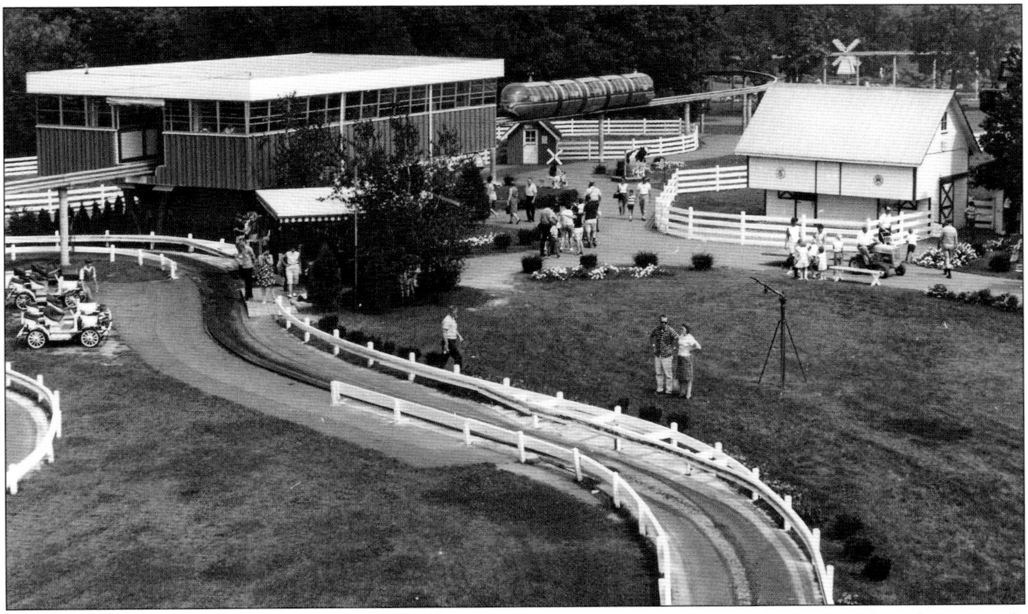

The monorail, the Little Dutch Farm, and the original Turnpike cars can be seen in this photograph from the late 1960s. In front of the monorail station is the Turnpike's loading area with a tentlike covering. A station and a queue line were built a few years later. (MC.)

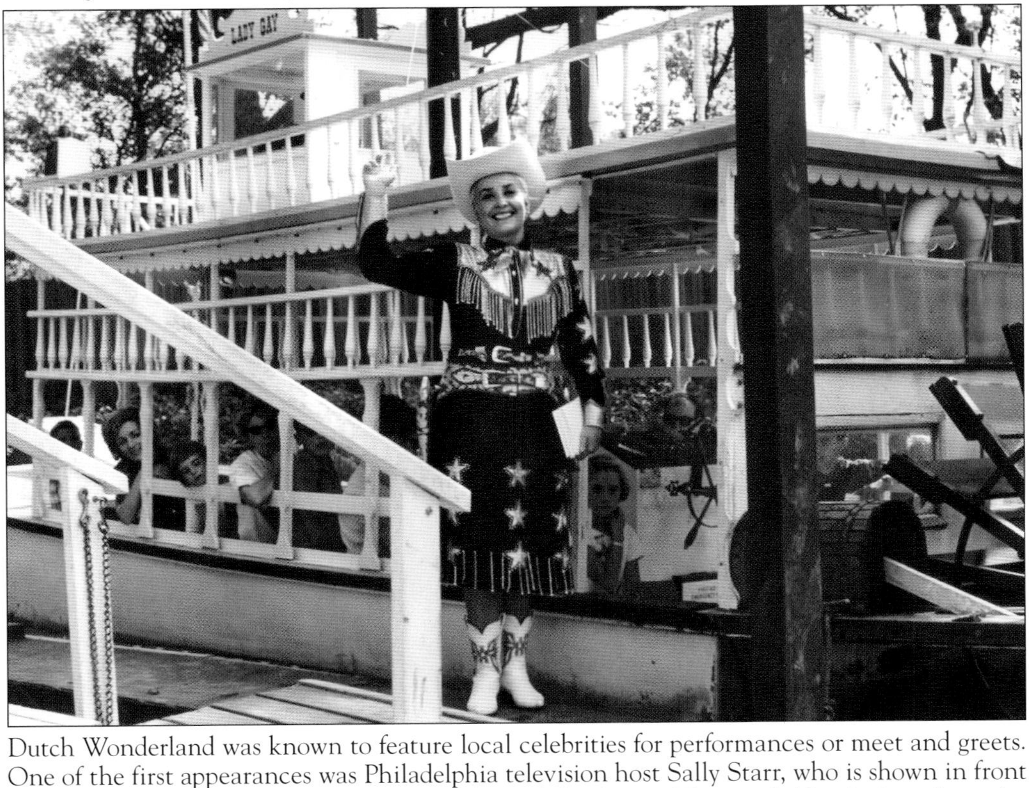

Dutch Wonderland was known to feature local celebrities for performances or meet and greets. One of the first appearances was Philadelphia television host Sally Starr, who is shown in front of the Lady Gay River Boat in 1963. Starr hosted the *Popeye Theatre* children's show from the 1950s until 1971. (MC.)

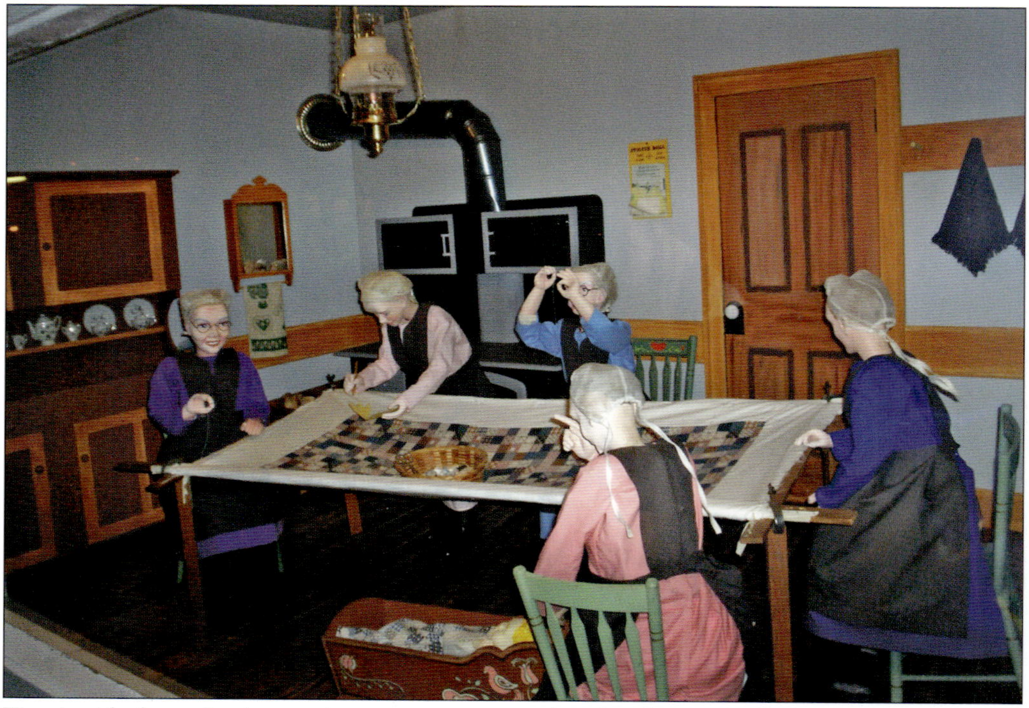

Two Amish-themed animatronic puppet scenes were handmade specifically for Dutch Wonderland by the Luft brothers of Wernersville, Pennsylvania. With the push of a button, the small Amish people would move and talk to each other. One scene showed Amish women sewing a quilt (above); the other showed Amish men crafting items in a wood shop. A few years later, two more puppet displays were added. One was located inside the Gingerbread House. It showed small animatronic candy makers hard at work (below), singing songs such as "The Chocolate Train" and Shirley Temple's classic "On the Good Ship Lollipop." John and Jim Luft began handcrafting puppets and performing shows in 1935. They performed at Dutch Wonderland on the weekends starting in 1963. With the popularity of their puppet show, they signed a contract to perform daily. The brothers retired from show business in 1988. (Both, AD.)

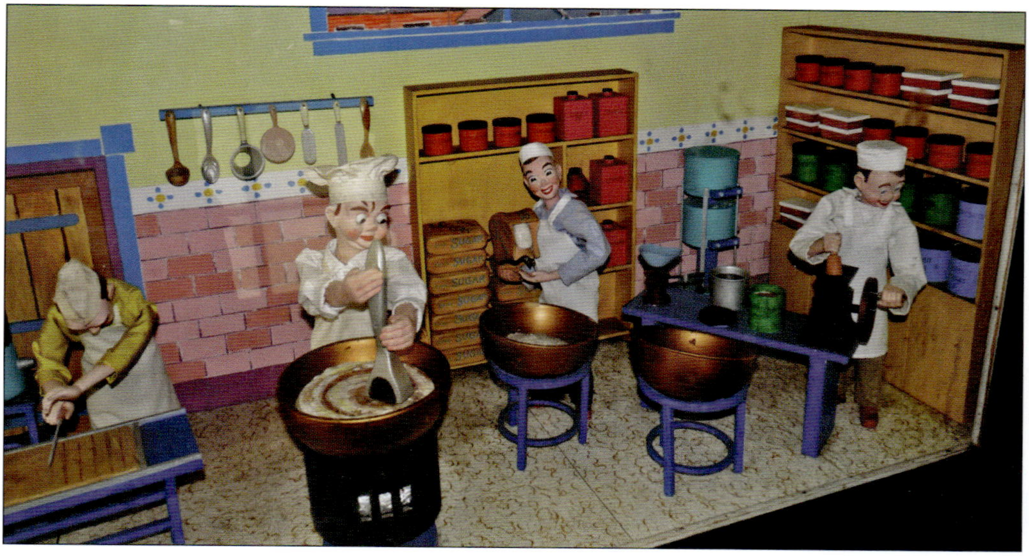

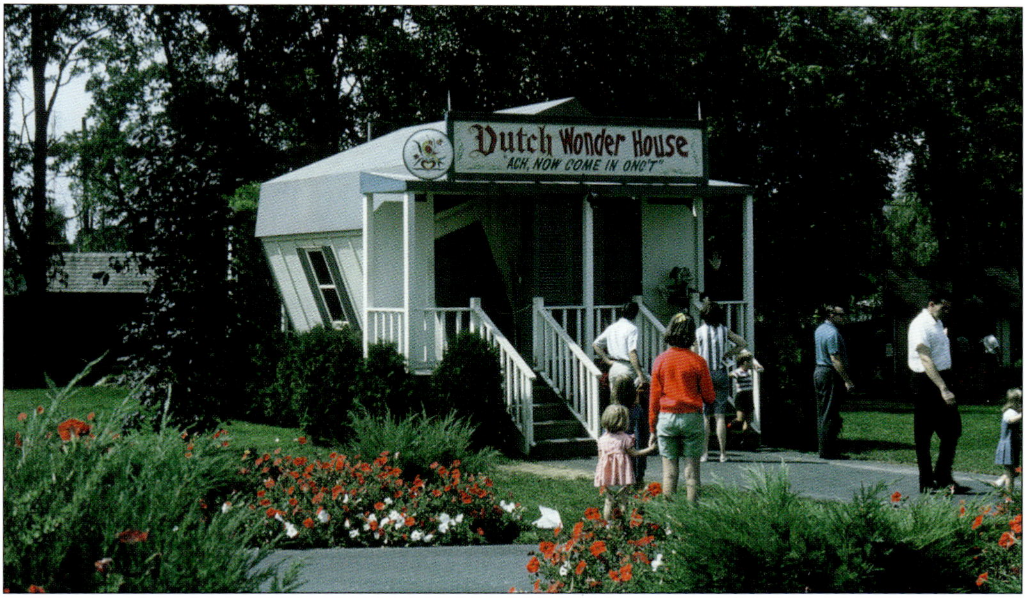

In 1964, the Dutch Wonder House was added near the park entrance. The new ride was designed and built by Earl Clark, along with his friend, a Mr. McFadden. It was based on the Haunted Swing created by Amariah Lake, which was first seen in the 1890s in Atlantic City, New Jersey. The house would rotate around those seated on a stationary bench, which gave the illusion of spinning upside down. In 1984, the Dutch Wonder House was relocated to accommodate the Space Shuttle ride. (DW.)

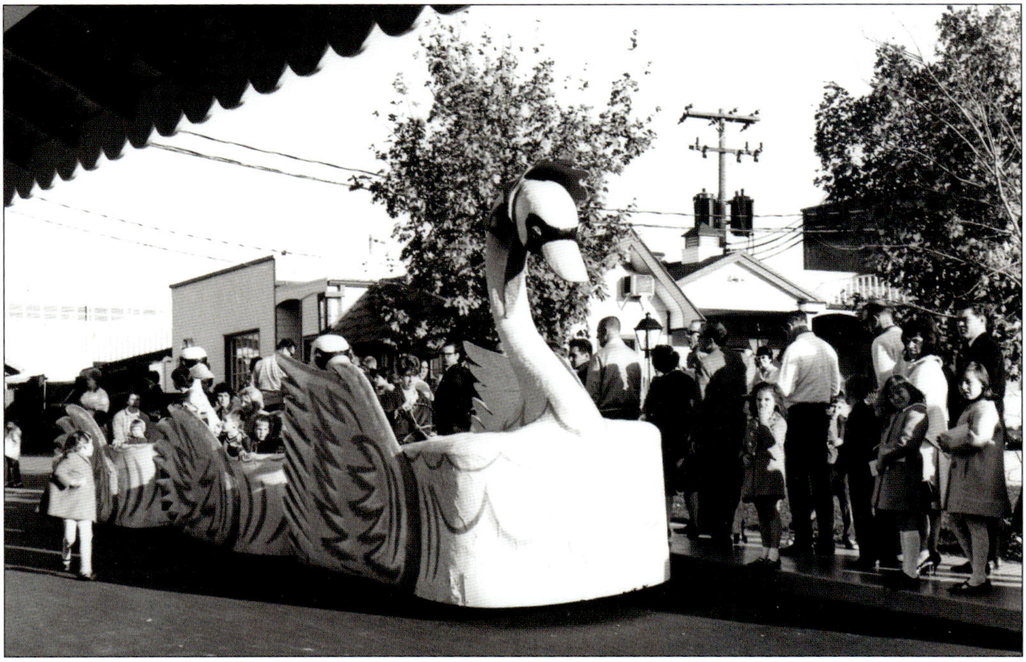

A unique tram-like ride with a swan design was introduced in 1965. Beneath the swan overlay, the ride's framework consisted of a farm tractor with two trailers that carried passengers throughout the park. The Gliding Swans, as they were referred to in a 1966 pamphlet, operated for only three seasons before being removed due to increased foot traffic. (MC.)

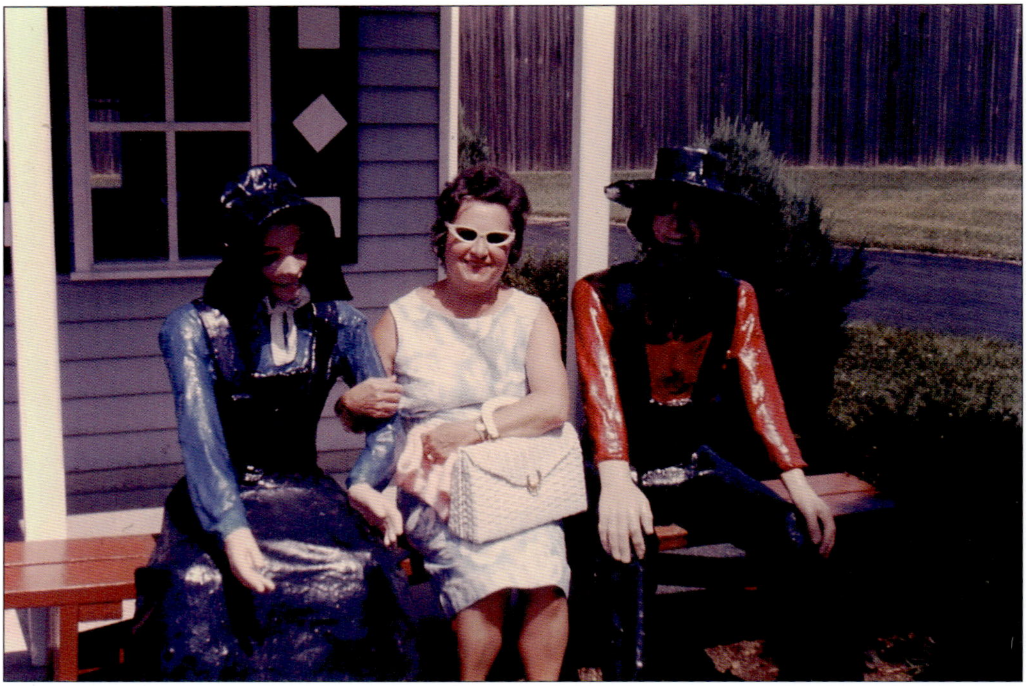

The Dutch section of the park featured the Amish Farmhouse, where guests could peer inside the windows of the replica house to see life-size wax figures of an Amish family. A fiberglass Amish couple also sat on a bench in front of the building. (CB.)

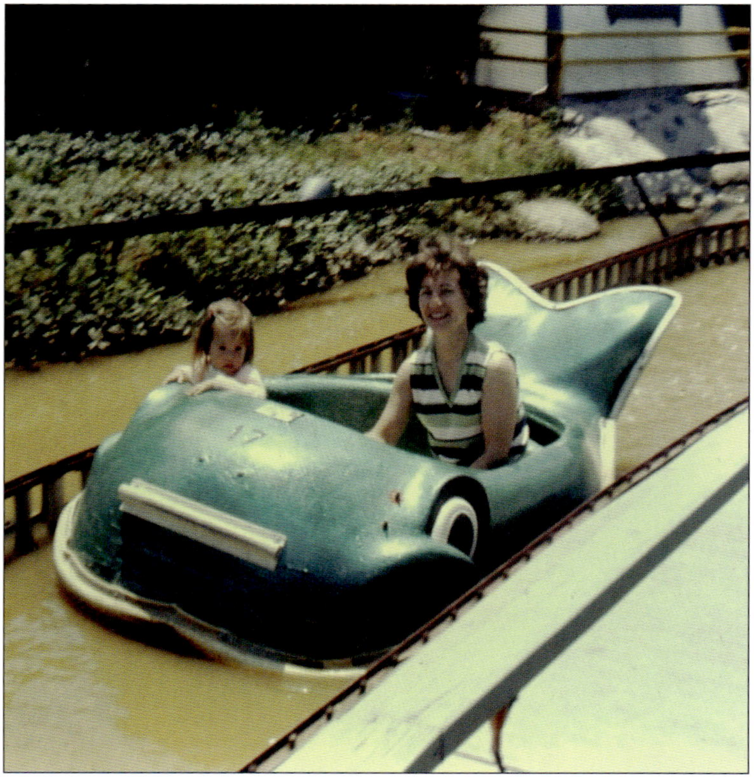

The exit area for the Wally the Whale Boats, one of Dutch Wonderland's original attractions, is seen here a few years after its opening. (CB.)

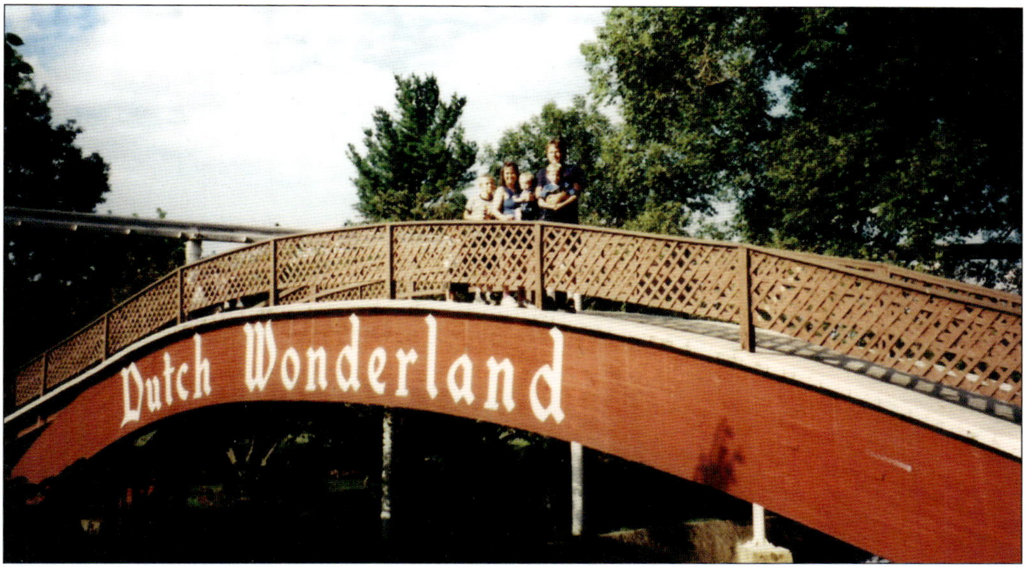

Part of the 1966 expansion included the International Botanical Gardens. Earl Clark's love of flowers inspired the creation of the gardens. A large bridge with the words "Dutch Wonderland" painted on the side served as the entranceway to the new five-acre section. The iconic bridge was a symbol of Dutch Wonderland for many years. (AD.)

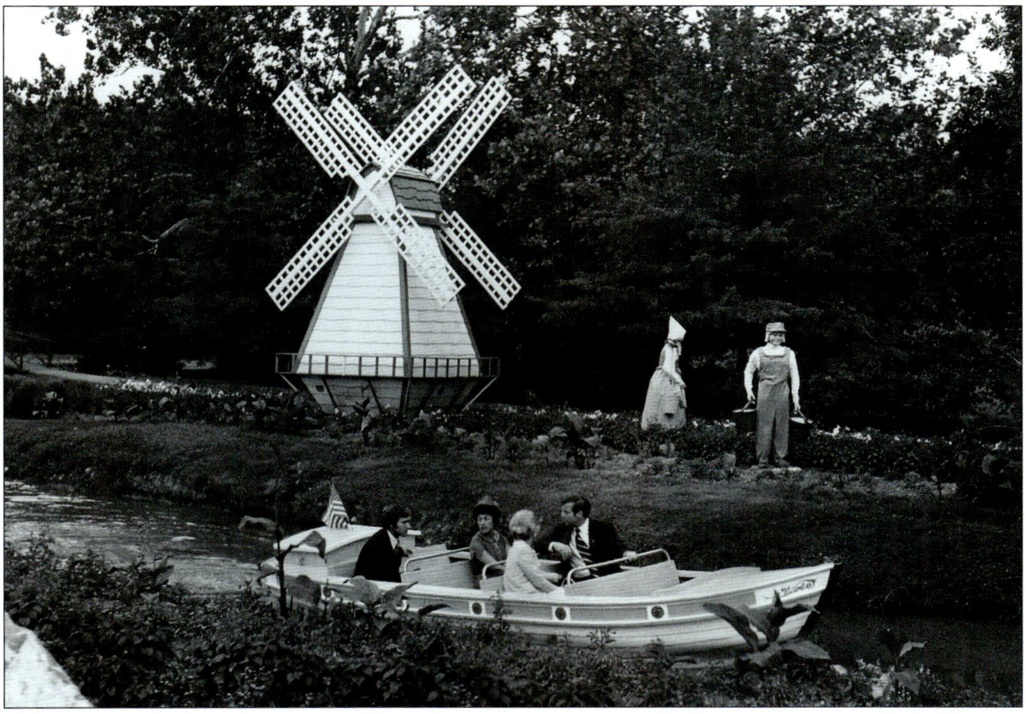

Winding through the island was the Gondola Cruise. Each of the 12-passenger boats, manufactured by Arrow Development, led riders on a relaxing journey though the International Botanical Gardens via a series of canals that passed underneath small bridges. Along the route, riders would pass the gardens' many replica structures, such as this Holland scene. Riding in the center of the boat seen here is TV personality Pixanne, played by Jane Norman. (MC.)

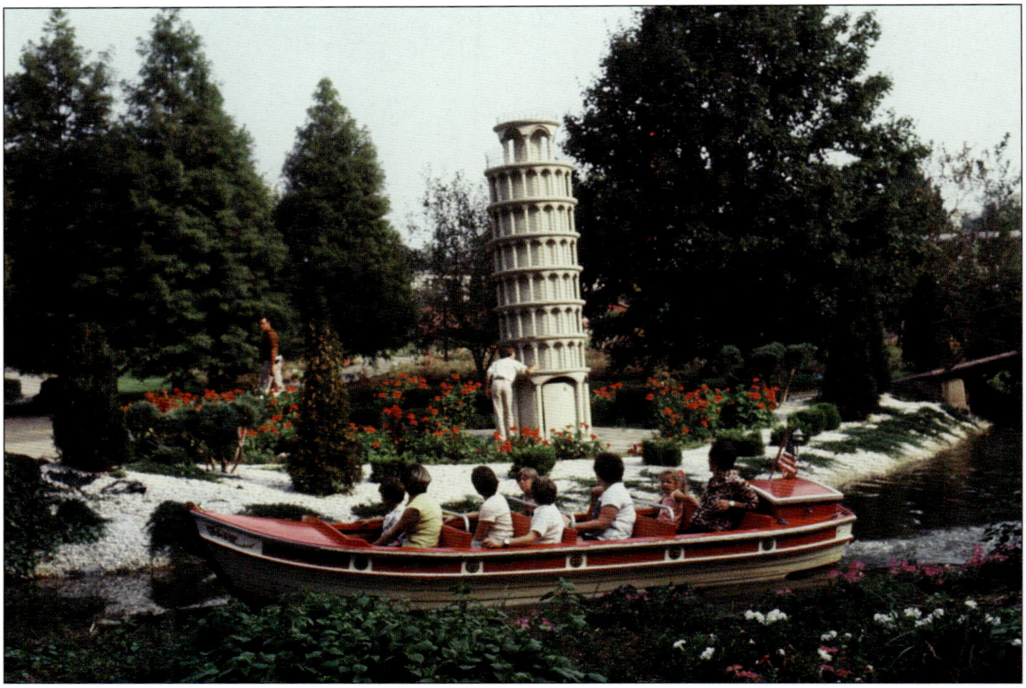

Clark's attention to detail was apparent in each country's scene, which featured various plants and flowers native to that area. Here, juniper, cypress, scarlet sage, and marigolds surround Italy's Leaning Tower of Pisa. Over the course of one year, more than 300,000 flowers would bloom throughout the gardens. Visitors could tour the gardens at three distinct points throughout the year, and the look of the plants would be completely different each time. (DW.)

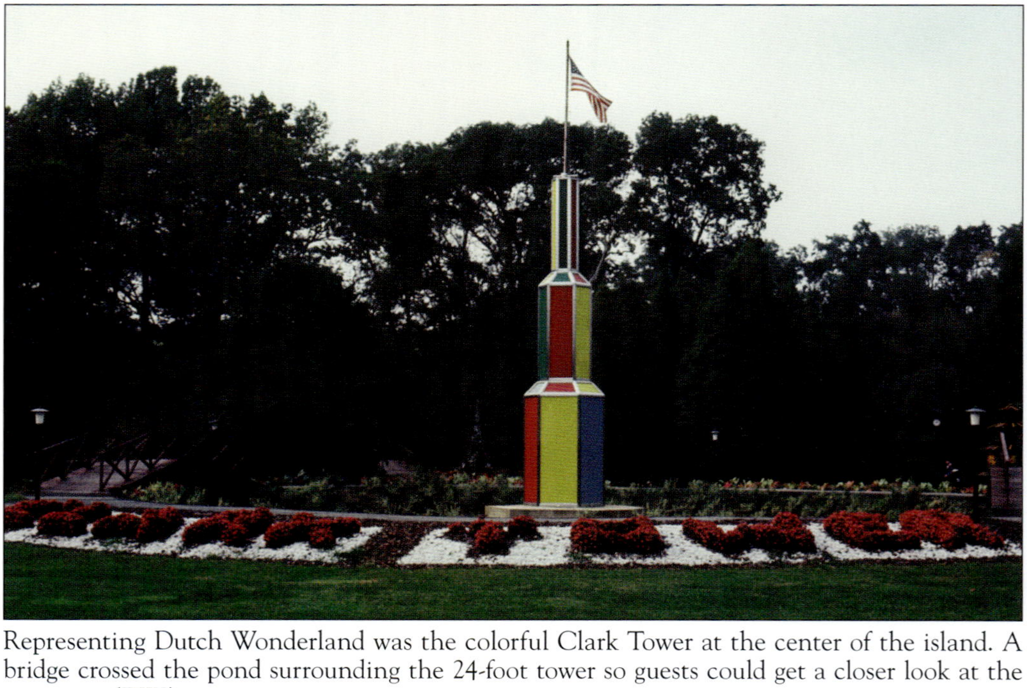

Representing Dutch Wonderland was the colorful Clark Tower at the center of the island. A bridge crossed the pond surrounding the 24-foot tower so guests could get a closer look at the structure. (DW.)

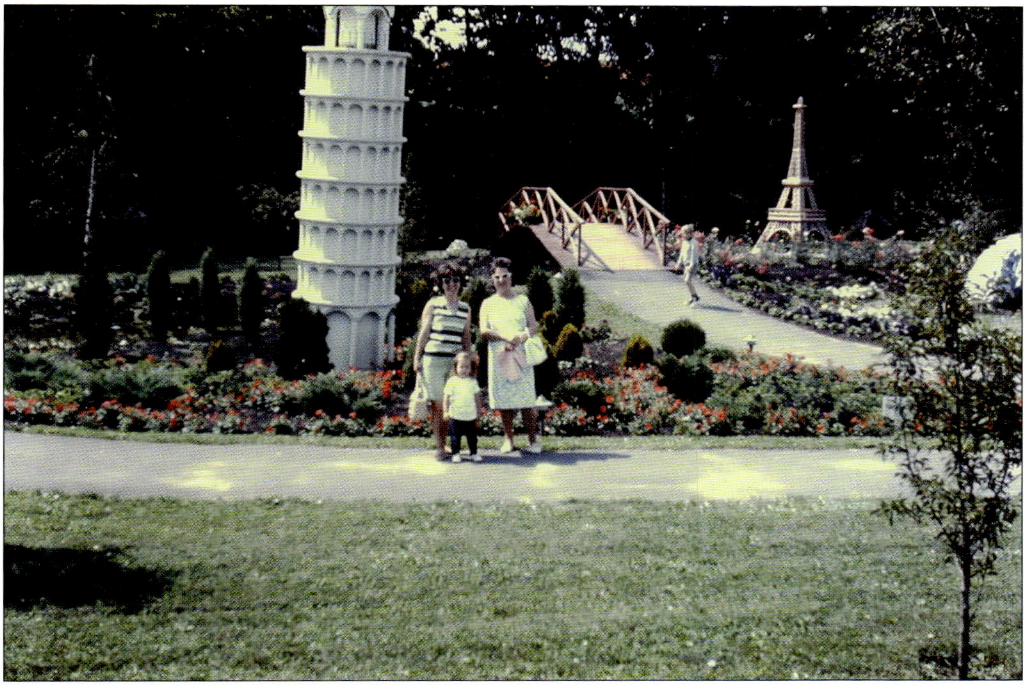

In this photograph, taken the year after the gardens opened, are miniature replicas of Italy's Leaning Tower of Pisa and France's Eiffel Tower, which was surrounded by hundreds of French roses. (CB.)

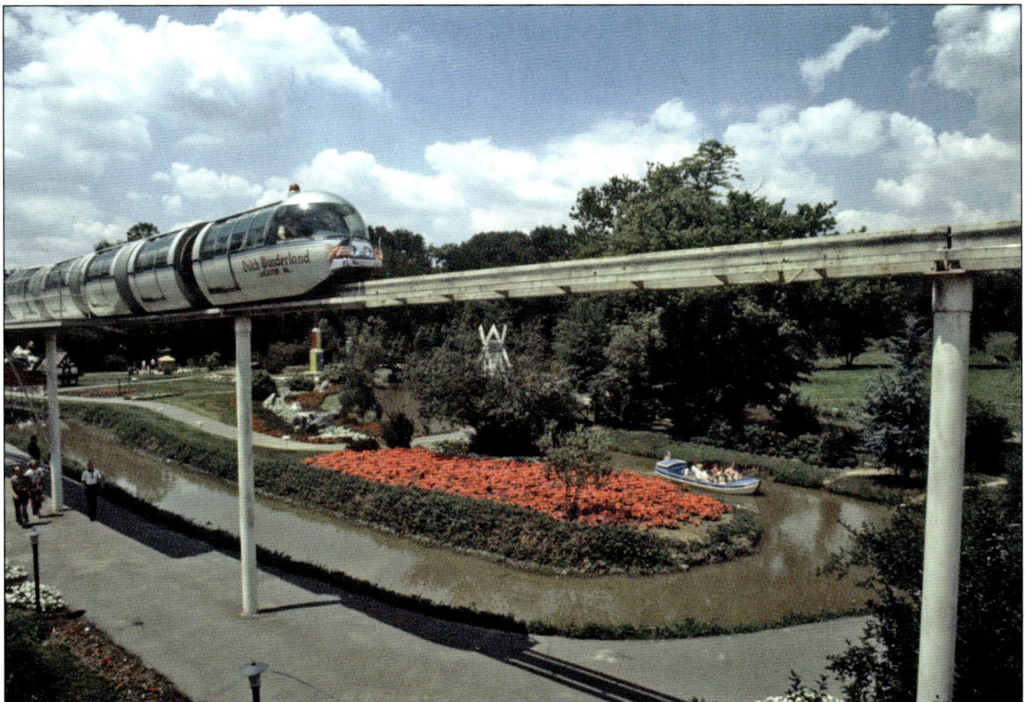

Other representations included a rock mountain with a Swiss chalet for Switzerland, a grass hut for Hawaii, an English garden with the Big Ben clock tower for England, and a pagoda for Japan, seen here at the center of the image. The monorail overhead was also added in 1966. (DW.)

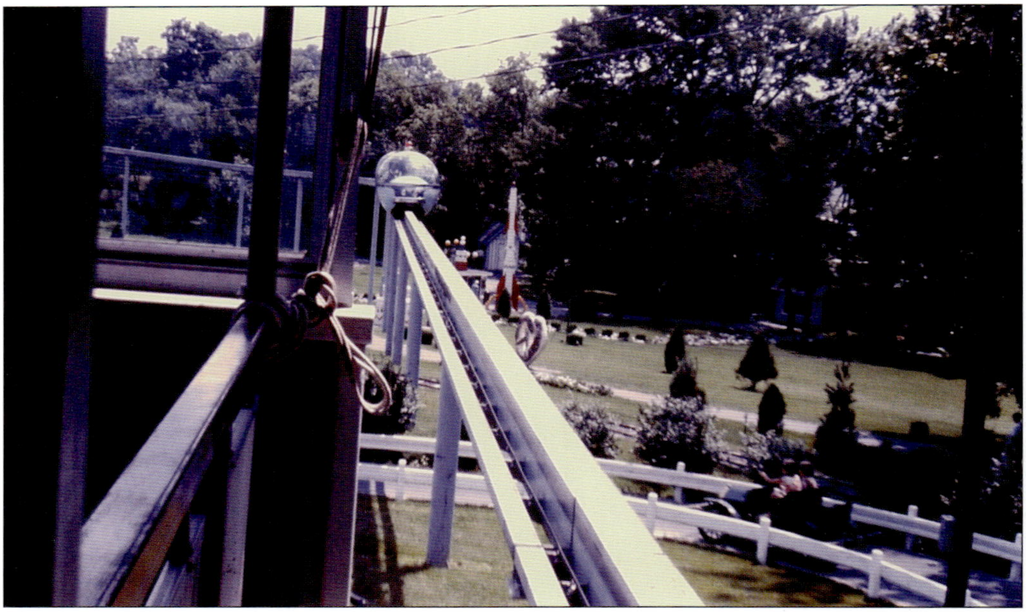

Three 50-passenger monorail trains travel over a mile-long track throughout the park. Disneyland had one of the first monorails in the United States when it was added in 1959. Thus, when Dutch Wonderland's monorail system was installed less than a decade later, it garnered national attention for the park. People came from everywhere just to ride the state-of-the-art monorail, which had a separate admission price. The monorail could be accessed from two stations: one inside the park and one in the parking lot. The separate admission price for the monorail was discontinued after Hershey Entertainment bought the park. During the final year of charging extra for the ride, the monorail could be boarded at the parking lot station for $2 and at the in-park station for $1. (CB.)

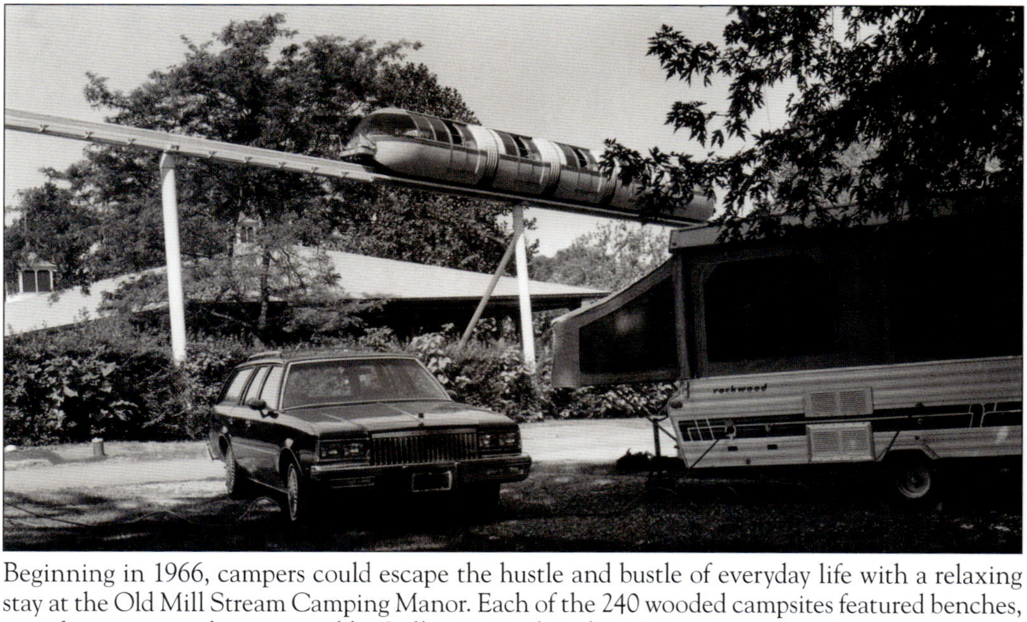

Beginning in 1966, campers could escape the hustle and bustle of everyday life with a relaxing stay at the Old Mill Stream Camping Manor. Each of the 240 wooded campsites featured benches, a cookout area, and a picnic table. Still in use today, the 15-acre campground borders the Mill Stream and Amish farmland on the east side of Dutch Wonderland. (DW.)

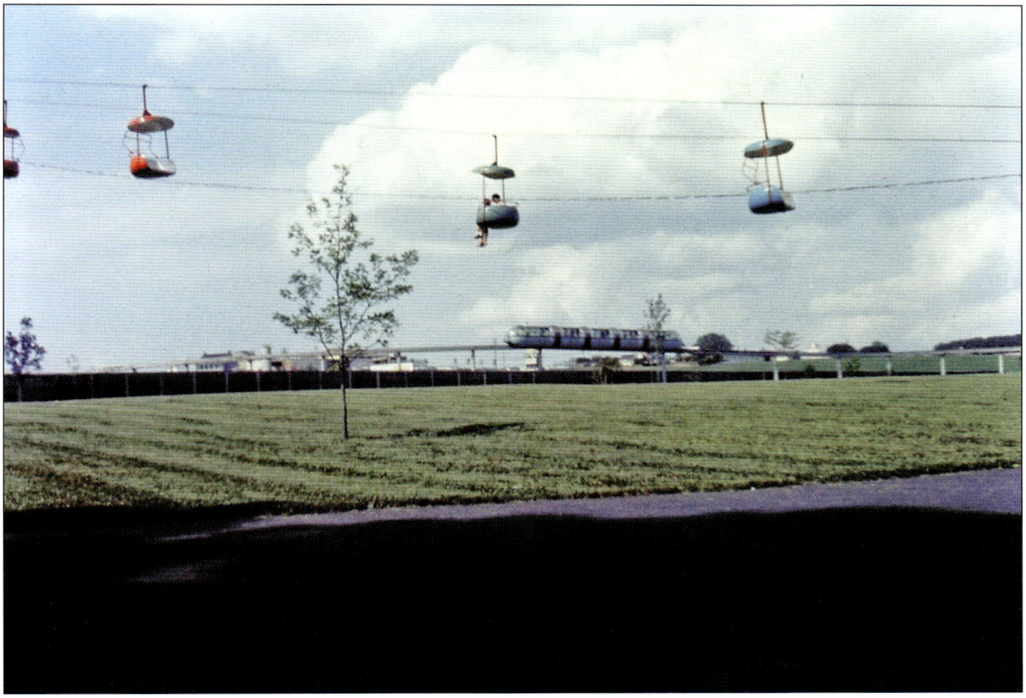

The Sky Ride made its debut in 1967. The new ski lift–style ride was manufactured by Universal Design, the same company that had built the park's monorail a year earlier. Transporting guests across the park via 32 suspended bench seats, this attraction provides a relaxing way to travel from one side of the park to the other. Below is a view of the park as seen from the Sky Ride. Both photographs were taken during the ride's inaugural year. (Both, CB.)

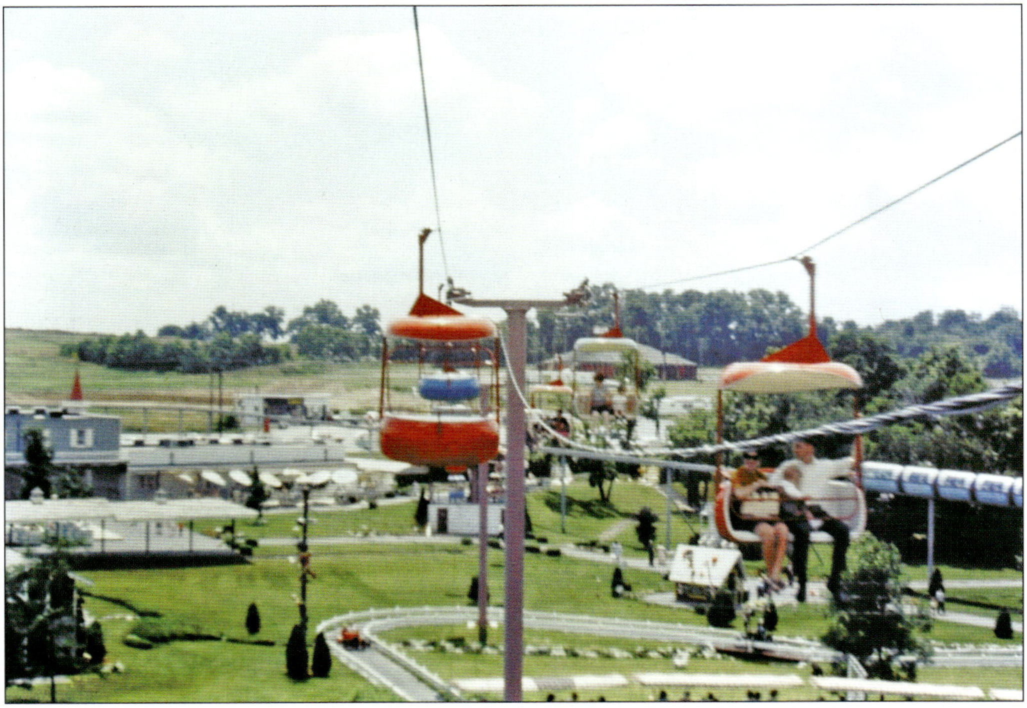

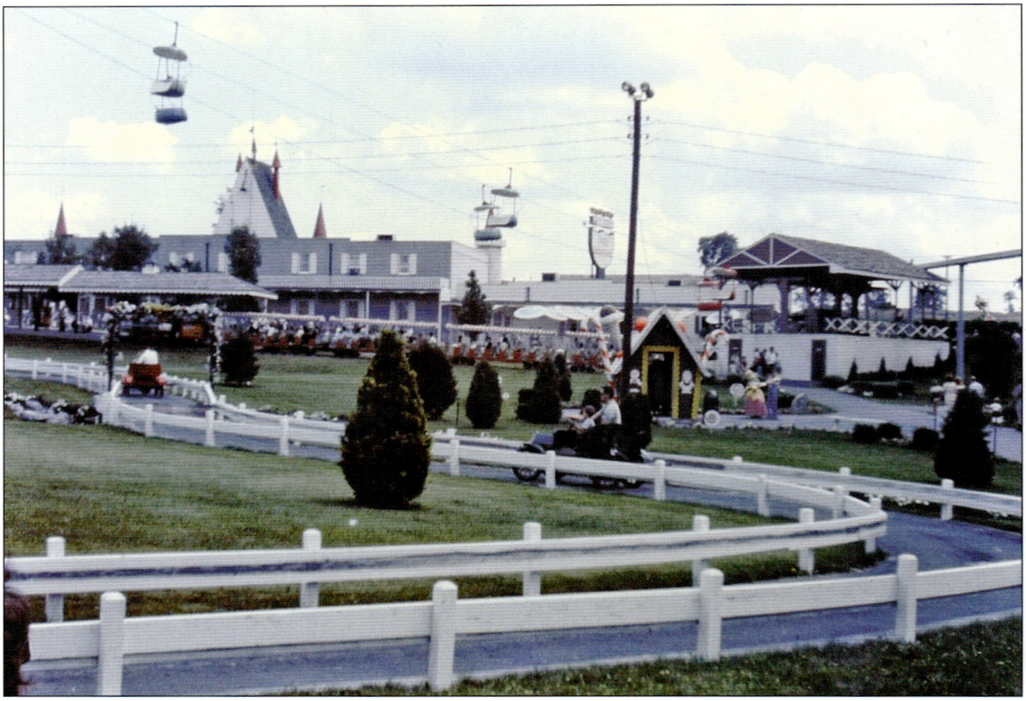

This c. 1967 photograph shows the original Turnpike ride with its side guardrails. In the background are the Allan Herschell train, the Gingerbread House, and the Sky Ride. (CB.)

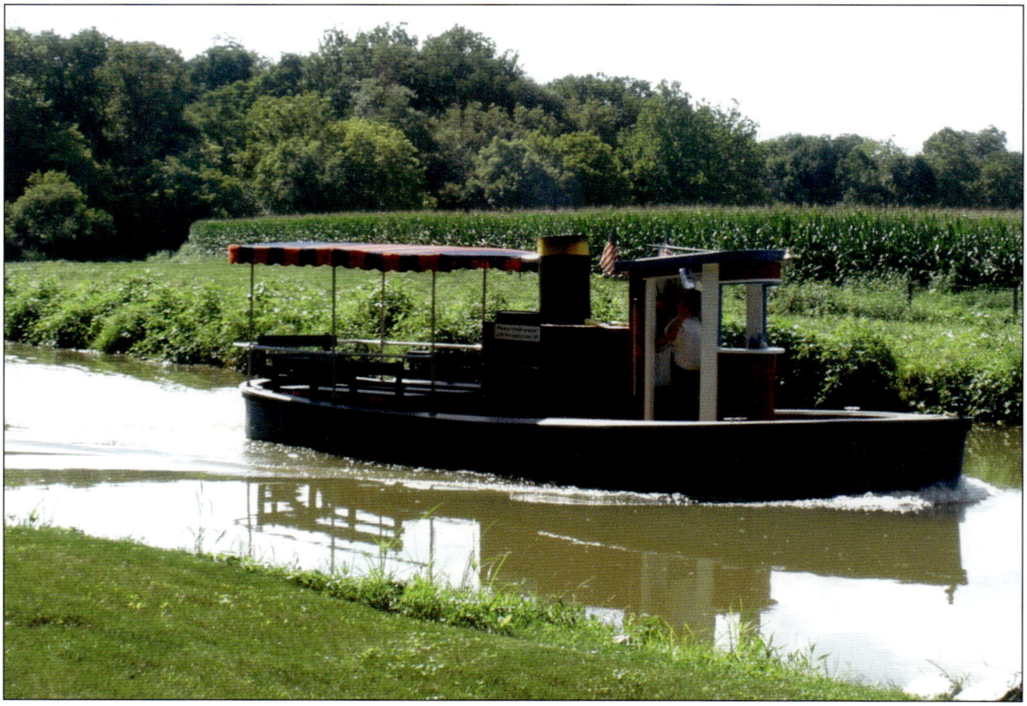

In 1967, the park added another boat ride manufactured by Sanford Company, the Molly C. Tug Boat. The new vessel was named after Earl Clark's wife, Molly Clark. Over the years, its appearance has changed. The photograph above shows the Tug Boat during the 2010 season. (AD.)

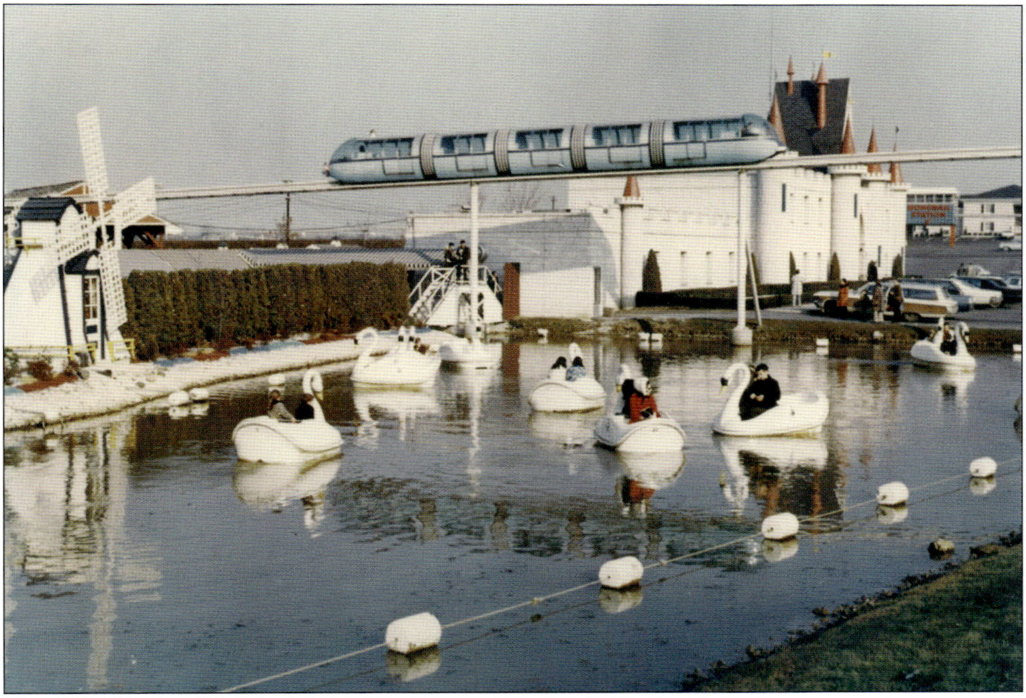

The first of the park's original four rides to be modified was the boats in Castle Lake. The Wally the Whale Boats were removed and replaced with swan boats in 1968. Like the whale boats, park guests could steer the vessels around Castle Lake. Earl Clark bought the new boats for his wife, Molly, because of her love for swans. (MC.)

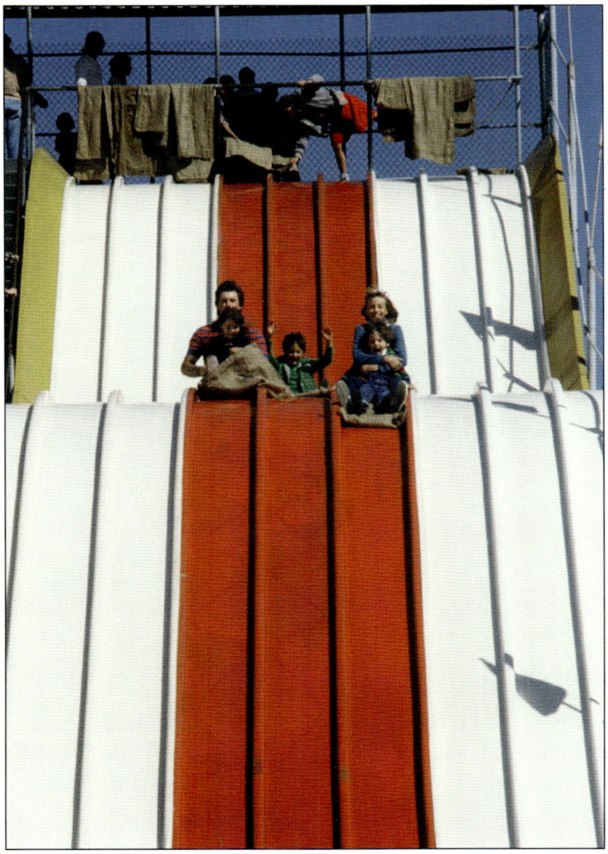

Giant slides were very popular in the late 1960s and early 1970s. Almost every park in the country had one, and Dutch Wonderland was no exception. The red-and-white Giant Slide opened in 1968 at a cost of about $25,000. Manufactured by Whitehouse Plastic Corporation, the nine-lane slide was 165 feet long, with 60 steps to reach the top. The burlap sacks hanging from the railing above were used to facilitate the ride down. (DW.)

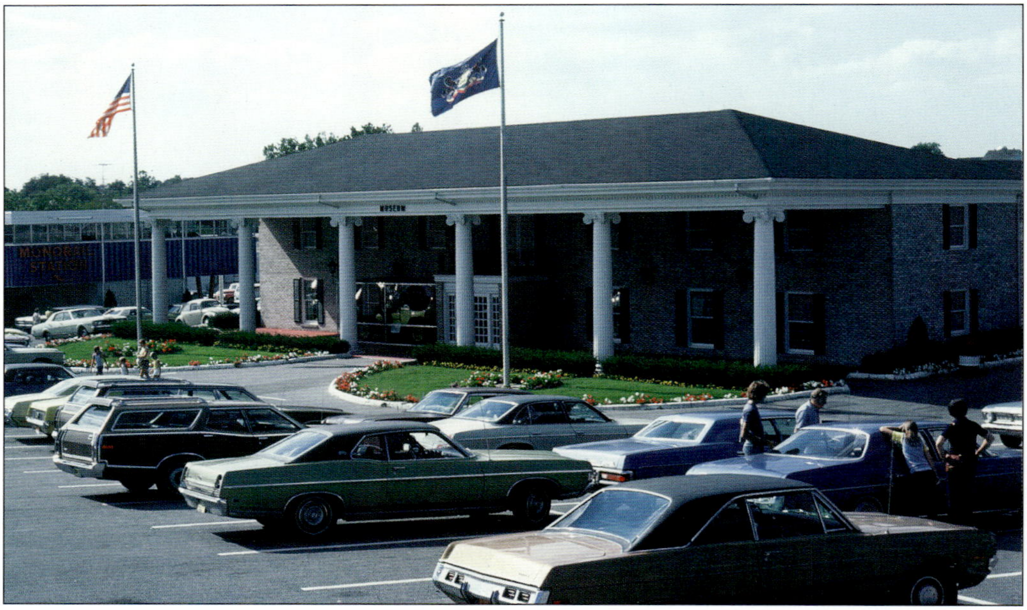

Earl Clark designed the wax museum with the help of six local historians to depict major Lancaster County events. The realistic figures in each of the scenes were made by Dorfman Museum Figures of Baltimore, Maryland. Nearly 50 construction workers were assigned to the project from October 1968 to April 1969 to have the museum ready for Easter weekend. After six months of work, the National Wax Museum of Lancaster County Heritage opened on April 6, 1969. After 37 years, the museum was permanently closed in December 2006. (DW.)

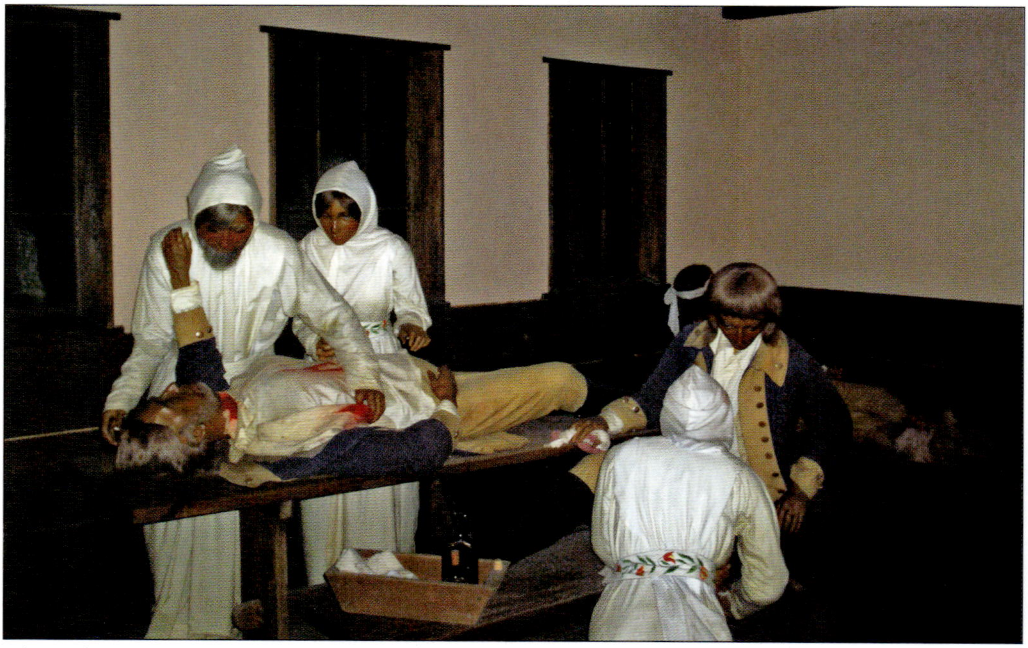

The Ephrata Cloisters were a German Seventh Day Baptist religious community led by Conrad Beissel. They lived in Ephrata, Pennsylvania, and were known for their musical ability. In 1777, during the American Revolution, members of the Ephrata Cloisters opened their doors to help wounded soldiers from the Battle of Brandywine. (AD.)

In 1861, the Lititz Pretzel House opened as the first commercial pretzel bakery in America. This scene shows handmade pretzels being baked in a brick oven. The same technique for making the pretzel knot is still in use today. Developed by a monk in the seventh century, the shape depicts a child's arms in prayer. At the time, Christians prayed by crossing their arms over their chest. (AD.)

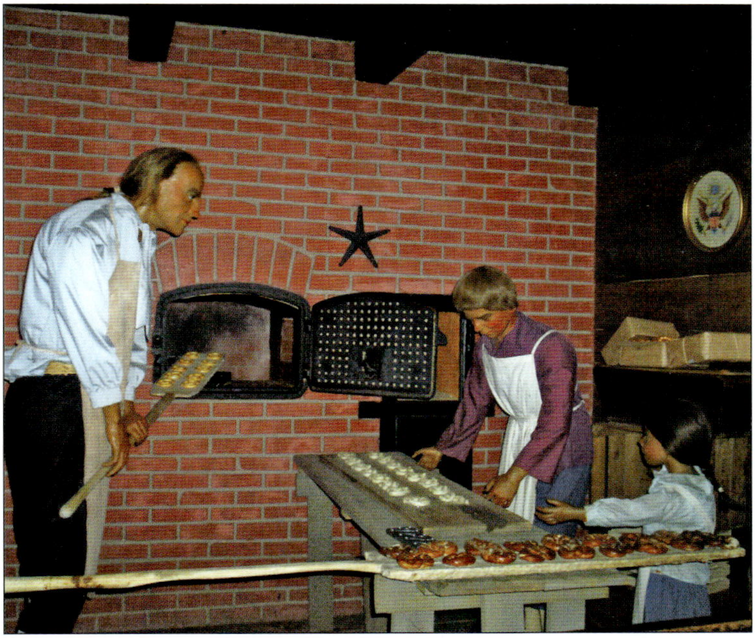

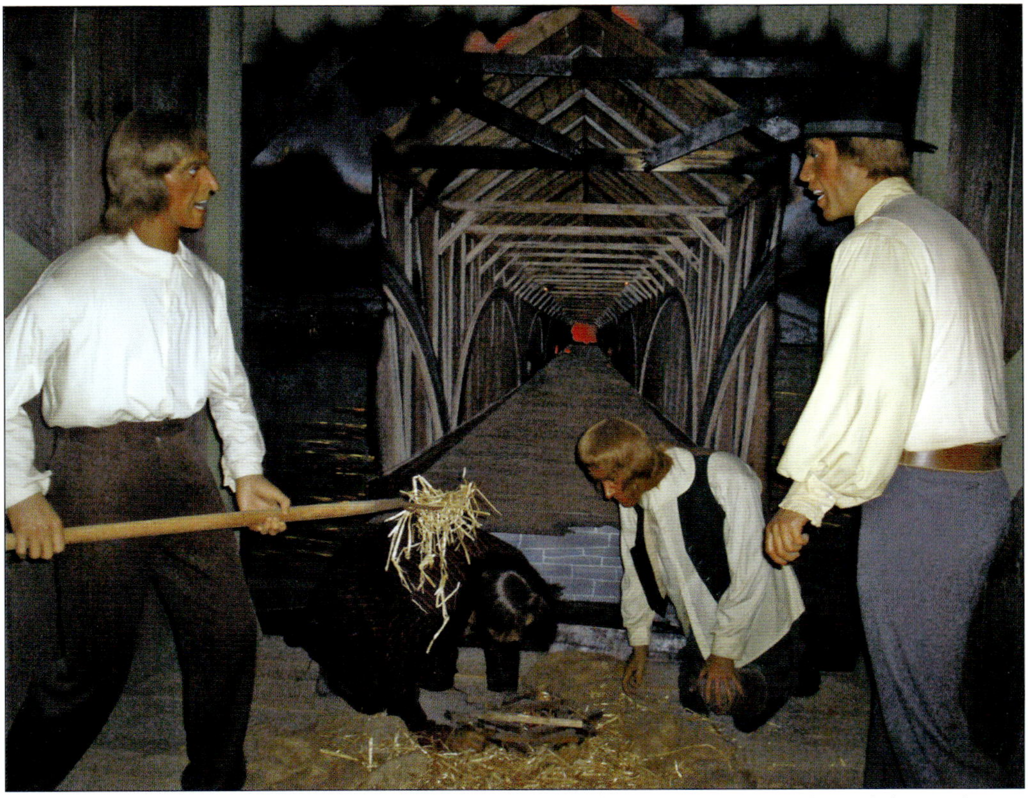

During the Civil War, Lancaster County was threatened by an invasion of Confederate forces. On June 28, 1863, a group of citizens from Columbia, Pennsylvania, burned the covered bridge that led into the area over the Susquehanna River, forcing Confederate troops to head west to Gettysburg. (AD.)

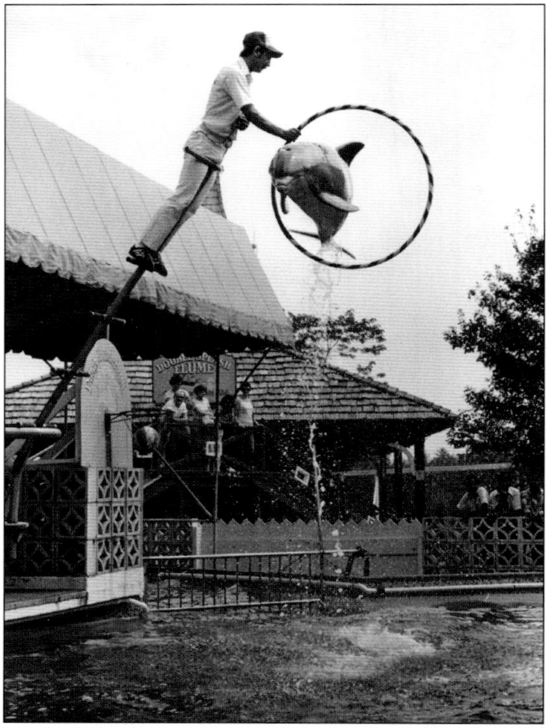

In the late 1960s, Dutch Wonderland expanded its entertainment to include a dolphin show. The show started out small. Originally, the dolphins swam in a portable pool surrounded by a wooden stage, and spectators would watch from an awning in front of the pool. The show ended up being extremely popular, and it was not long before it was expanded. The park constructed a nine-foot-deep concrete pool and a 600-seat stadium. Throughout the show, the dolphins would perform a variety of tricks, such as jumping through a hoop, waving, leaping 12 feet in the air, and even singing and dancing. After each trick, the trainers would reward the dolphins with a treat in the form of fish. The two resident dolphins were named Dutchie and Dutchess. Later, the show was expanded again, with the addition of sea lions. (Both, MC.)

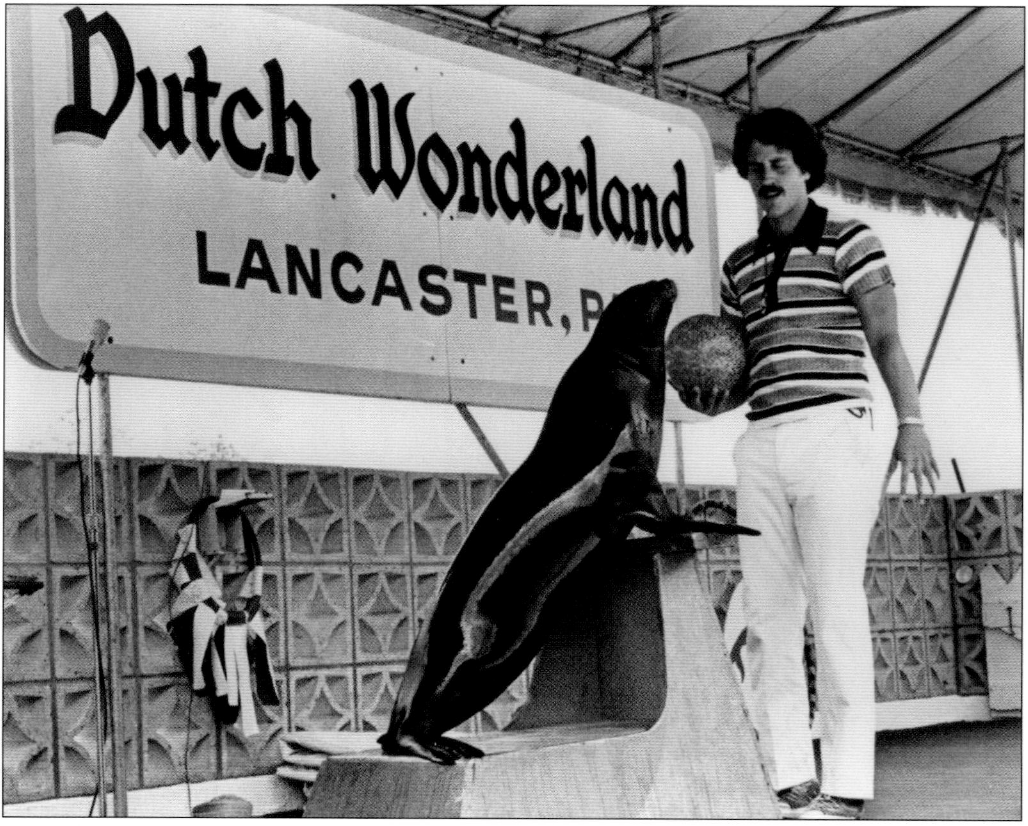

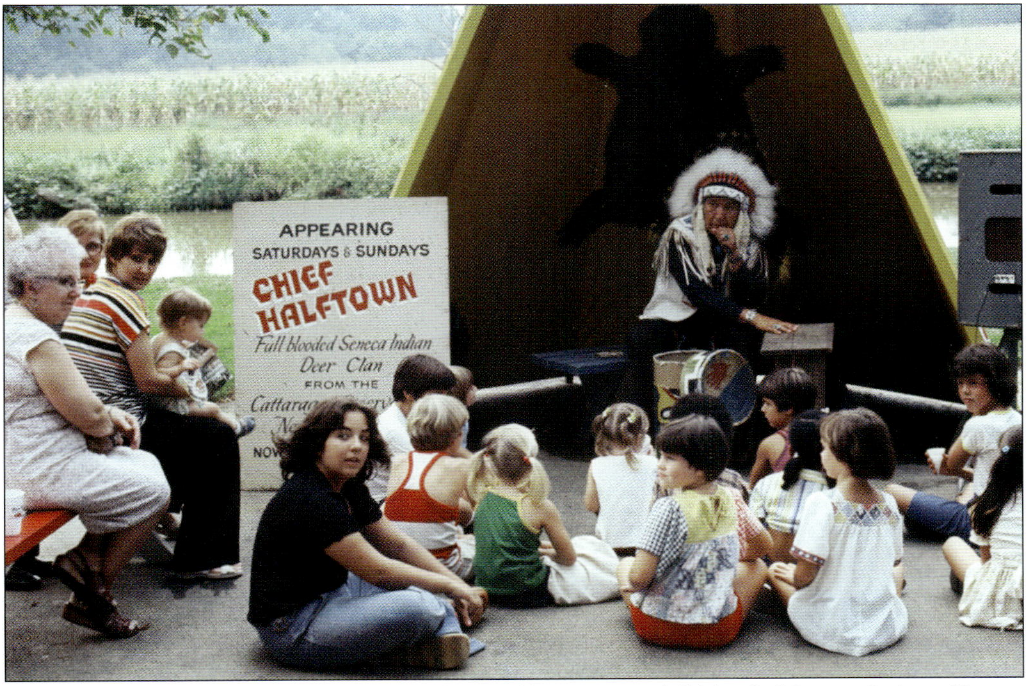

Traynor Ora Halftown, better known as Chief Halftown, was a full-blooded Seneca Indian. He was born on a Seneca reservation in Upstate New York in 1917. Chief Halftown was a popular children's television host in Philadelphia, Pennsylvania. His show aired on WPVI-TV from 1950 to 1999. The *Chief Halftown Show* was the longest-running children's television show in the Philadelphia area. Three generations of children watched his show, making him a well-known local celebrity. He came to the park almost every weekend from 1969 until 2001. He would sit on a wooden bench in the park's Indian Village, entertaining guests by telling stories and educating them about American Indian culture. With over three decades of appearances, he became a park icon. (Both, DW.)

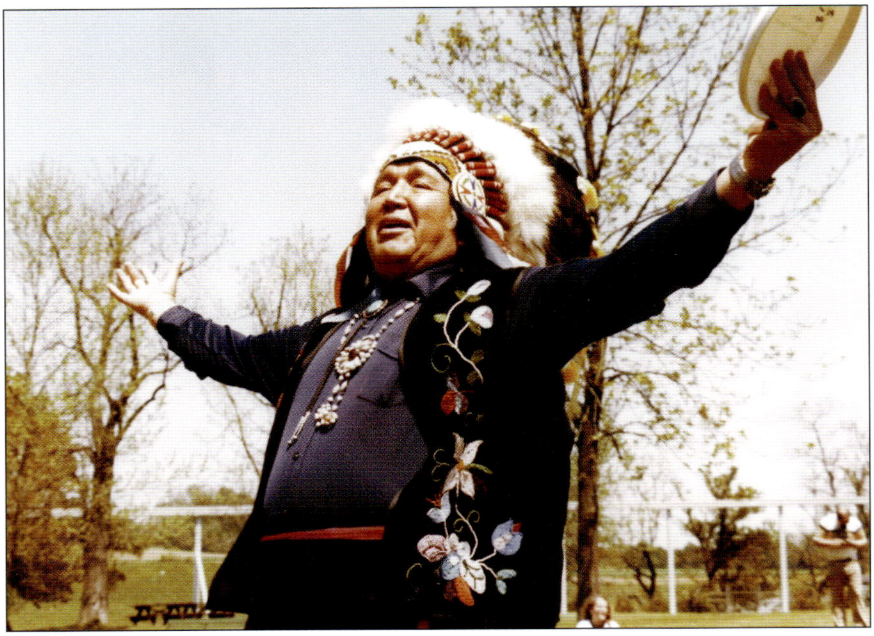

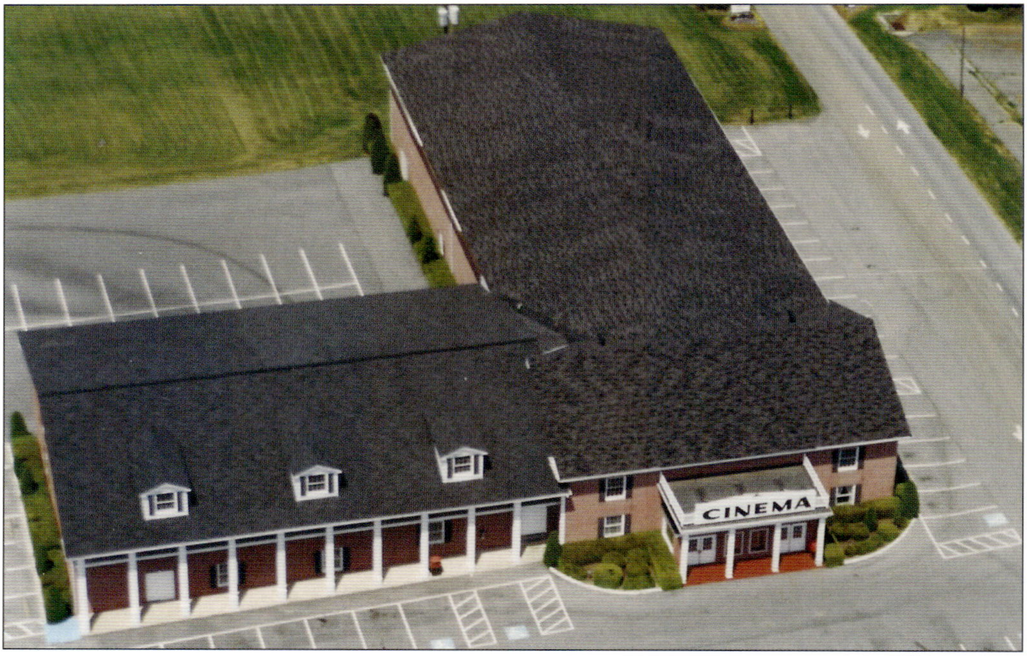

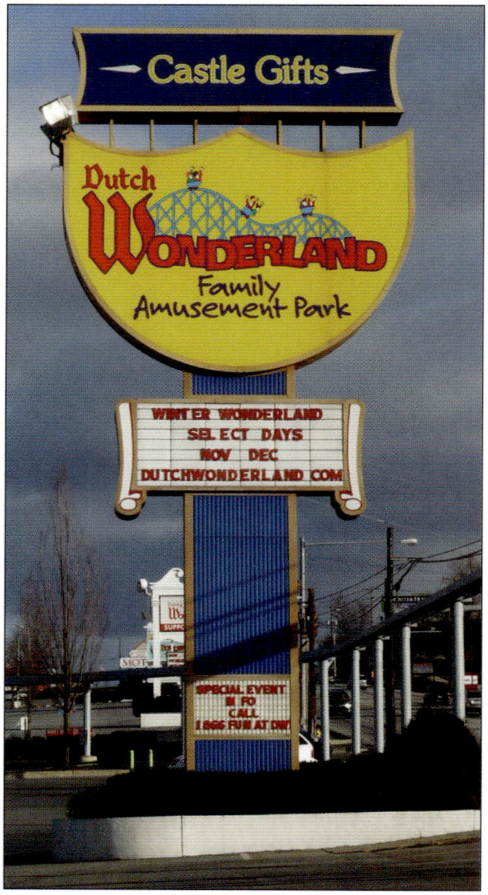

The Wonderland Cinema officially opened with one theater around 1970. *Popi* was one of the first movies to premiere. Due to its popularity, the building doubled in size with the addition of a second theater in 1971. This theater was a bit bigger and ran parallel to the highway. In 1977, the original theater was twinned, meaning it was divided to create two theaters, each with 280 seats. In 1986, the second theater was also twinned to hold 390 and 410 viewers, respectively. The cinema could now show four movies at once. The Clark family owned the theater, which was run by Budco Theaters. In early 1987, AMC acquired Budco Theaters and would continue to run the cinema until it closed on September 6, 2001. *Pearl Harbor* and *Rush Hour 2* were among the last movies to ever play at the theater. The theaters were used as storage for the park from 2002 to 2014, then were demolished in March 2015. (DW.)

Each attraction on the park's property had a large sign visible from Route 30. Over the years, the position of the Dutch Wonderland sign and the monorail track has changed. As shown in the photograph at left, the sign was updated in the 1990s to include the park's new logo. (AD.)

Two

The Dream Continues 1970–1989

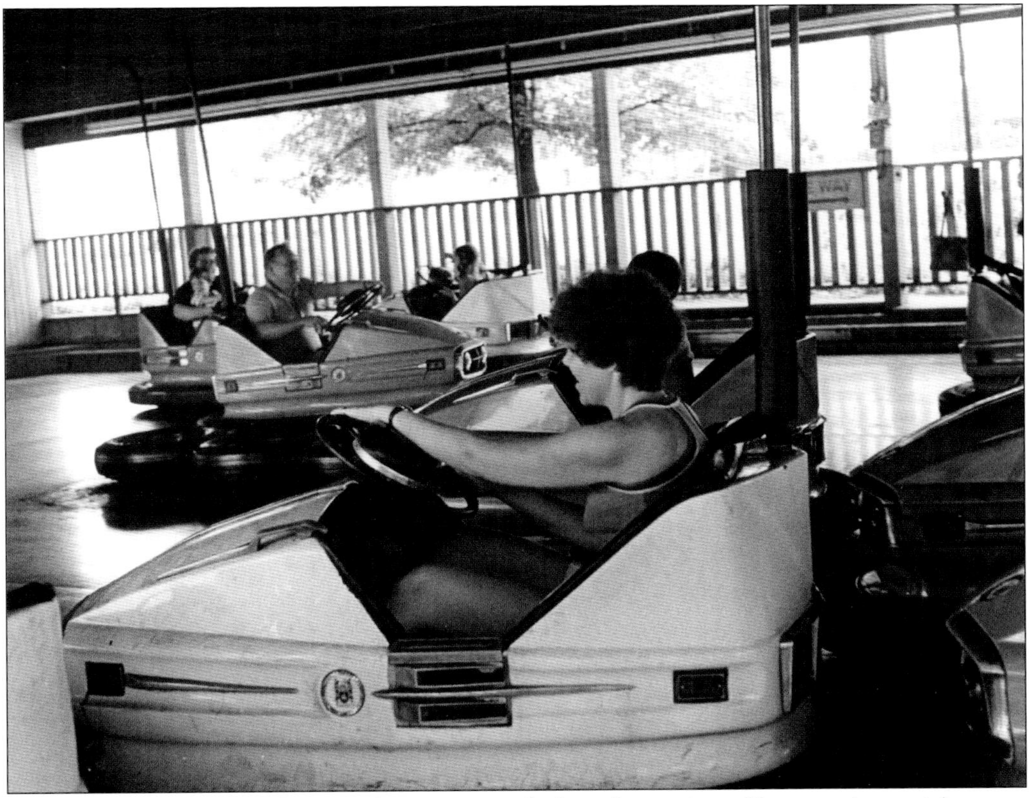

The 1970s started off with a new bumper car ride from Lusse Auto Skooter, along with a new structure to house it. Each bumper car could hold up to two riders. (MC.)

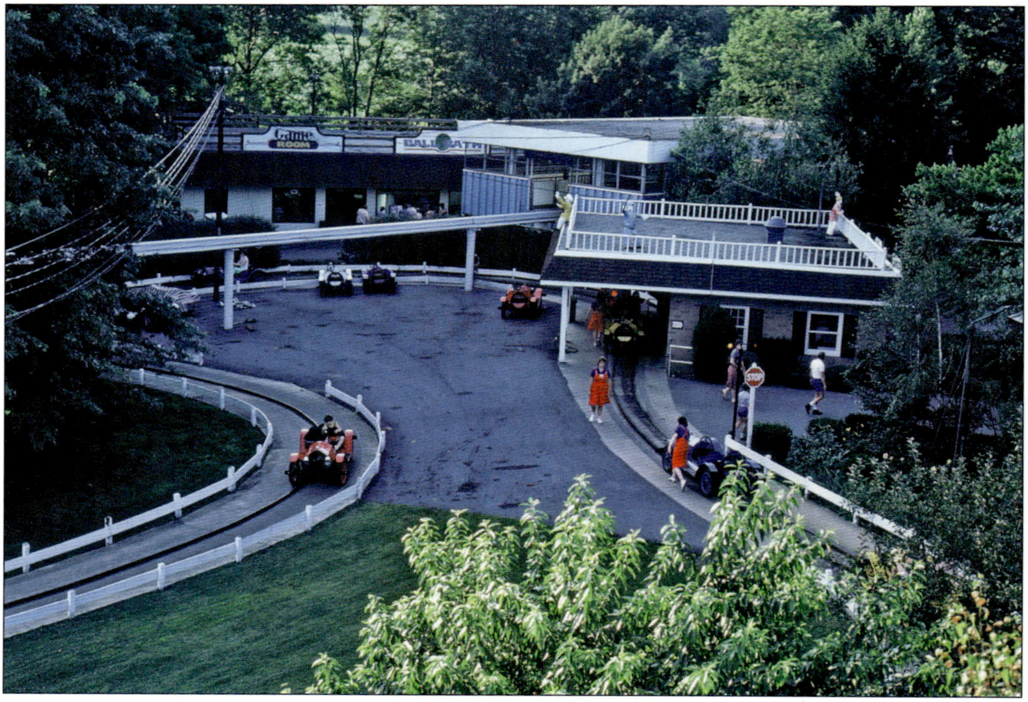

In 1972, the original 1910 Buick-style cars of the Turnpike ride were replaced with new models based on the 1916 Mercer. With the new vehicles, manufactured by Arrow Development, came a center guideline to keep drivers from bumping the guardrails. Below, the park's original bear mascot joins a guest for a ride on one of the new Turnpike cars. (Both, DW.)

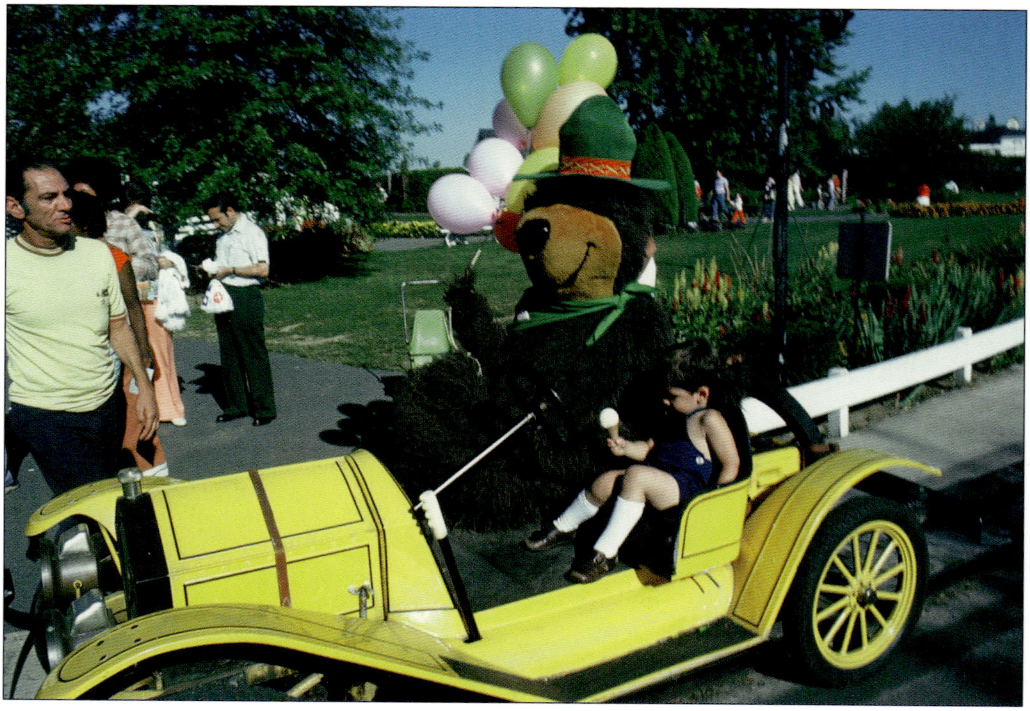

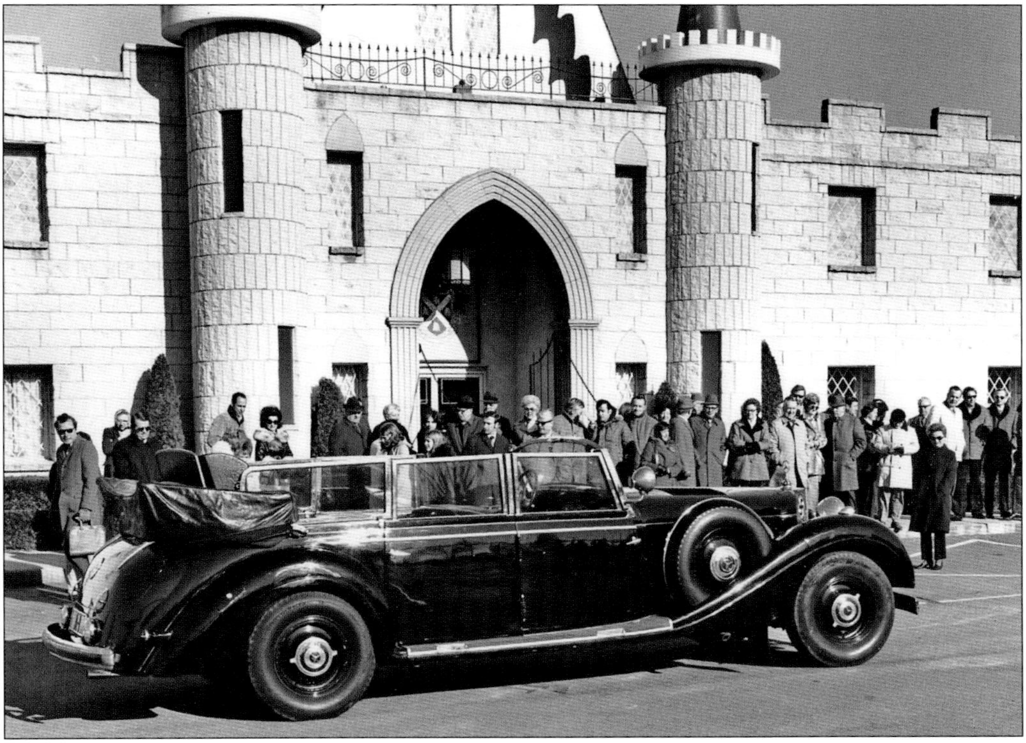

In addition to running a successful amusement park, Earl Clark was an avid car collector. Every fall, Clark would hold car auctions in Dutch Wonderland's parking lot. In 1973, he bought Adolf Hitler's 1940–1941 Mercedes-Benz 770K parade car for $153,000 from an auction in Scottsdale, Arizona. At the time, it was the most money ever paid for a car at auction. A building (now a snack stand) was constructed beside the castle where the car could be viewed for 50¢. The car, which took almost a year to manufacture, included bulletproof glass and a raised floorboard designed to make Hitler appear taller. It was resold nine months later for $176,000 at Dutch Wonderland's car auction. Below, members of the Clark family pose with a Duesenberg that was also owned by Earl Clark. (Both, MC.)

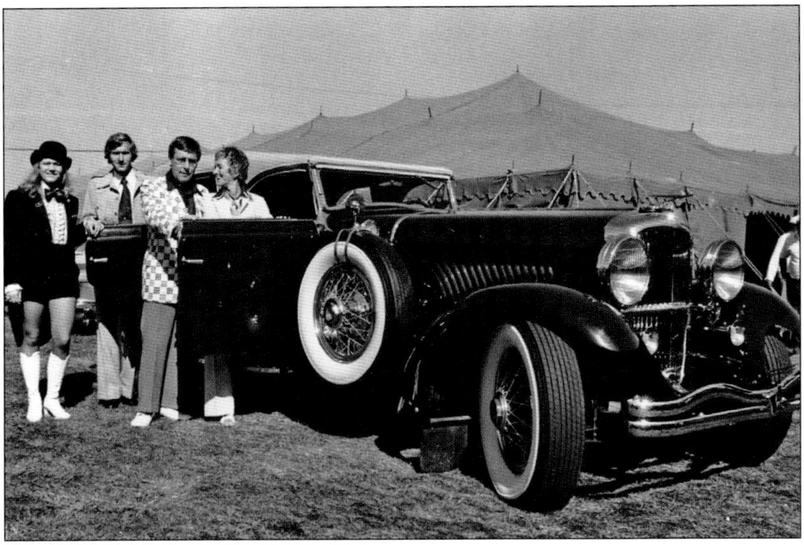

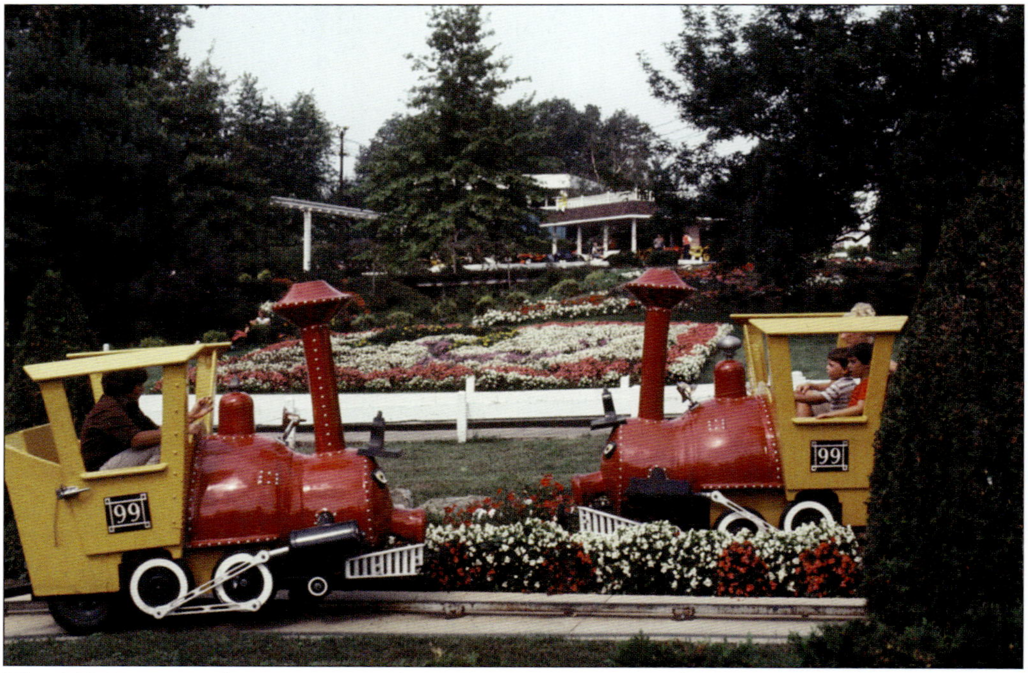

The Old 99 train ride was integrated in a large area between the Wonderland Special and the Turnpike in 1974. Each train engine was painted either red or black and had a cartoonlike face. Although riders could not steer the trains as they whipped around the track, they enjoyed ringing the bell that was hooked up to each car. There were also a few surprises along the route, such as a cow that jumped out of the bushes. The Old 99 was produced by Chance Rides, which discontinued the attraction not long after it was installed at Dutch Wonderland. (Both, DW.)

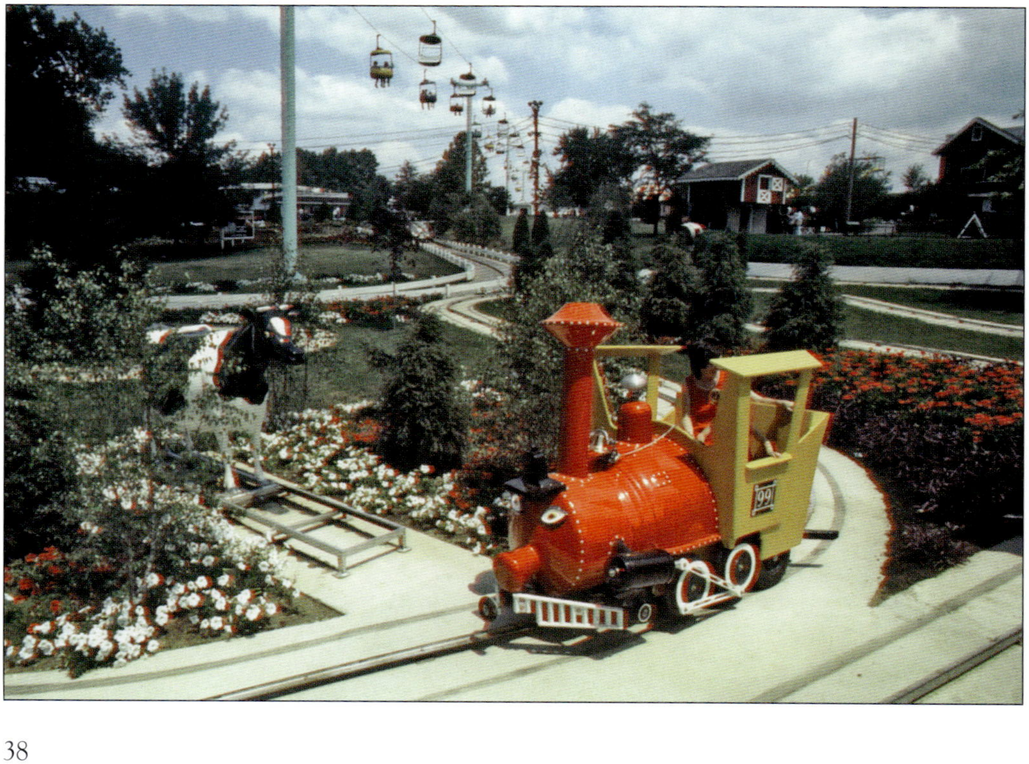

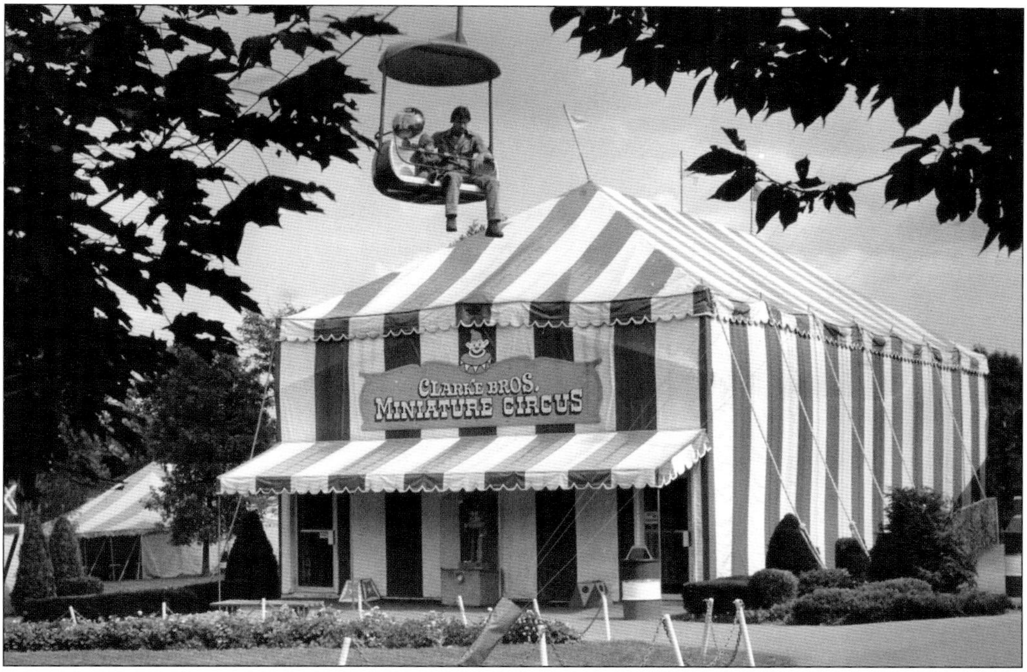

The Clarke Brothers Miniature Circus opened in 1975. Inside the huge red-and-white tent were over 5,000 hand-carved circus figures displayed on a 12-foot-by-48-foot platform. Robert Clarke, an Arizona native who traveled with the circus as a child, spent more than 10 years in the 1920s and 1930s carving and painting the set, including animals, clowns, and sideshow performers. An incredible amount of detail went into each individual piece, some of which were mechanical. Every scene was based on real circus attractions from that time period. (Both, DW.)

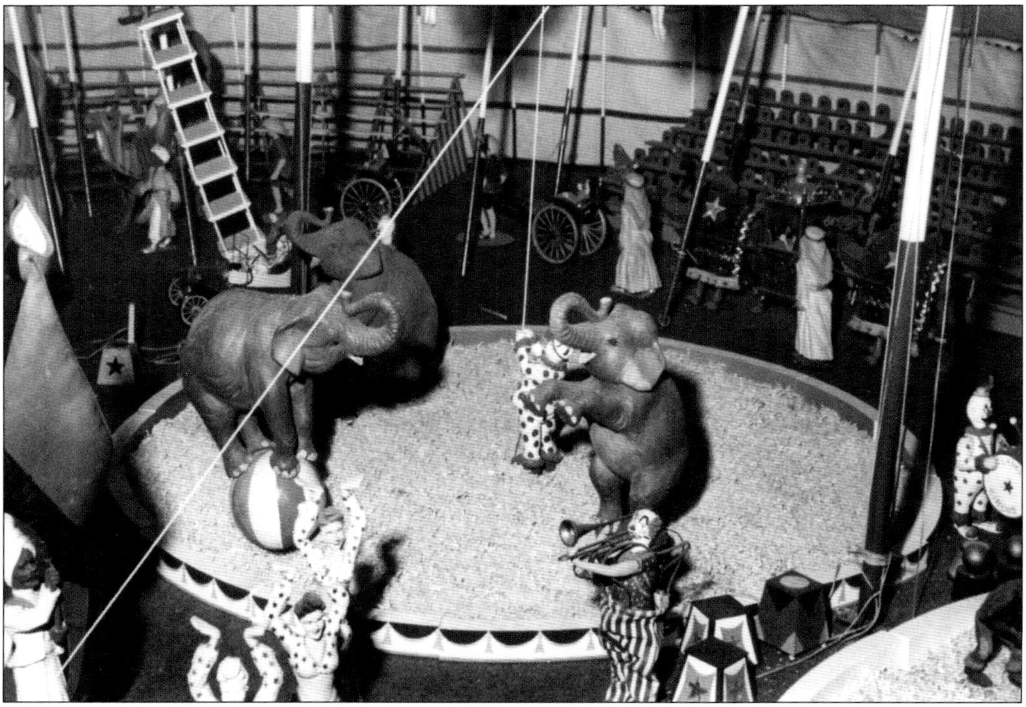

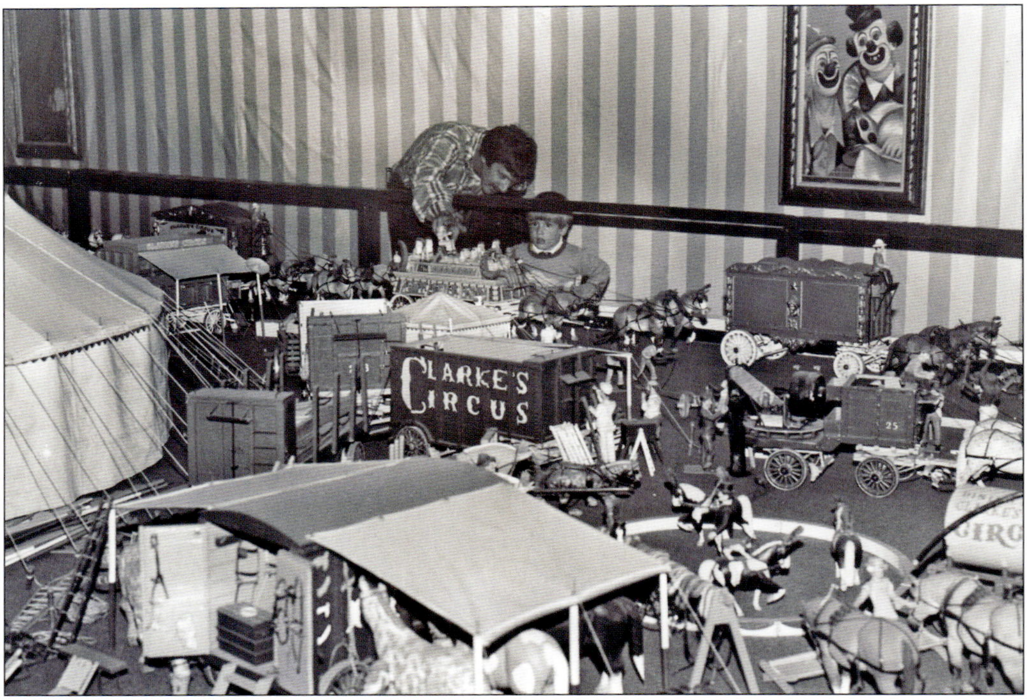

When Robert Clarke visited the park in 1973, he realized that the miniature circus, which was on display in Phoenix at the time, was better suited to Dutch Wonderland. He offered to sell his creation to the park, so Murl Clark traveled to Arizona to see it. He purchased the circus and had it shipped to Dutch Wonderland, where it was set up two years later. (DW.)

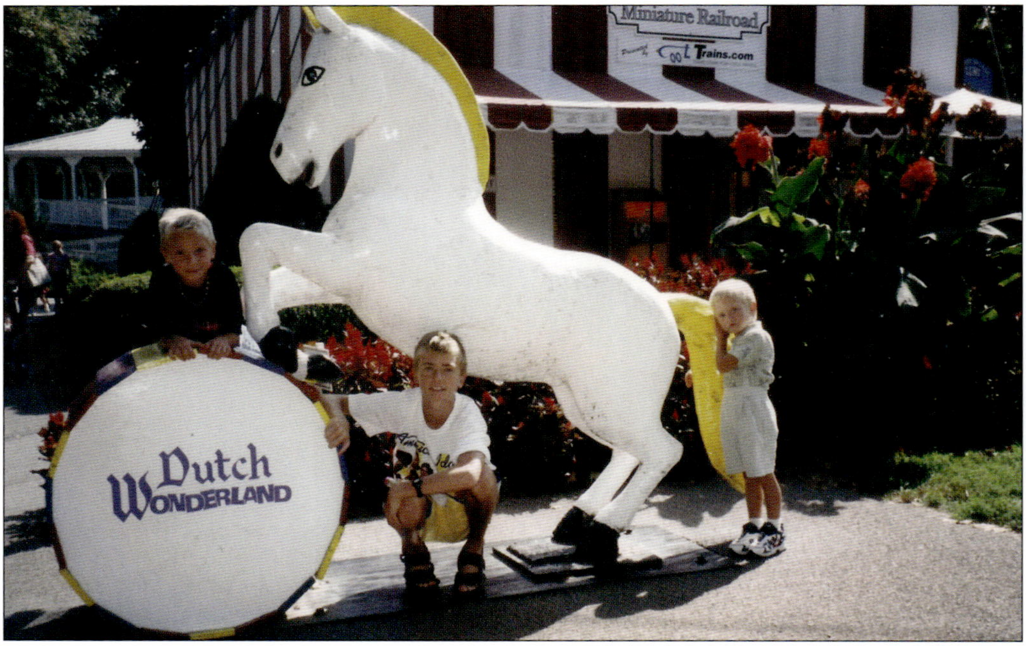

The iconic Dutch Wonderland circus horse has been a fixture at the park since 1963. It stood in front of the circus tent for many years before being moved to the island in the early 2000s. The horse was removed from the park in 2012 to make room for Exploration Island in 2014. (AD.)

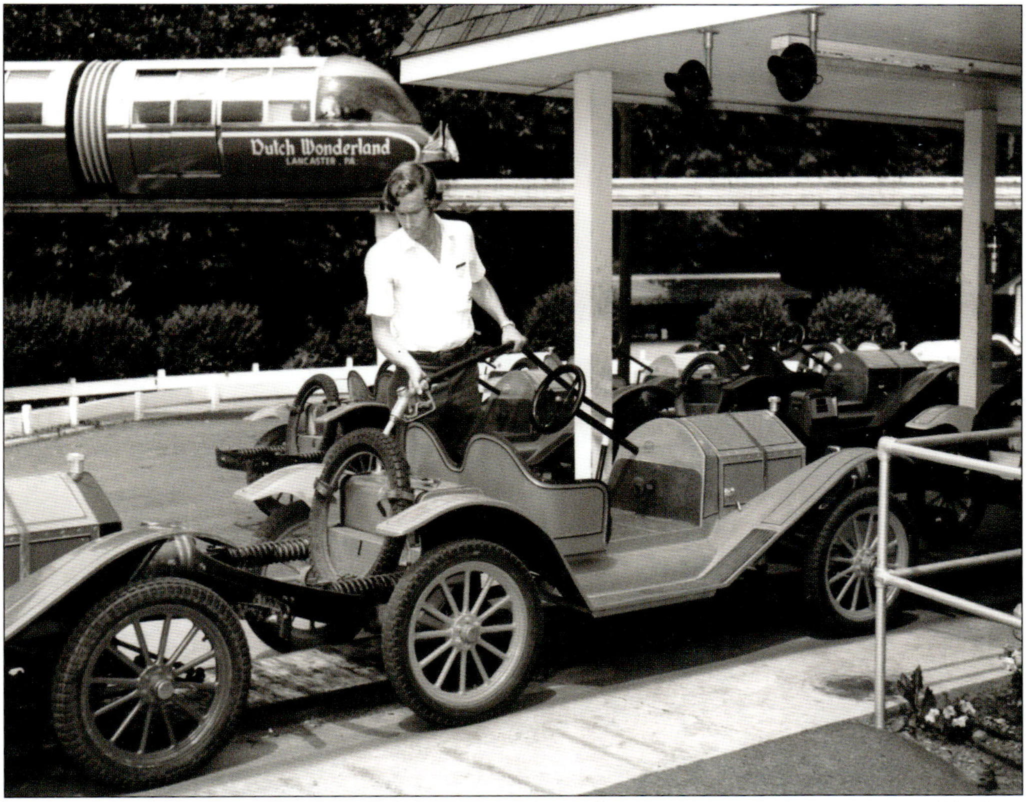

Earl Clark's oldest son, Murl, played a large role in the park's operation. Murl was 11 years old when Dutch Wonderland opened. He started out by emptying trash cans and cleaning restrooms. Here, he is shown pumping gas for the Turnpike cars. Murl worked his way through the park, quickly moving into the position of general manager to oversee the entire complex. (MC.)

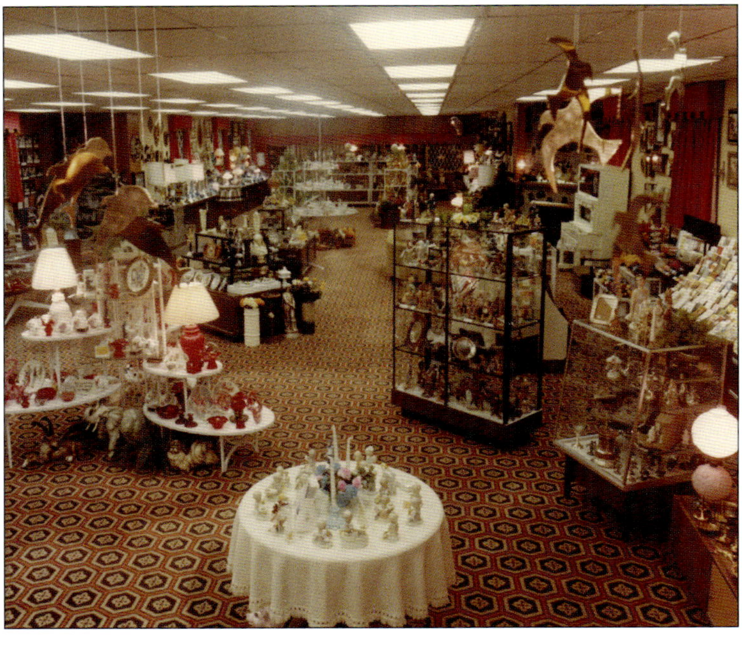

Molly Clark ordered and managed all the items for the Castle Gift Shop, which featured not only Dutch Wonderland souvenirs but also unique items from all over the world. The Clarks' youngest son, Brad, would eventually help his mother with managing the gift shop. (DW.)

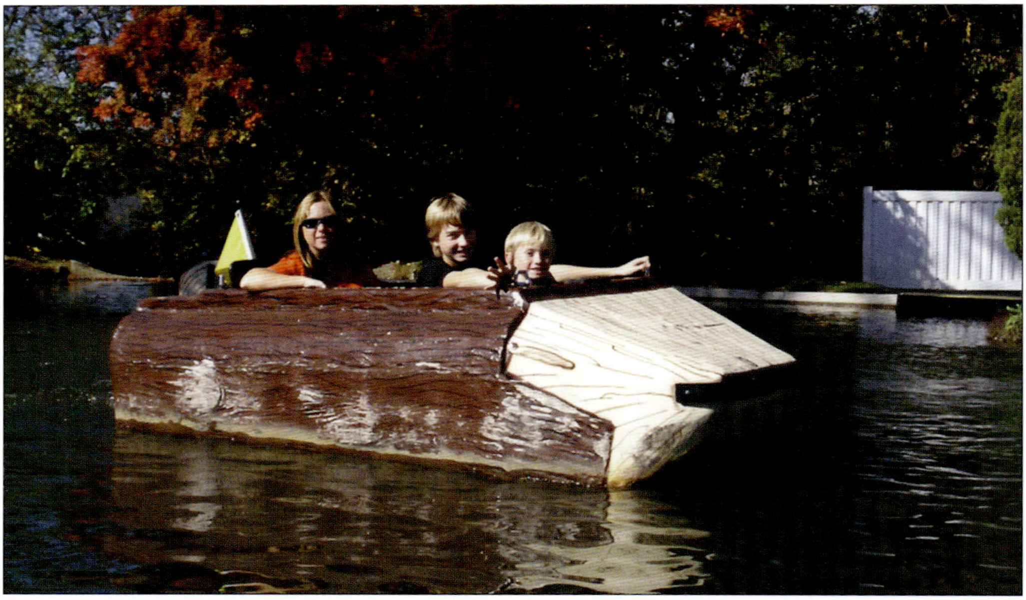

In 1975, the swan boats were removed and replaced with log boats manufactured by International Amusement Devices. Still enjoyed at the park today, the log boats run on a track underneath the water in an attraction known as Dragon's Lair. (AD.)

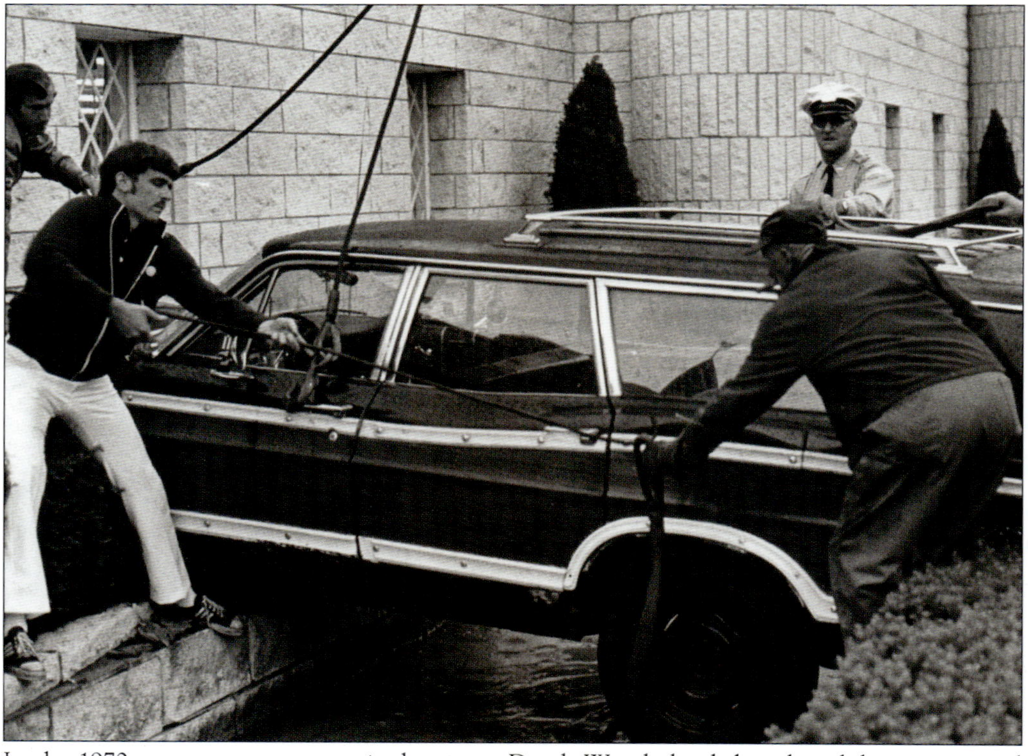

In the 1970s, someone was so excited to go to Dutch Wonderland that they did not stop until they hit the park, literally. Here, workers carefully remove the car from the castle moat. General manager Murl Clark (back left) assists his crew, along with the help of longtime park security guard Harold Nonnenmocher (back right). (DW.)

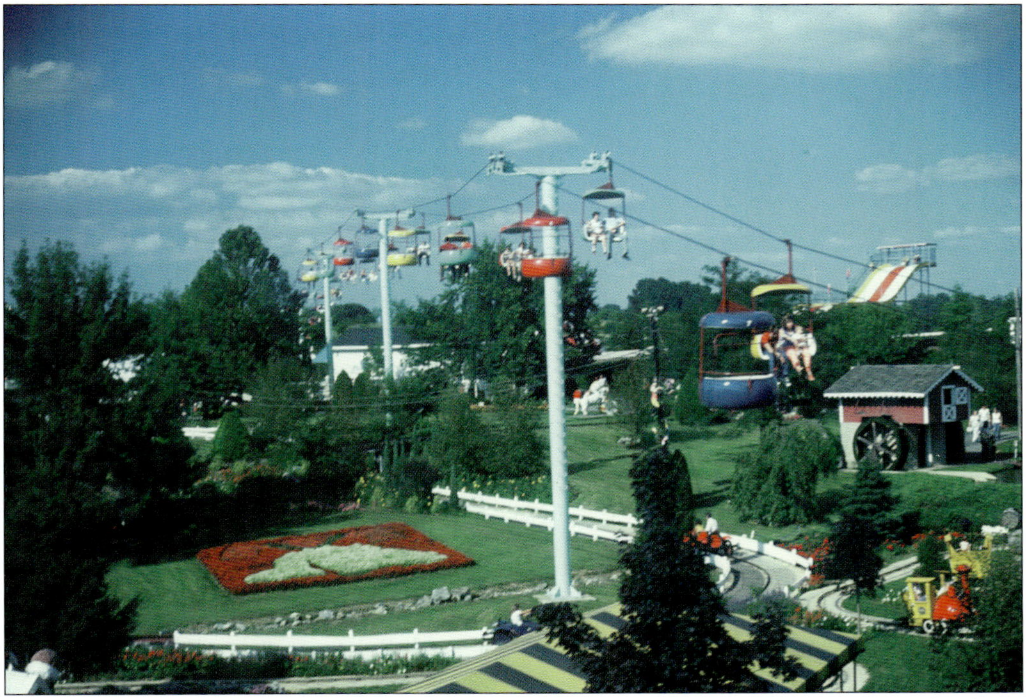

Dutch Wonderland celebrated America's bicentennial in 1976 by planting flowers in the shape of the Liberty Bell. The floral display was located within the Turnpike ride, where it could be seen from the Sky Ride. (DW.)

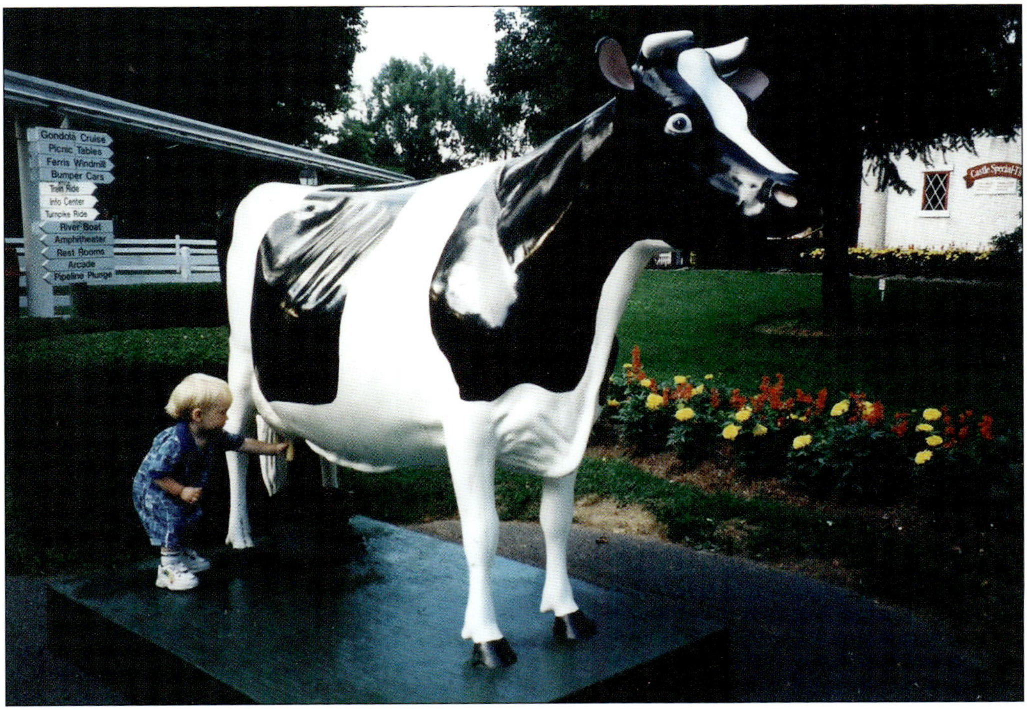

Bossy the Cow continued to be a park favorite. Murl Clark had the cow completely rebuilt in order to preserve it for many more years. (AD.)

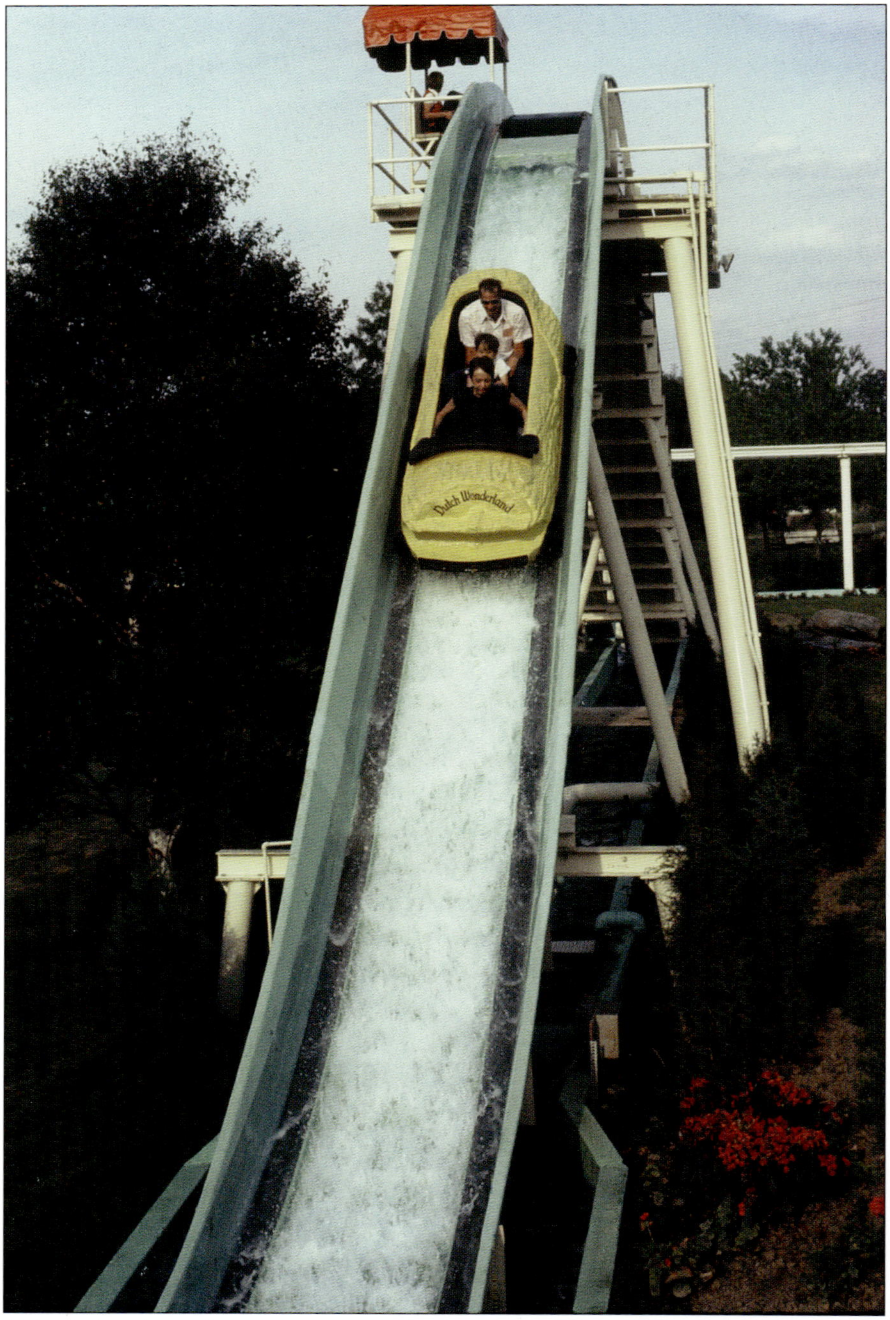

Dutch Wonderland sought to incorporate a water ride that would cool off riders during the hottest days of the year. In 1976, the leading manufacturer of log flumes, Arrow Development, was approached to help build the perfect ride. Murl and Earl Clark attended Great Adventure in Jackson, New Jersey, to research the log flumes there. The layout was finalized in December 1976. Unlike other log flumes with an elevated trough that winds through the treetops, such as Great Adventure's Saw Mill Log Flume and Hydro Flume, Dutch Wonderland's Double Splash Flume remains at ground level except when climbing its two hills. The ride that the Clarks designed was a perfect fit for Dutch Wonderland. (DW.)

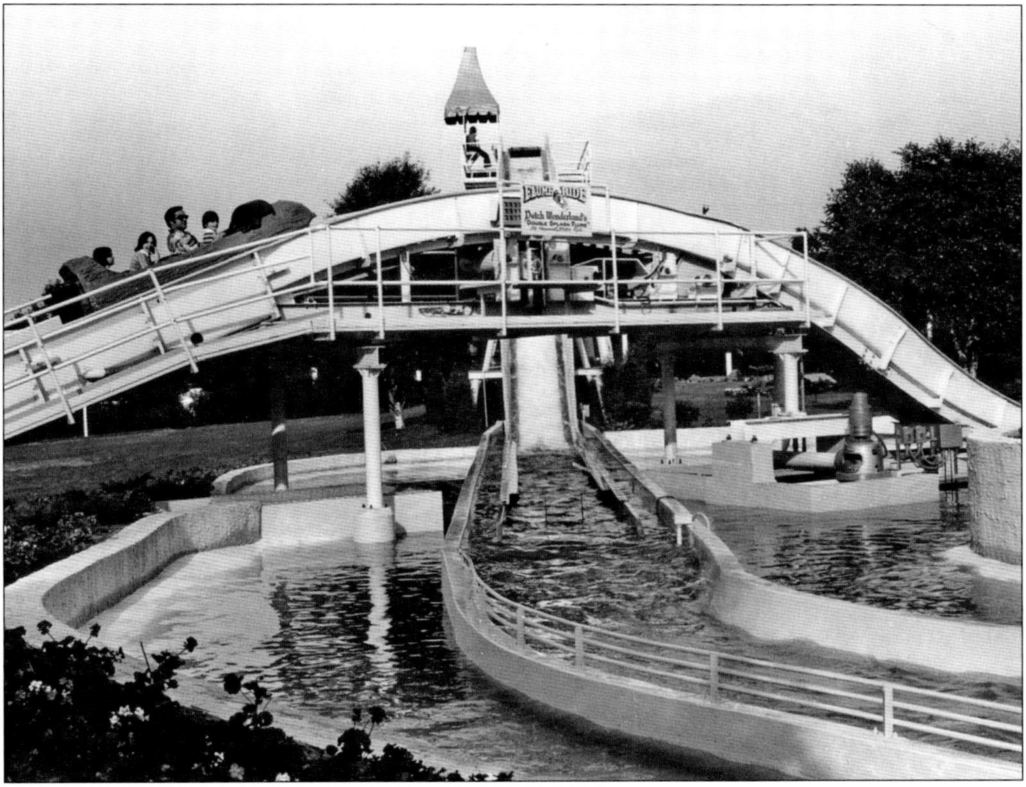

Dutch Wonderland's log flume opened to the public on May 28, 1977. The 120,000-gallon Double Splash Flume is 807 feet long with two hills. The first hill has a 12-foot drop; the second hill has a 25-foot drop. Originally, the log boats were multicolored; now they are painted brown to look like an actual log. (DW.)

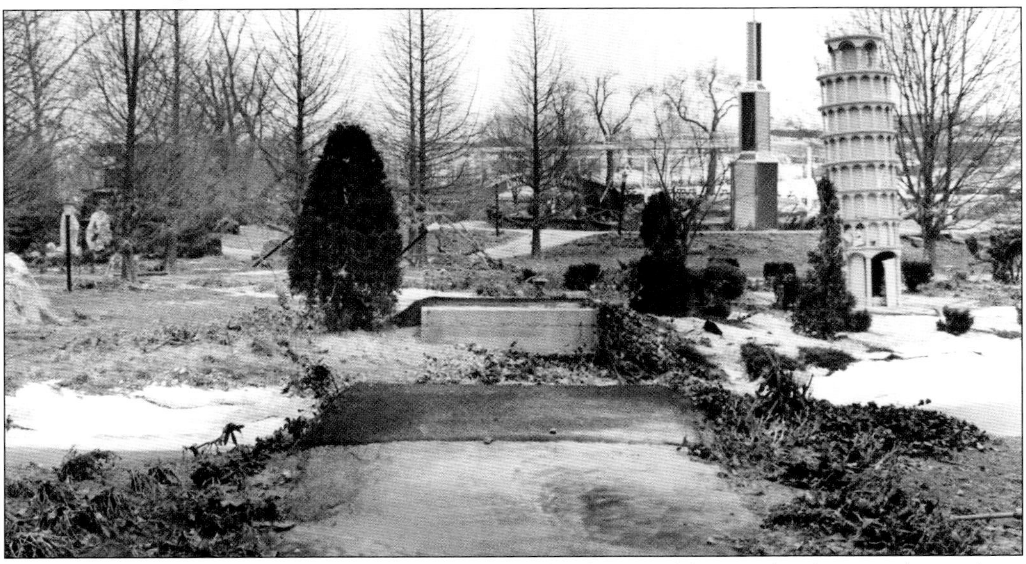
The park's location along a stream often causes flooding problems. The damage shown here occurred on January 23, 1978, as a result of heavy rain and melting snow. The International Botanical Gardens and the Indian Village got hit the hardest by the rising waters. (DW.)

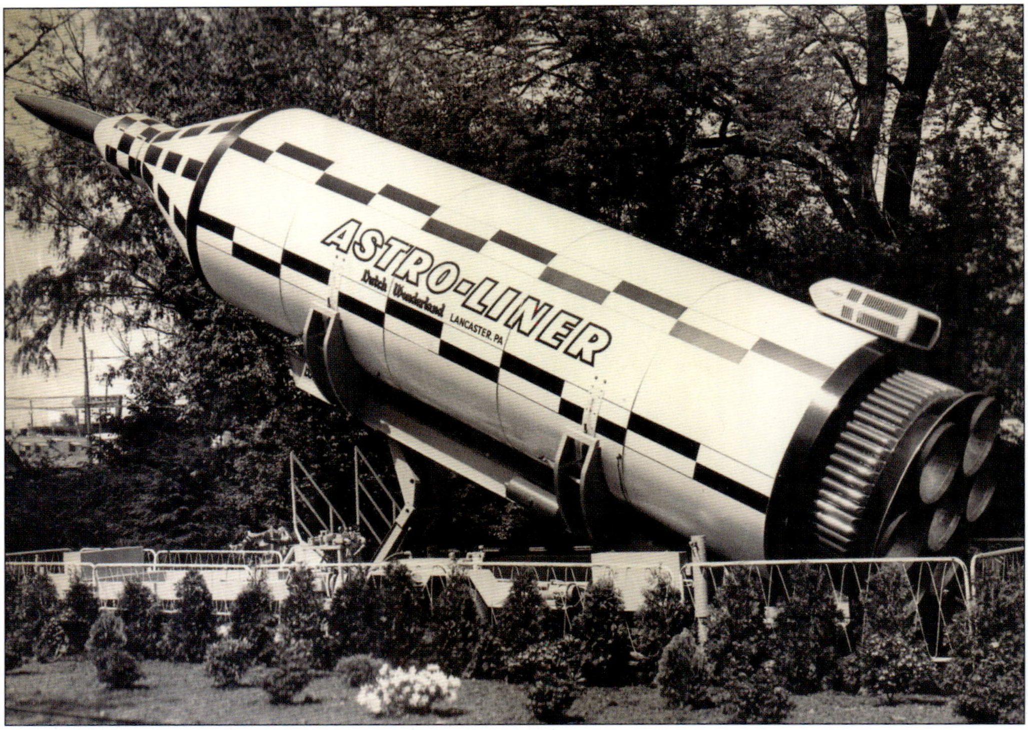

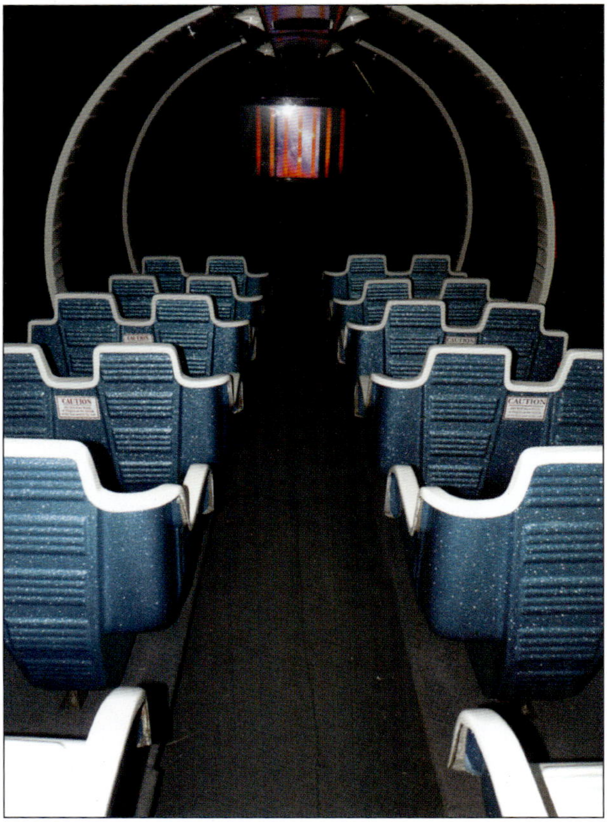

The space-themed Astro-Liner landed in Dutch Wonderland in 1978. Wisdom Rides created the first simulator ride made specifically for amusement parks, and Dutch Wonderland was first in line to buy the new state-of-the-art attraction. Once inside the 39-foot-long, 40-passenger rocket ship simulator, a space adventure film is shown. The rocket then rises to a 60-degree angle and tilts back and forth based on the action in the movie. The ride operator controls the movement with a joystick in the rear cockpit. Shot with 35-millimeter film, the movie was played on a rear-projection screen. Many years later, the projection screen was replaced with a slightly smaller monitor. The movie was digitized for compatibility with a DVD player connected to the new monitor. (Above, DW; left, AD.)

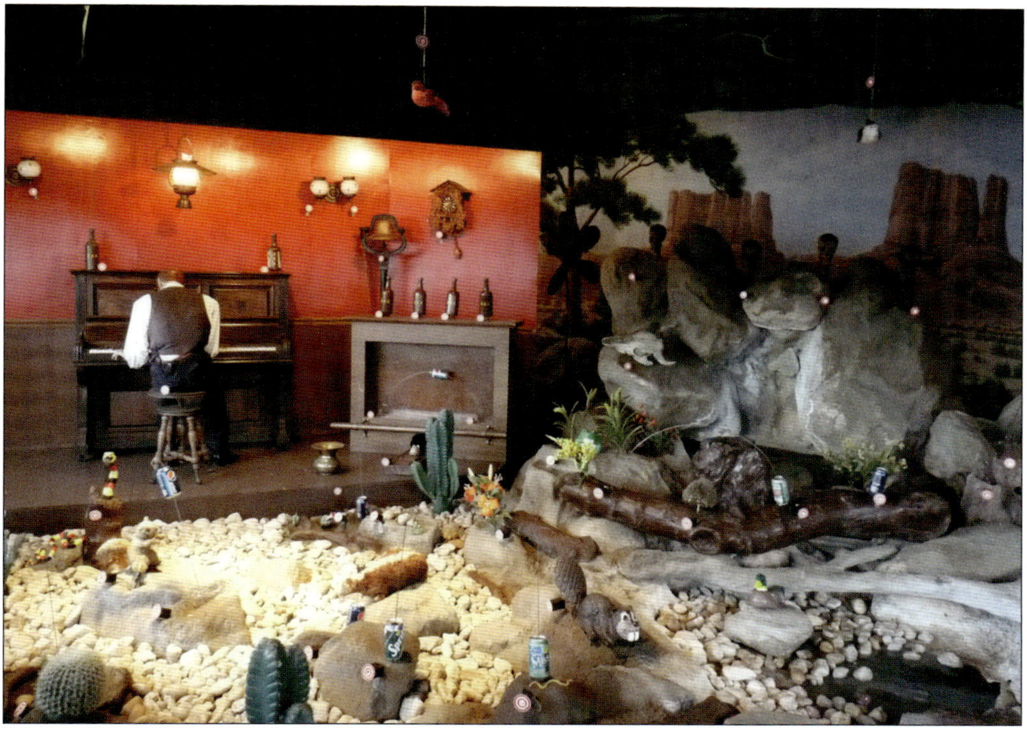

The Phoenix Bonanza Shooting Gallery was established in 1978. The shooting gallery was located in a new Western-themed building near the Turnpike entrance. Guests would shoot at various objects using coin-operated guns. If they hit a target, the object nearby would move. Most of the shooting gallery consisted of a desert landscape, as well as a barroom complete with a piano player. The fiberglass cowboy at right stood next to the building. In 2010, half of the shooting gallery was removed to make room for a gift shop. (Both, AD.)

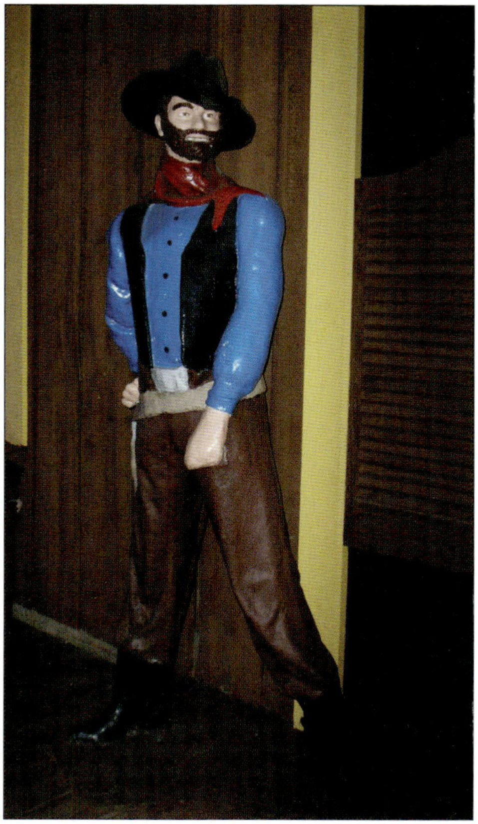

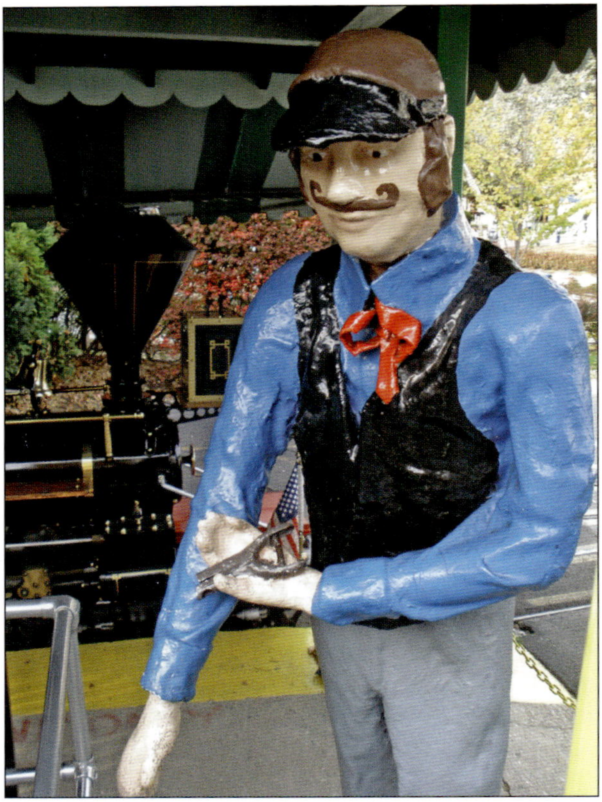

Throughout Dutch Wonderland's history, there have been over 50 fiberglass figures, most made specifically for the park by local artist Rod Shutt or artist Irv Lichty. The figures were modeled using a chicken wire frame, then coated with fiberglass and painted. The cowboy on the previous page even had real blue jeans and boots applied to its frame. Among the figures, many of which are now gone, were storybook characters, such as Little Miss Muffet; cartoon characters, including Yogi Bear and Popeye; and animals, like the llama seen below. At left is a figure that was referred to as the Wonderland Special ticket taker. Below, the girl holding the umbrella used to stand in a fountain near the park entrance; water would run off her umbrella and into the fountain. (Both, AD.)

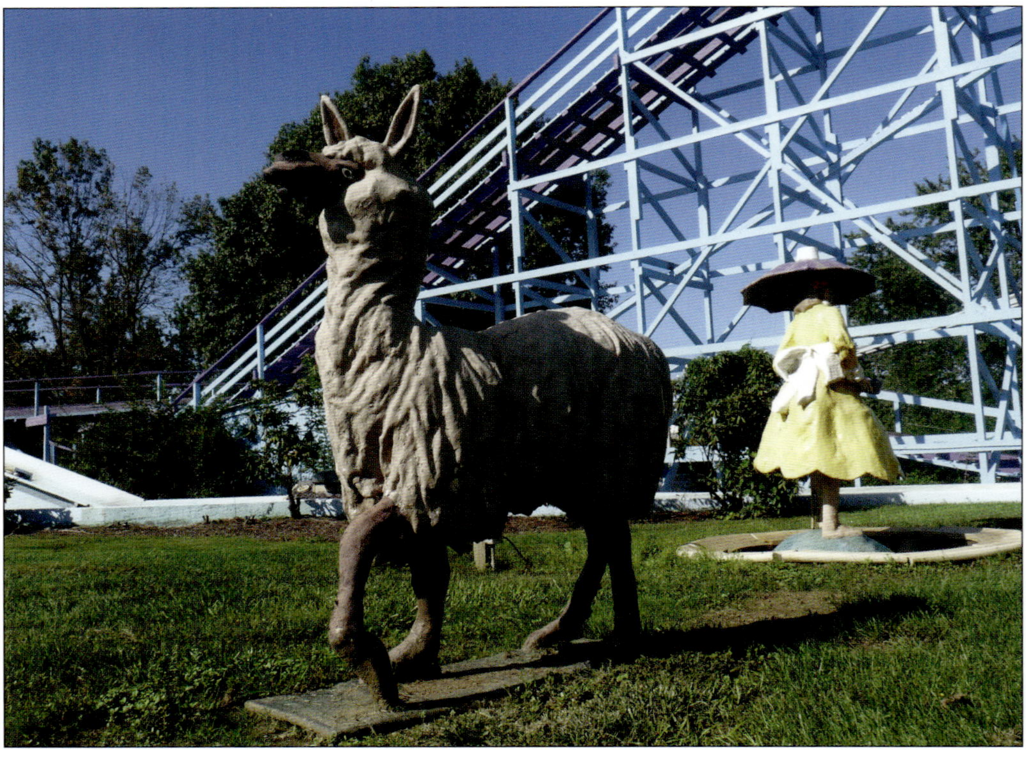

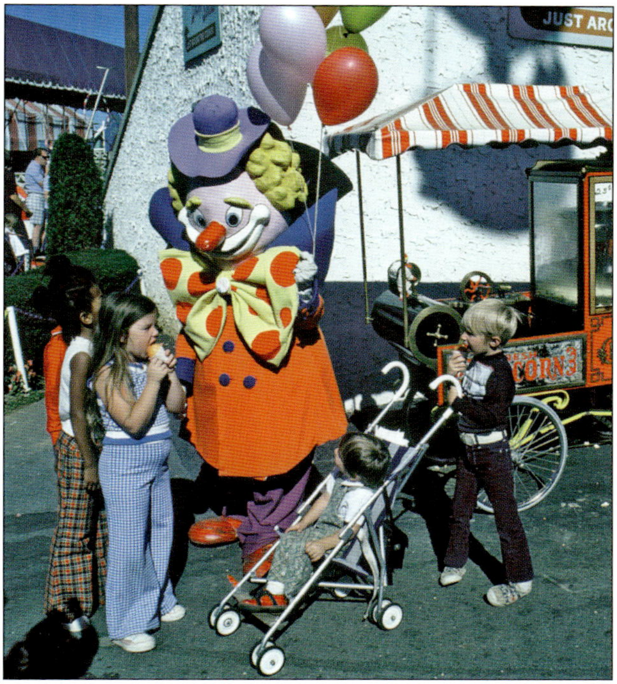

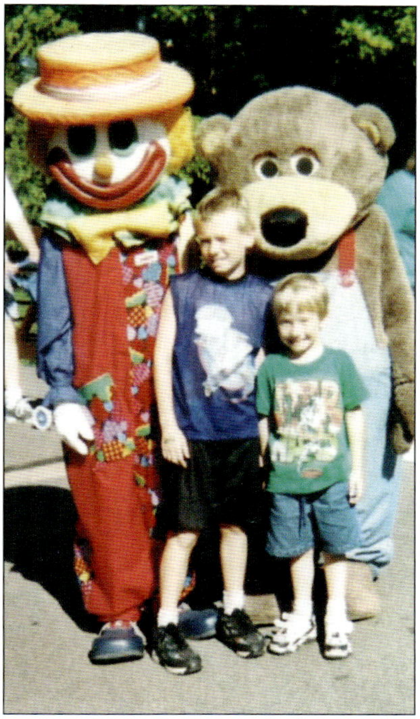

The park has outfitted a variety of costumed characters throughout the years. Above, at left, Sparky the Clown greets park visitors before one of the dolphin shows in 1978. Smiles the Clown and Bubba Bear are also shown above, at right. Below, Hinkle the Chicken and Papa Bear take a ride on the Double Splash Flume. (Above left, DW; above right, AD; below, DW.)

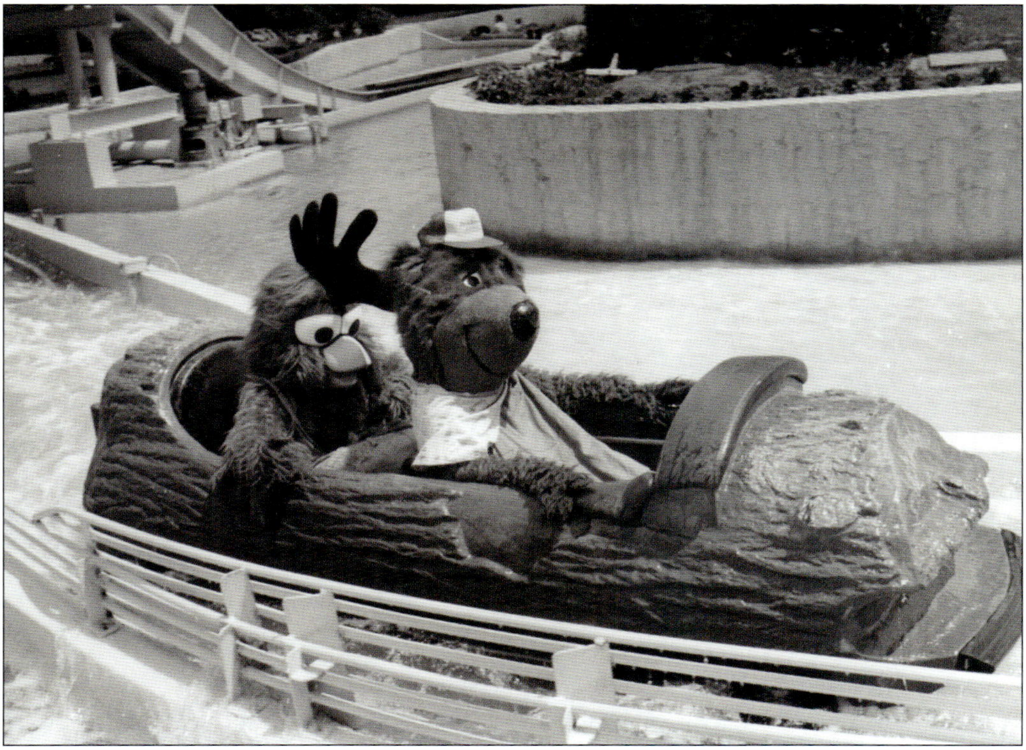

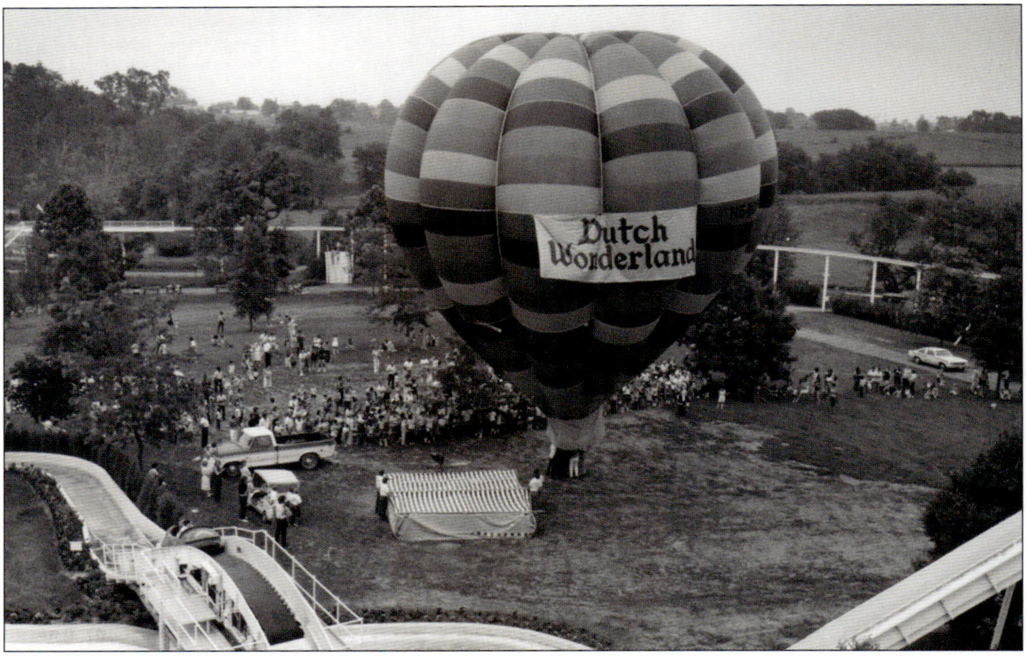

Balloon Blast Days was an annual tradition at Dutch Wonderland when thousands of helium balloons would be released, many of them with prizes inside. In this image, expert balloonist Richard Hess is about to launch a hot air balloon high in the sky above Dutch Wonderland to round out the event in 1979. (DW.)

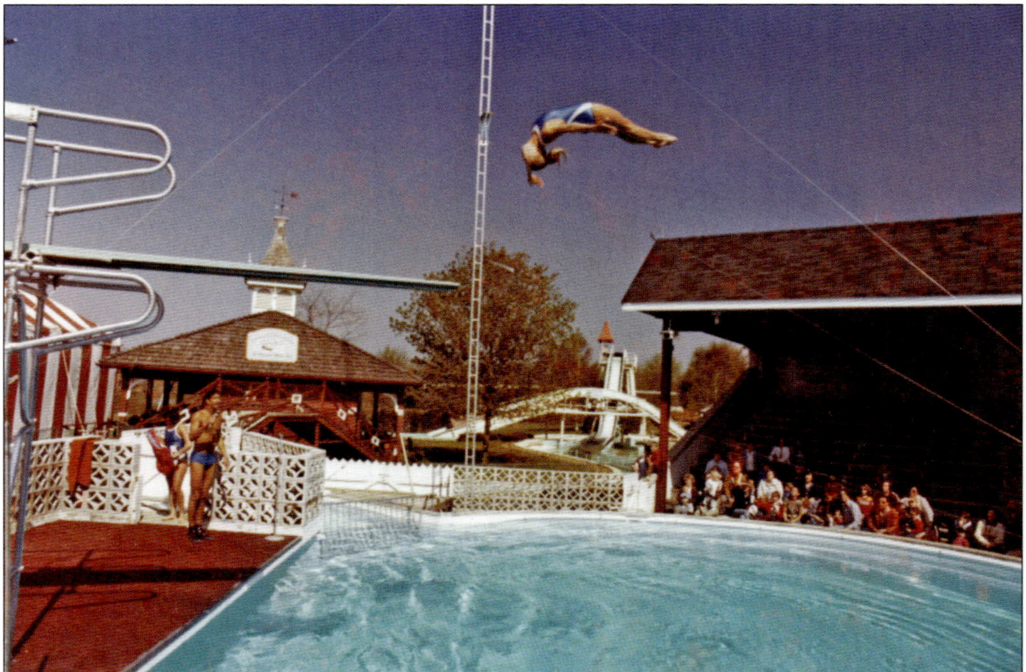

In 1981, the dolphin and sea lion show was replaced with "The Great American High Diving Show." During its inaugural year, the show featured six champion divers. Throughout the show, the divers performed comedic and professional dives into a nine-foot-deep pool. (DW.)

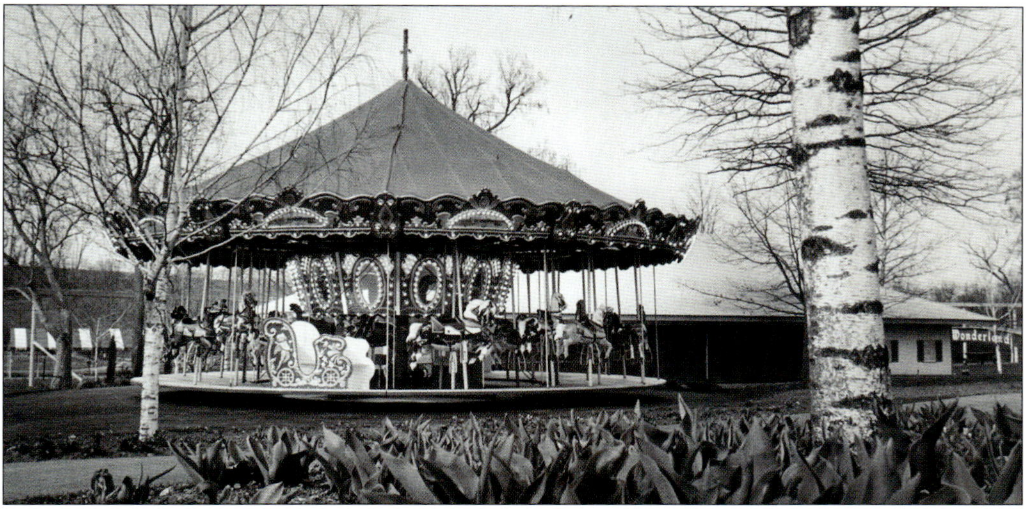

Before 1981, Dutch Wonderland did not have a carousel at the park. According to Murl Clark, "My father was not fond of circular rides because they reminded him of carnivals. After the carousel was installed and he saw our guests enjoying it, he admitted to me that he was wrong." (DW.)

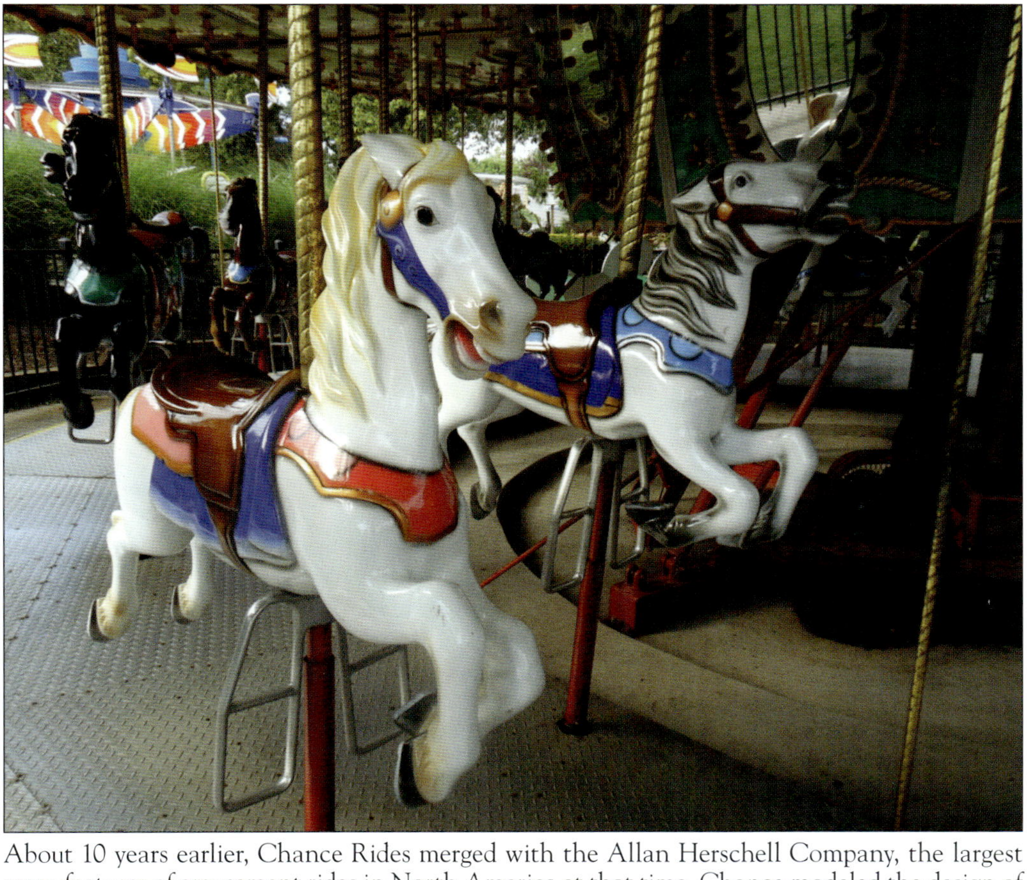

About 10 years earlier, Chance Rides merged with the Allan Herschell Company, the largest manufacturer of amusement rides in North America at that time. Chance modeled the design of its carousel horses after Allan Herschell's famous antique wooden horses. Dutch Wonderland's Chance carousel features 30 fiberglass horses and two chariots. (AD.)

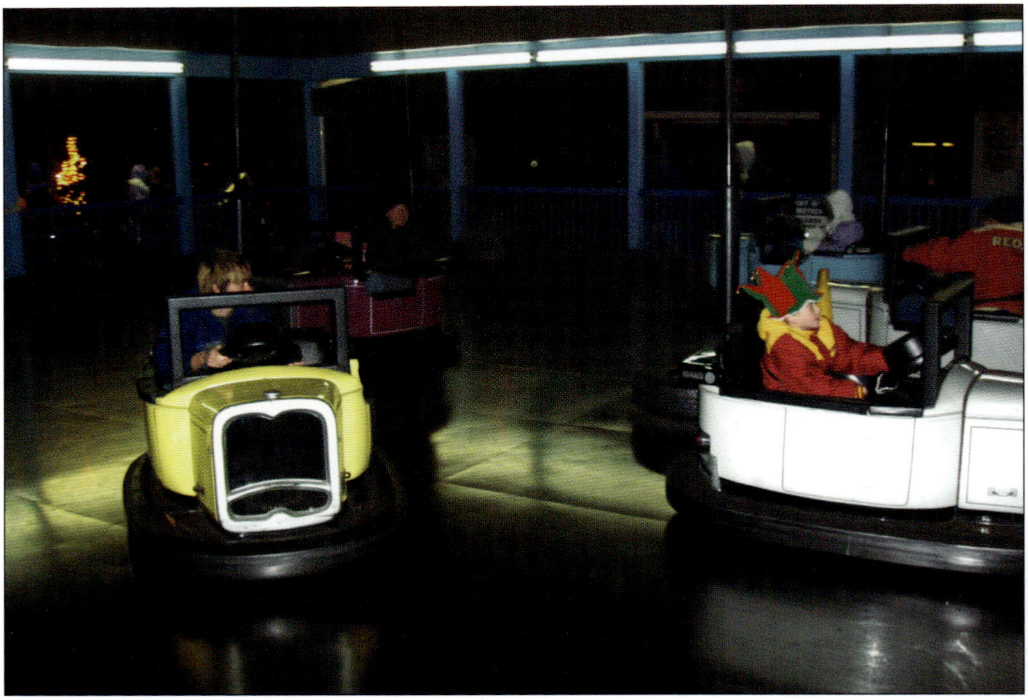

In the early 1980s, Lusse offered Dutch Wonderland a new model of bumper cars; thus, the original cars were replaced. The new cars resembled the classic antique look that Lusse was known for. (AD.)

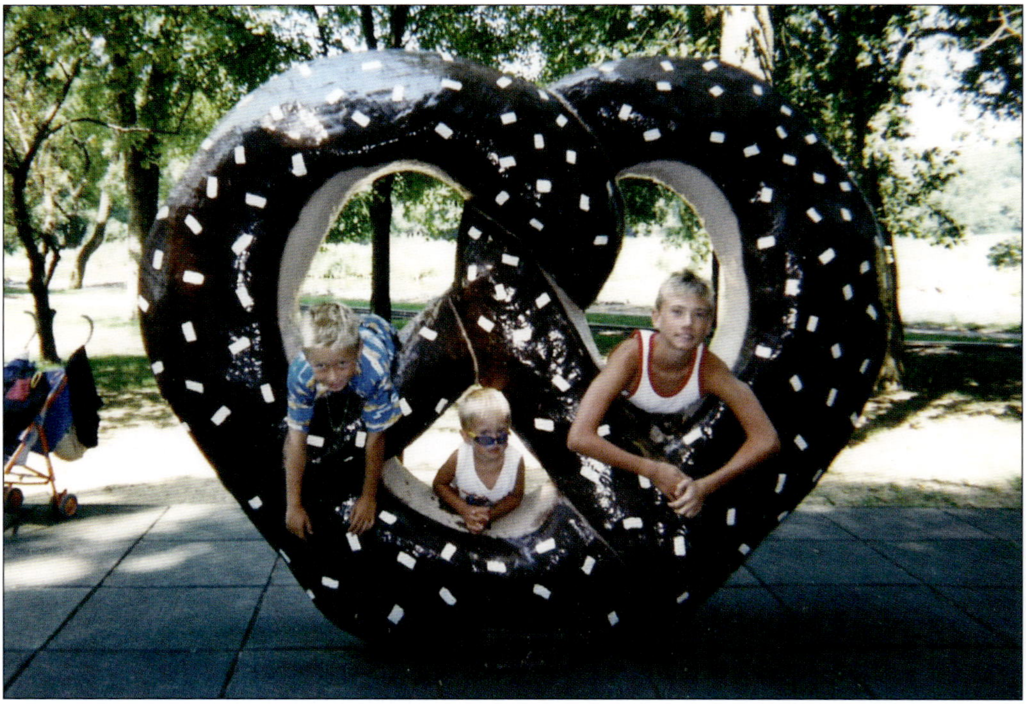

The classic Dutch Wonderland pretzel has been a park icon since 1963. Though its location and appearance has changed throughout the years, parkgoers still enjoy having their picture taken with the giant pretzel over 50 years later. (AD.)

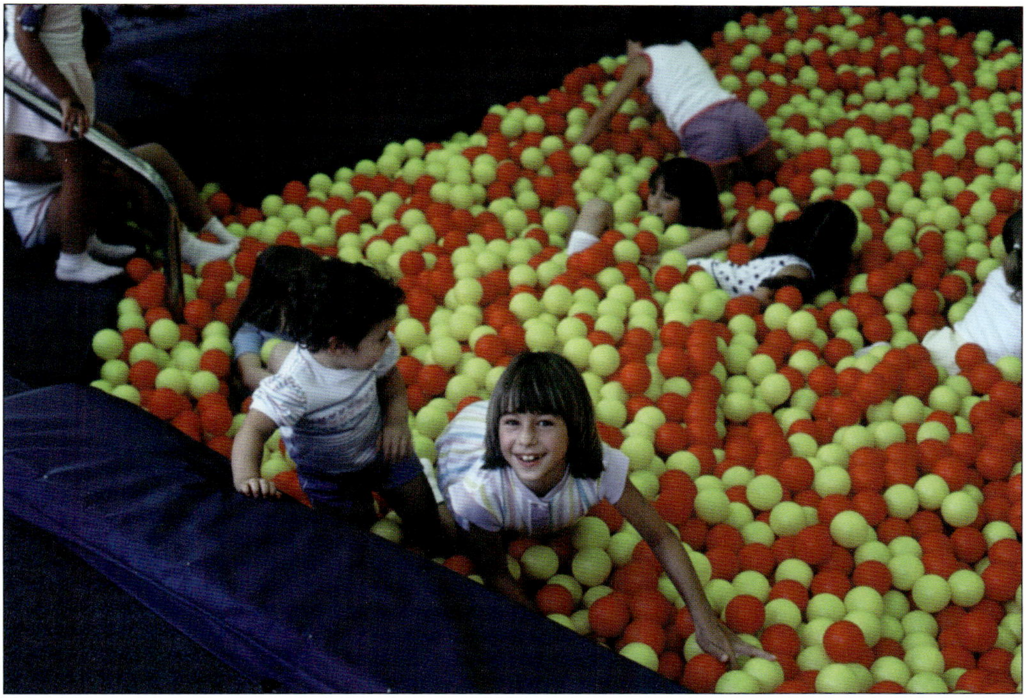

In 1982, the Ball Bath was added to the park. Kids enjoyed taking off their shoes and jumping into a pool of over 1,000 red and yellow balls. The Ball Bath was removed in the early 2000s and replaced with a pizza restaurant. (DW.)

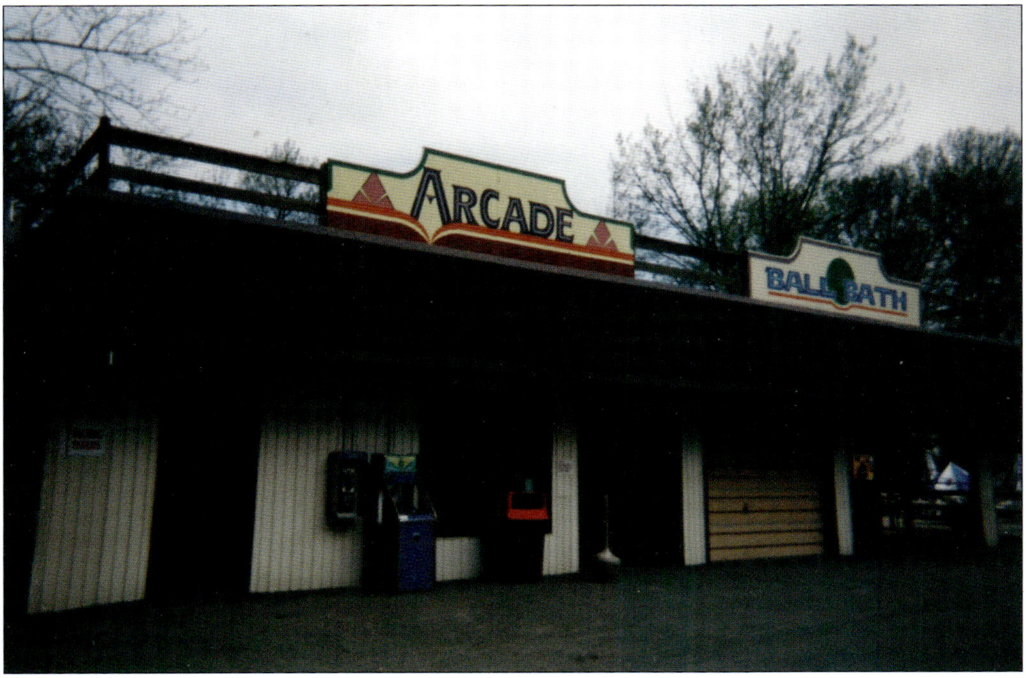

Next to the Ball Bath was an arcade where guests could win prizes. One of the most popular games in the arcade was skee ball. The arcade was removed in 2003 and replaced with a birthday party room. (DW.)

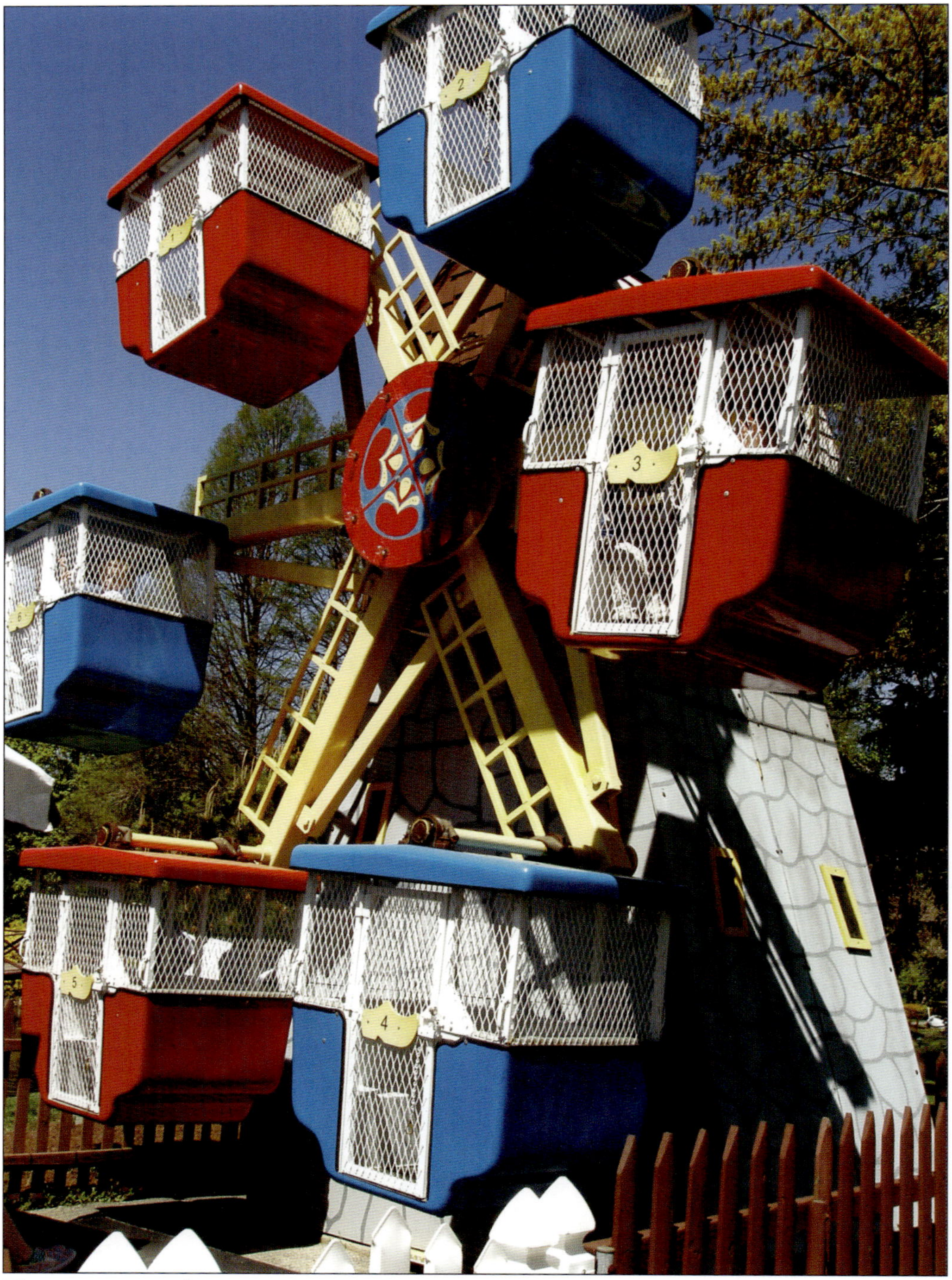

The International Botanical Gardens was still a popular section of the park, but it needed something new to attract more people. The windmill in the Holland section was demolished in 1981 to make room for a new attraction that would open the following year. Murl Clark worked with International Amusements to create a custom ride for the area. The result was the Ferris Windmill, a kiddie Ferris wheel with a Holland windmill theme. The new ride had three blue cars and three red cars; each one could hold about four children. (AD.)

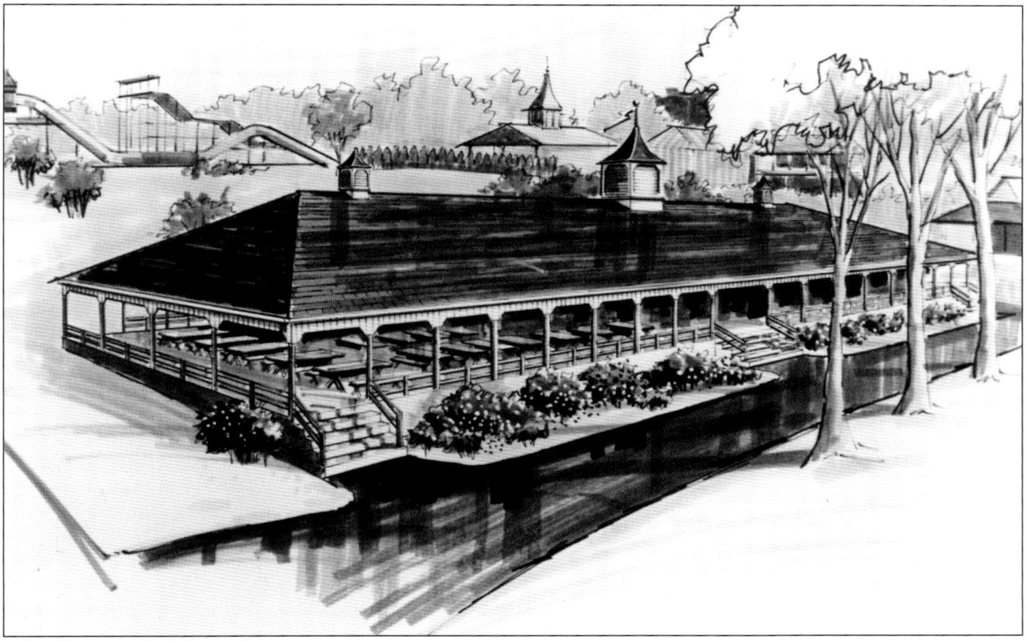

In 1983, Dutch Wonderland constructed a 12,180-square-foot multipurpose picnic pavilion to accommodate company picnics and large gatherings. Located near the bridge to the International Botanical Gardens, the 1,200-seat pavilion, known as the Park Place Cafeteria, featured a double-line cafeteria facility. It was later enclosed and renamed the Mill Stream Eatery. (DW.)

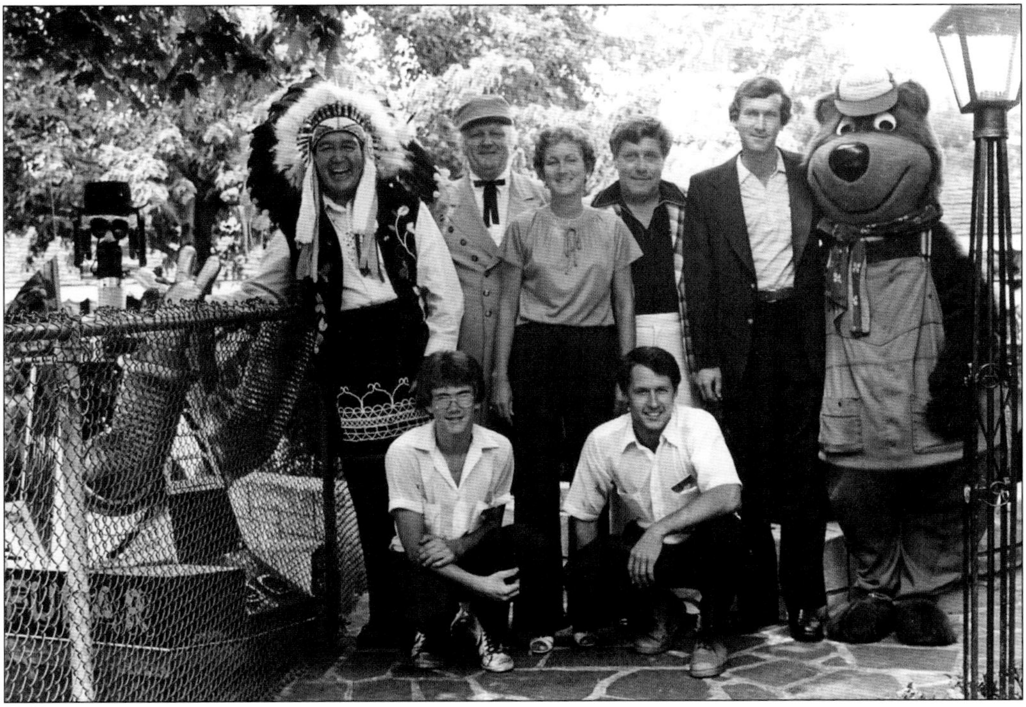

Gathered for the park's 20th anniversary are, from left to right, (first row) Brad Clark and operations manager Jim Werst; (second row) FUBAR the Robot, Chief Halftown, television personality Captain Noah, Molly Clark, Earl Clark, Murl Clark, and Papa Bear. (MC.)

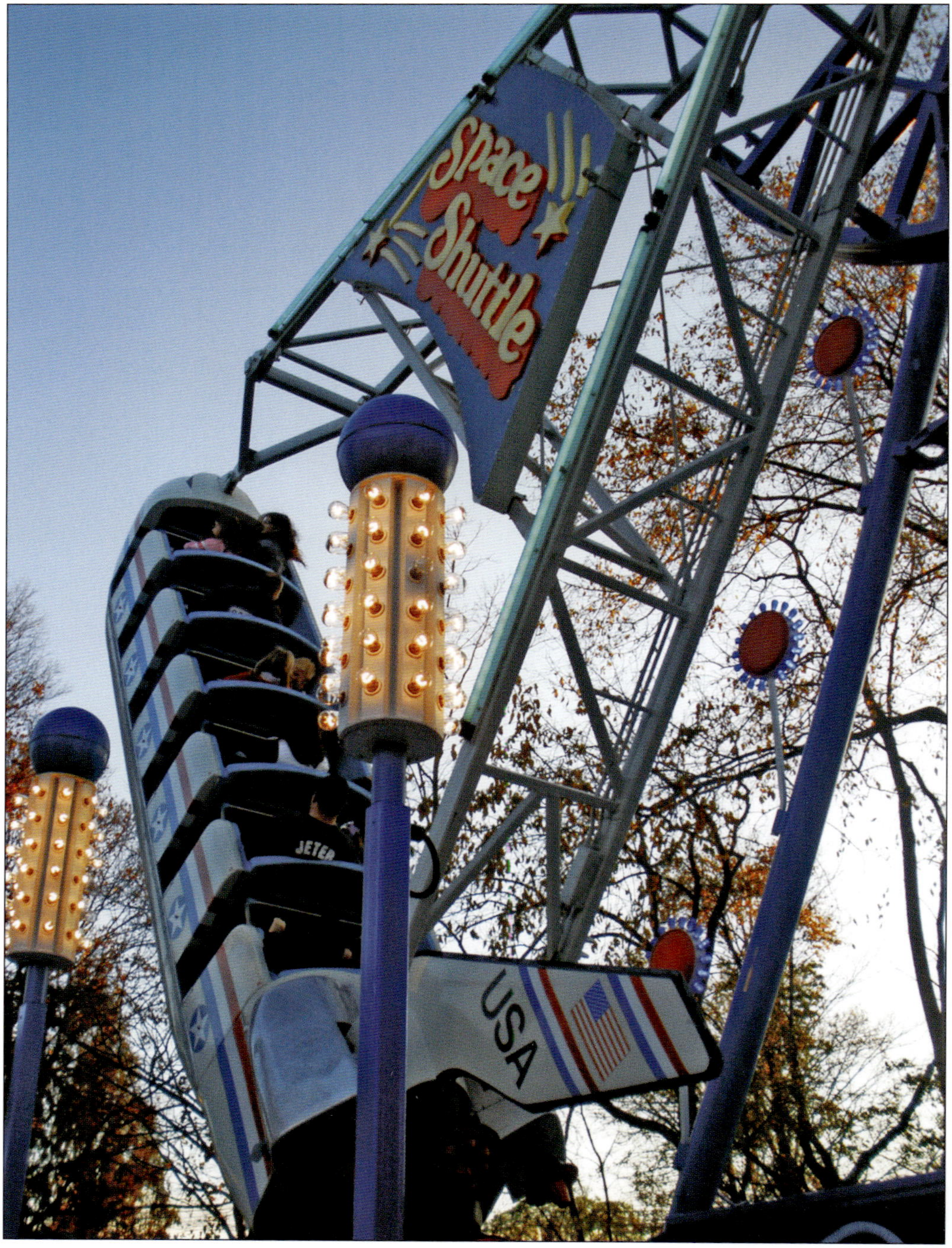

In 1981, Chance Rides designed its own version of the popular swinging ship ride. At the time, most of these rides were based on a pirate ship. Chance designed a swinging rocket ship called the Space Shuttle. While the ride is in motion, audio of a simulated space flight is played. Chance made the Space Shuttle ride portable so both amusement parks and traveling carnivals could install the ride. In 1984, Dutch Wonderland bought an early version of the ride. The two-minute ride swings up to 74 degrees. It has six rows of seats that each hold three adults or four children. The total weight of the ride when fully assembled is 35,600 pounds. (AD.)

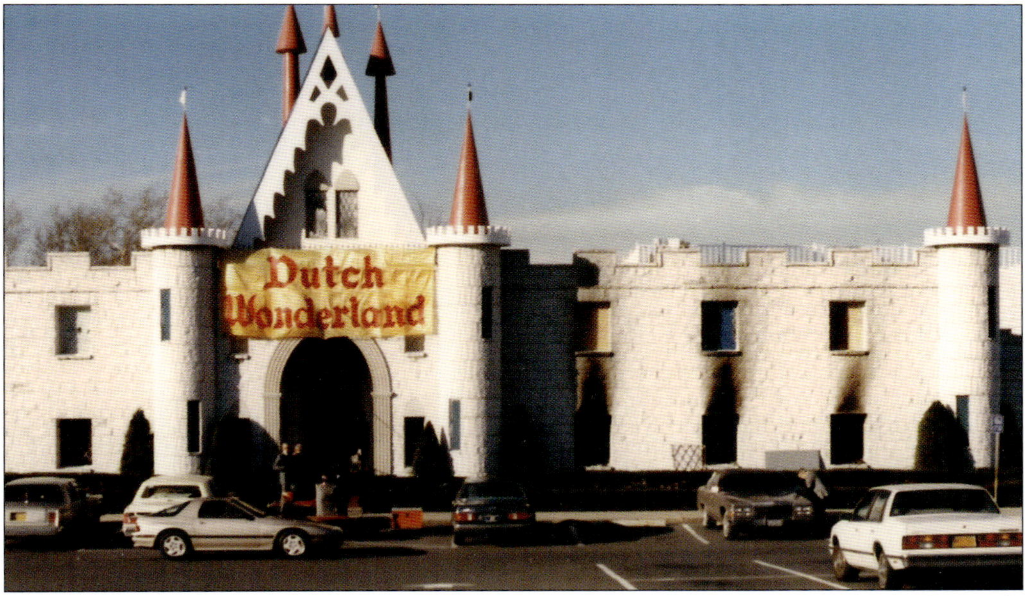

Two major fires occurred at the park during the 1980s. At 5:20 p.m. on November 8, 1985, the Castle Gift Shop caught fire. No one was hurt, but Murl Clark estimated that the fire had caused $600,000 in damages. On August 3, 1989, a fire broke out in the monorail's parking lot station. The fire destroyed both the red and white monorail trains, resulting in over $1 million in damages. (DW.)

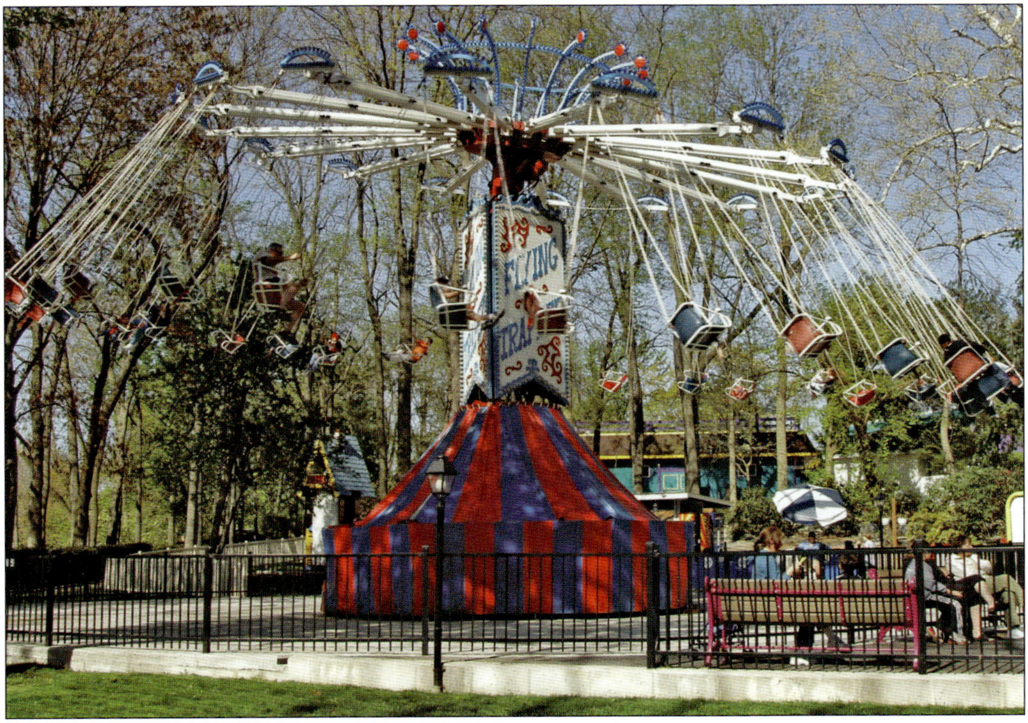

For the 1986 season, the park announced the addition of three new attractions, the most thrilling of which was the Flying Trapeze. This circus-themed version of the Yo-Yo by Chance Rides was adapted as such for placement near the circus tent. It holds 32 riders per cycle and travels counterclockwise. (AD.)

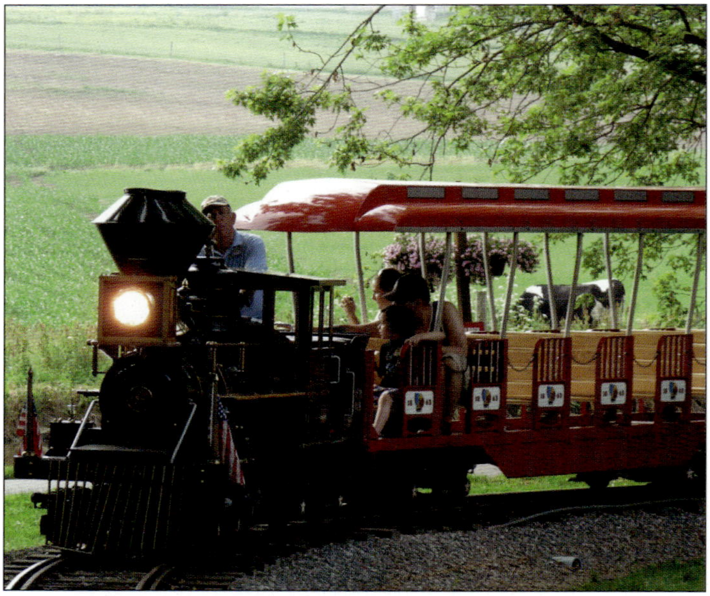

Also new for 1986 was another C.P. Huntington train, manufactured by Chance Rides. This No. 206 train, which replaced the original Iron Horse Train, shares the track with the No. 123 train from 1974. Both trains can carry up to 60 passengers each. The third new attraction of 1986 was the Flying Turtle Roller Racers, manufactured by Mason Corporation. Children powered and steered the 12 scooters by placing their feet on the handle and swiveling it from side to side. (AD.)

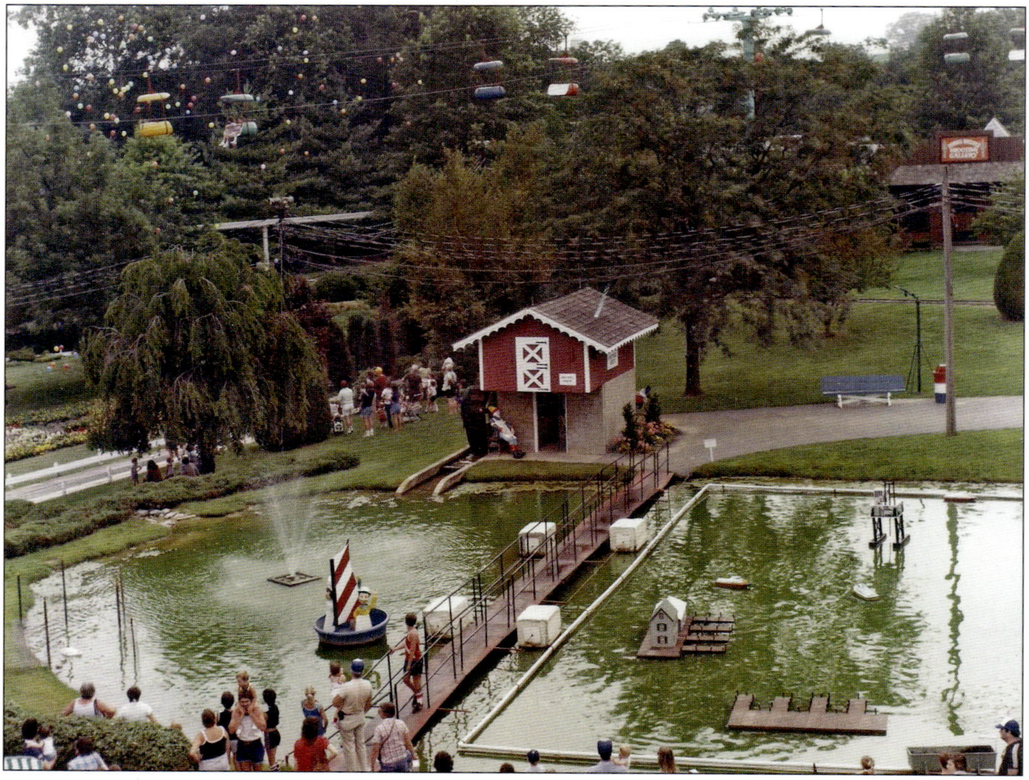

The Jolly Miller's Mill, with its working waterwheel, was an initial feature of Dutch Wonderland when it opened in 1963. The interior of the mill, which is now closed to guests, offered a look at the internal workings of a functioning mill. In addition to the mill, the Bobbing Bridge and the Three Men in a Tub display, all located at the pond near the front of the park, are other attractions from the park's first season. The remote-controlled boats shown here were added in the mid-1980s. (DW.)

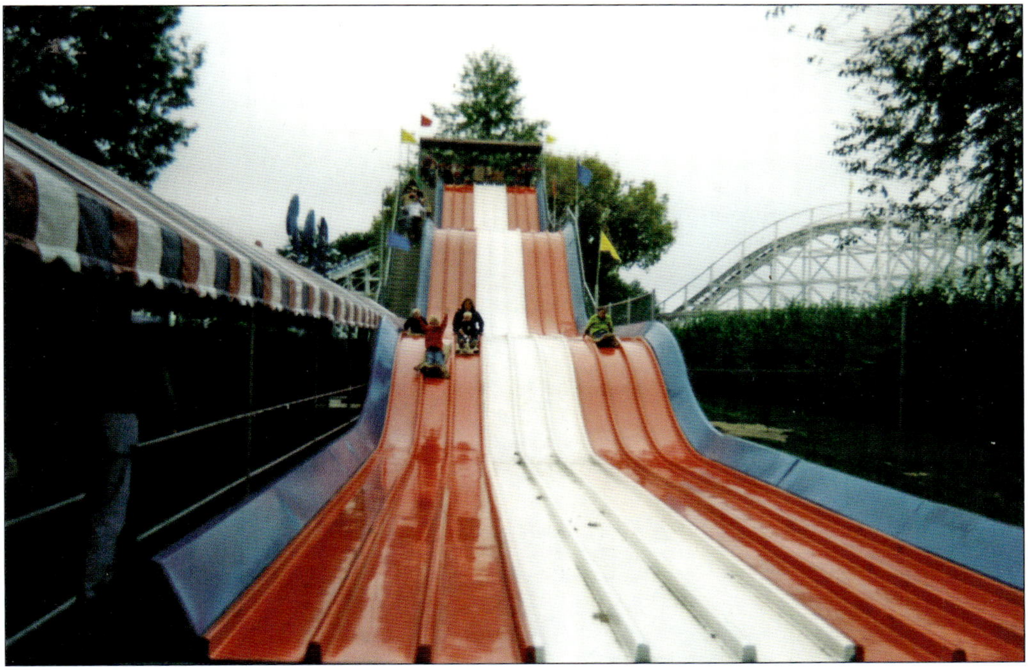

The Giant Slide was completely rebuilt in 1987. The park spent almost $100,000 in improvements to the attraction. A replacement slide was considered, but no companies could be found that still produced slides of that size. Molds were taken from the original fiberglass lanes to make new pieces. The support structure underneath was reinforced as well. The colors of the lanes were switched from white-red-white to red-white-red. (AD.)

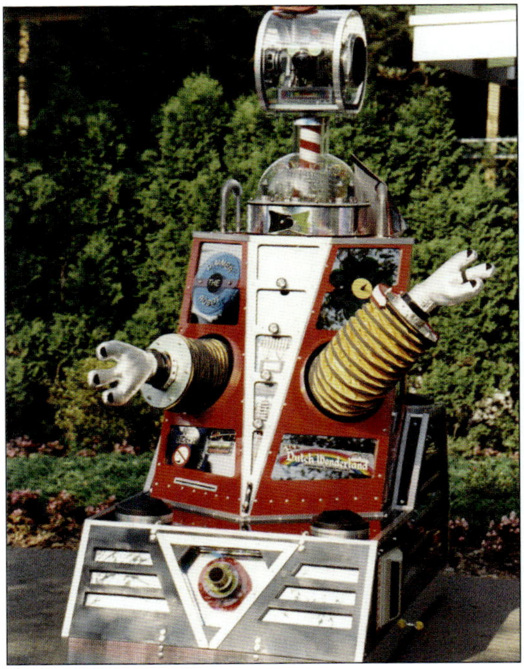

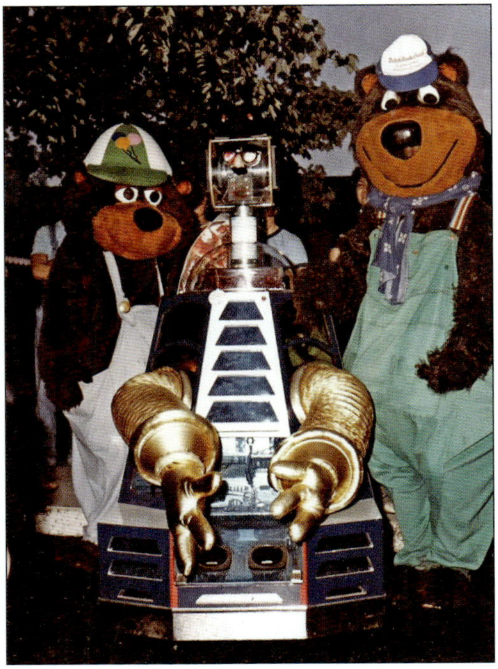

Throughout the 1980s, two interactive robots frequently visited the park. Seen here are Dimmer the Robot (left) and FUBAR the Robot (right), as well as Papa and Cubby Bear. (Both, DW.)

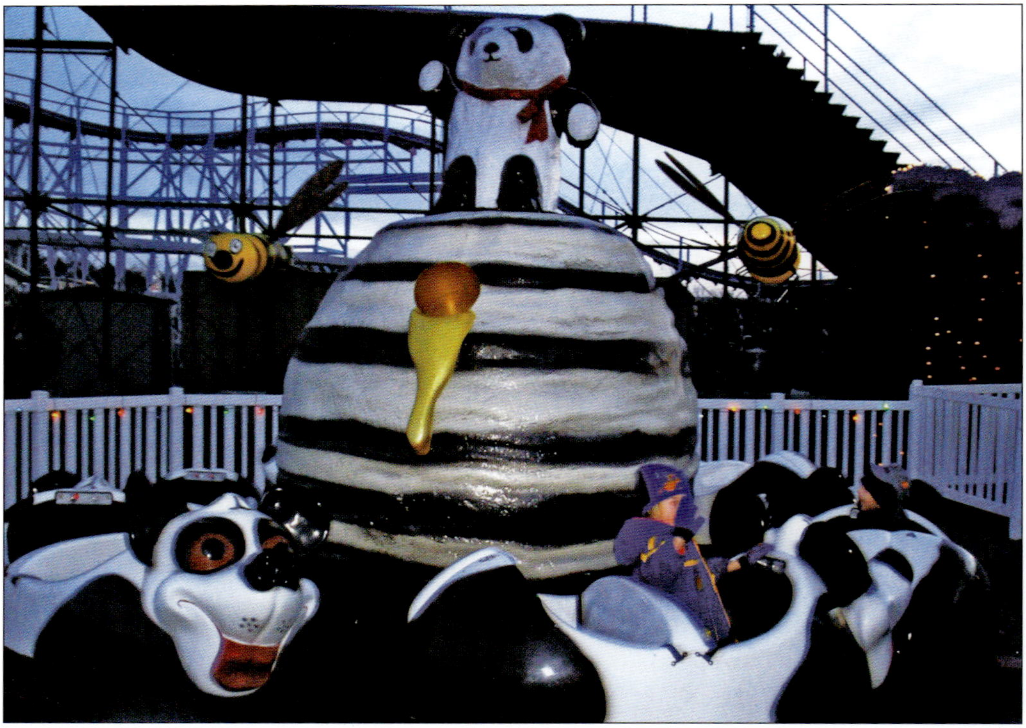

For the park's 25th anniversary in 1988, Dutch Wonderland added a kiddie ride called Panda Party, the highlight of which is pressing the loud buzzers as its six panda bears spin at 10 revolutions per minute. The Venture-manufactured ride was placed at the former site of Moonwalk, next to the Giant Slide. Moonwalk had been in the park since the late 1960s, but an increase in repair and insurance costs caused it to be decommissioned. (AD.)

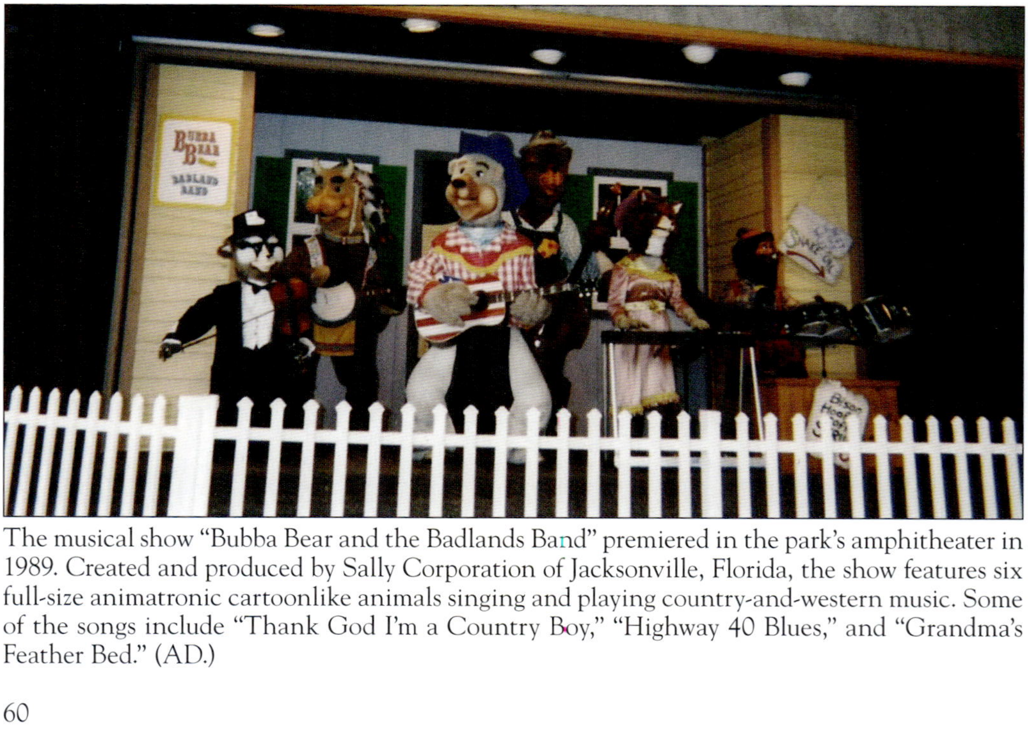

The musical show "Bubba Bear and the Badlands Band" premiered in the park's amphitheater in 1989. Created and produced by Sally Corporation of Jacksonville, Florida, the show features six full-size animatronic cartoonlike animals singing and playing country-and-western music. Some of the songs include "Thank God I'm a Country Boy," "Highway 40 Blues," and "Grandma's Feather Bed." (AD.)

Three

ROLLING INTO THE 1990S
1990–2001

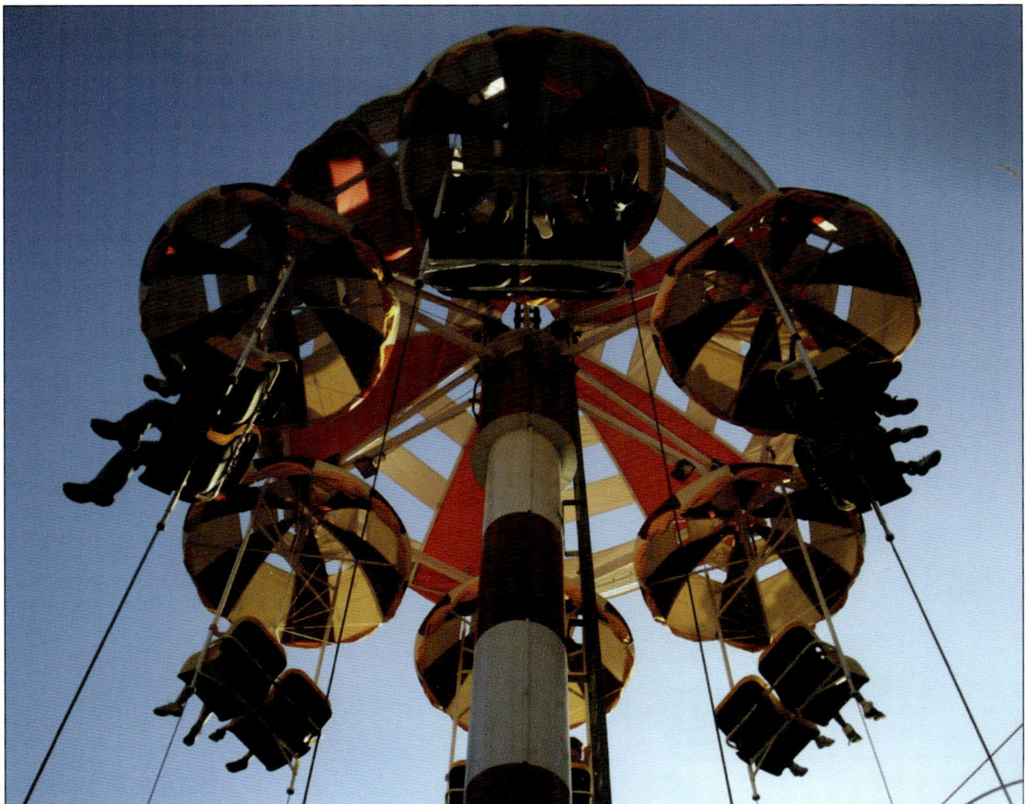

To kick off the new decade, the park introduced Ripcord, which raised passengers on one of six two-person parachutes up a 40-foot tower. Once the parachutes reached the top, they would slowly descend back down to the ground. The new ride was purchased from Venture Manufacturing. (AD.)

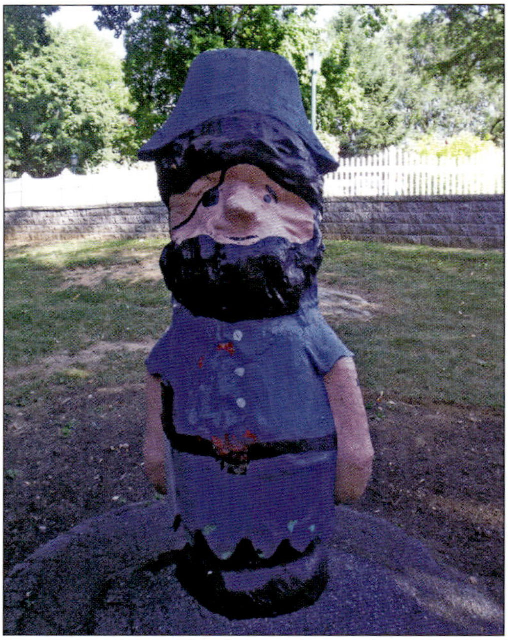

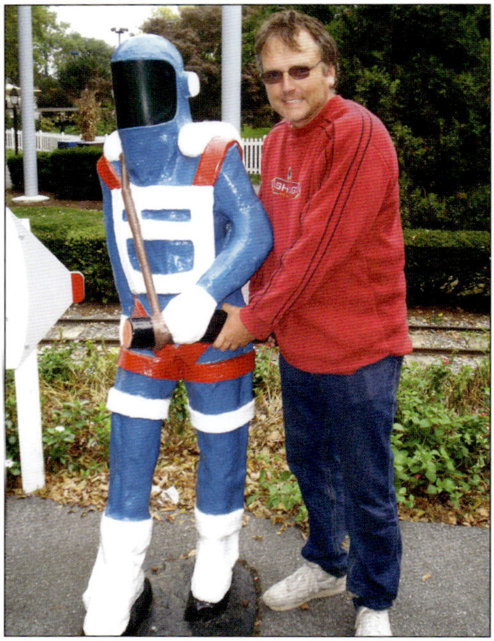

Throughout the years, the cartoon fiberglass figures had to be altered due to copyright issues, while others were modified for different purposes. As shown above, Fred Flintstone was adapted as a pirate (left), and the spaceman received a face shield during his later years (right). (Both, AD.)

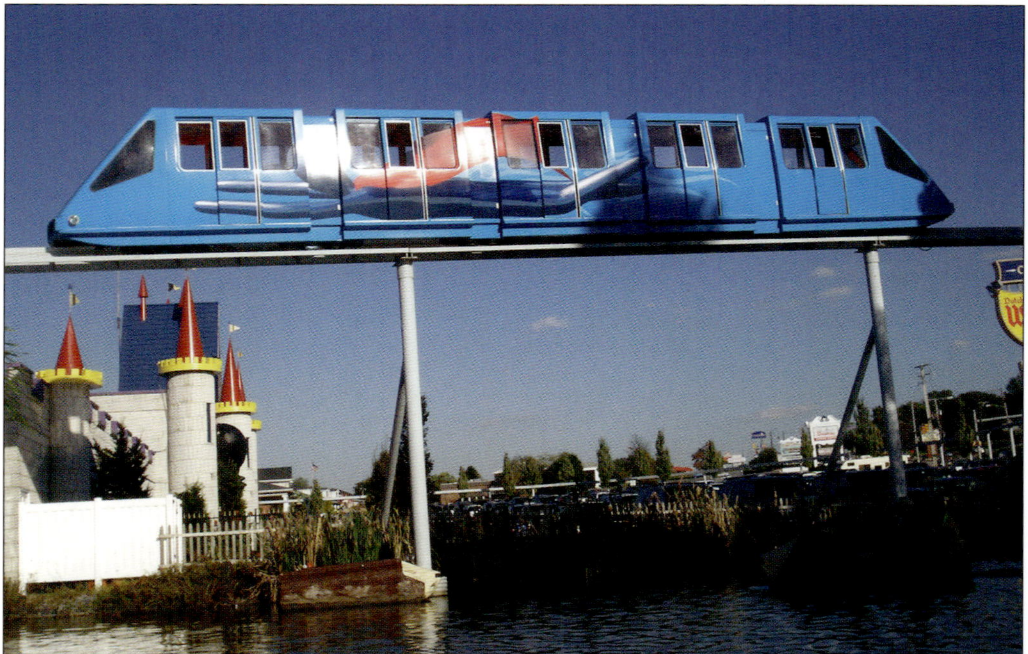

In 1992, Dutch Wonderland replaced the monorail trains that had been destroyed in the 1989 fire. Two new red and white monorail trains were purchased from Intermountain Design and United Monorail Company to join the older blue train, which was eventually taken out of operation. As seen here in 2007, the monorail trains were repainted from their original colors in the early 2000s. (AD.)

By 1990, Dutch Wonderland was nearly 30 years old. Times were changing, and the park was ready for a roller coaster. A smaller steel roller coaster was proposed first, although a wooden coaster was thought to look more impressive. When designing the new ride, the Clarks sought to create a roller coaster that would appeal to thrill-seekers of all ages. The end result was a wooden coaster named the Sky Princess. (DW.)

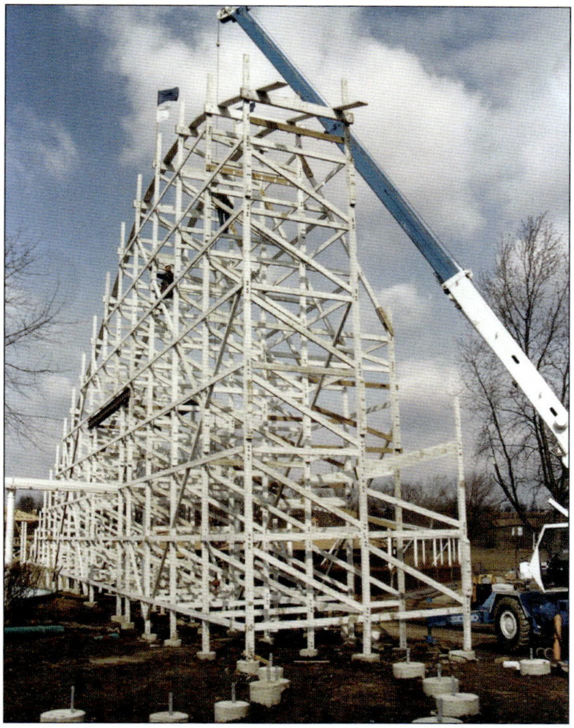

Both Earl and Murl Clark had ideas about which elements should be included. Murl Clark knew exactly what he wanted in the ride—a fan turn and a helix. The picture below shows the fan turn under construction. (DW.)

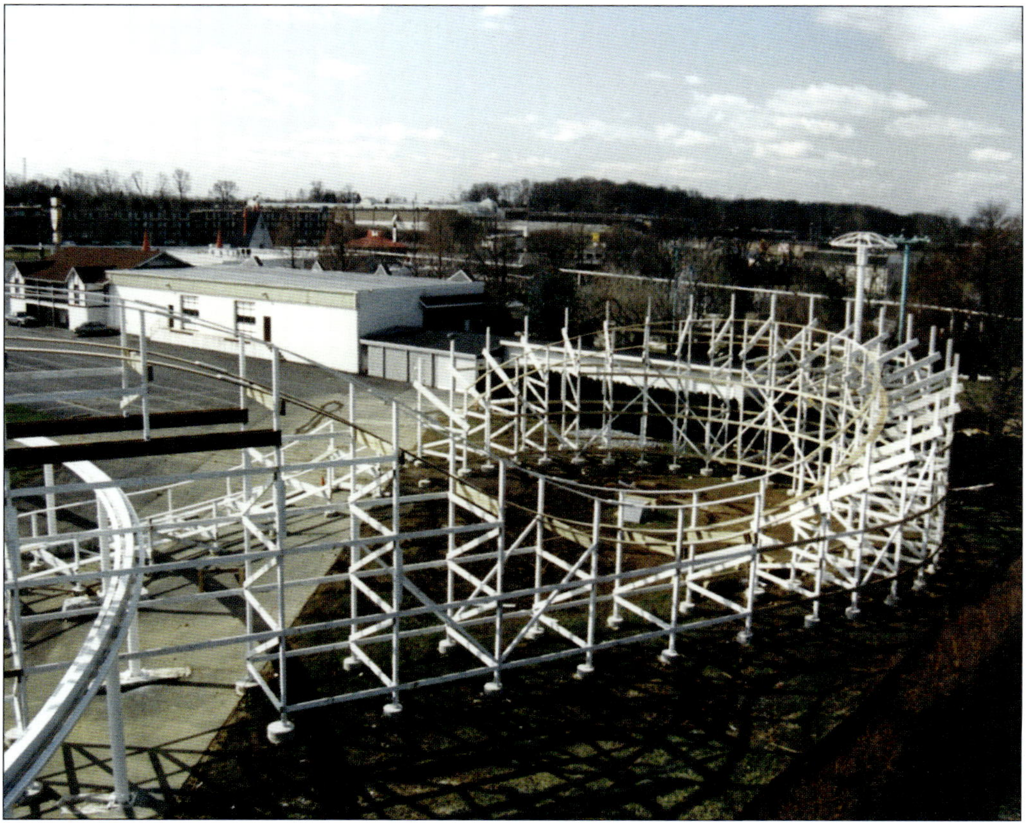

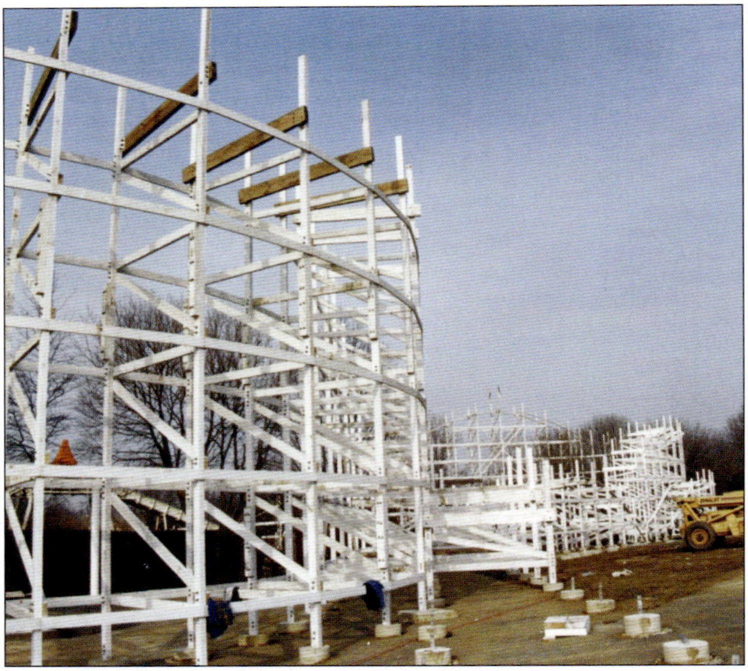

The integrated placement of the roller coaster is part of what makes the ride unique. The coaster forms an L-shape around the Double Splash Flume and the Fun Slides (formerly the Giant Slide), and within the wooden structure are two openings that allow the monorail to pass through the ride. It also runs along the park's overflow parking lot, where it is visible from the road. (DW.)

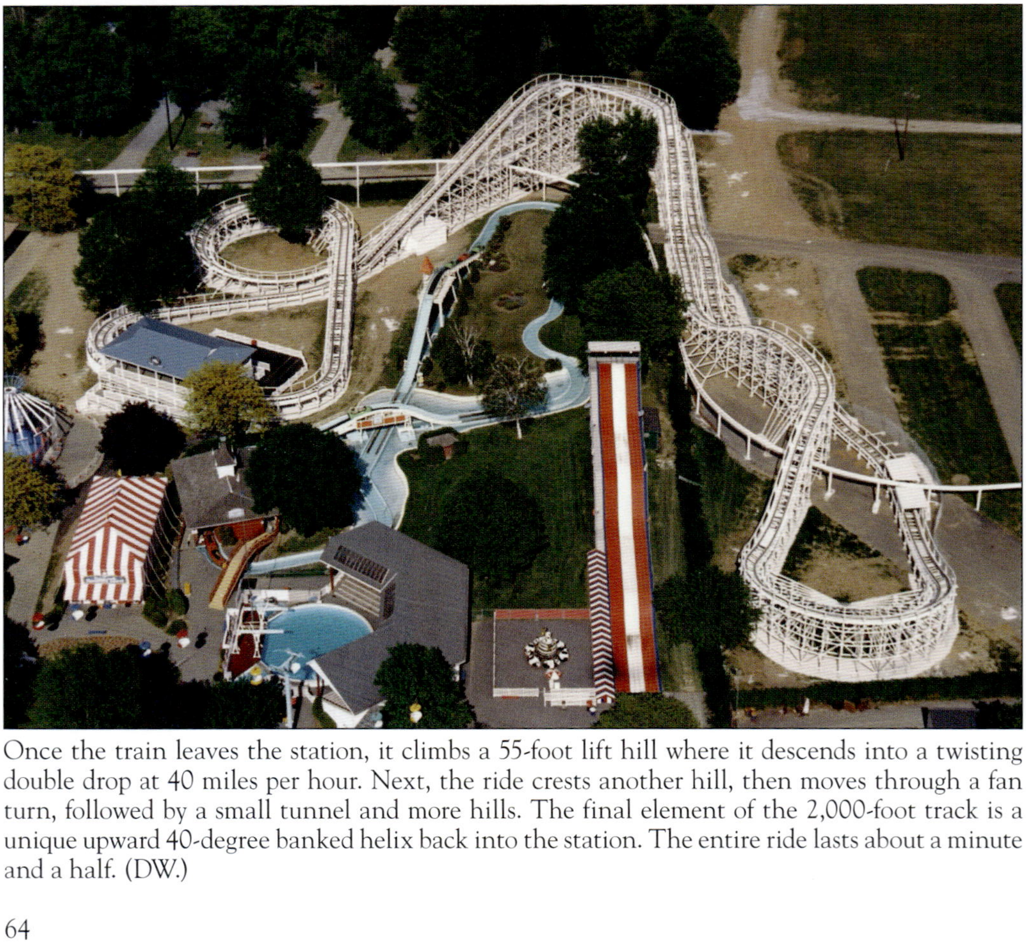

Once the train leaves the station, it climbs a 55-foot lift hill where it descends into a twisting double drop at 40 miles per hour. Next, the ride crests another hill, then moves through a fan turn, followed by a small tunnel and more hills. The final element of the 2,000-foot track is a unique upward 40-degree banked helix back into the station. The entire ride lasts about a minute and a half. (DW.)

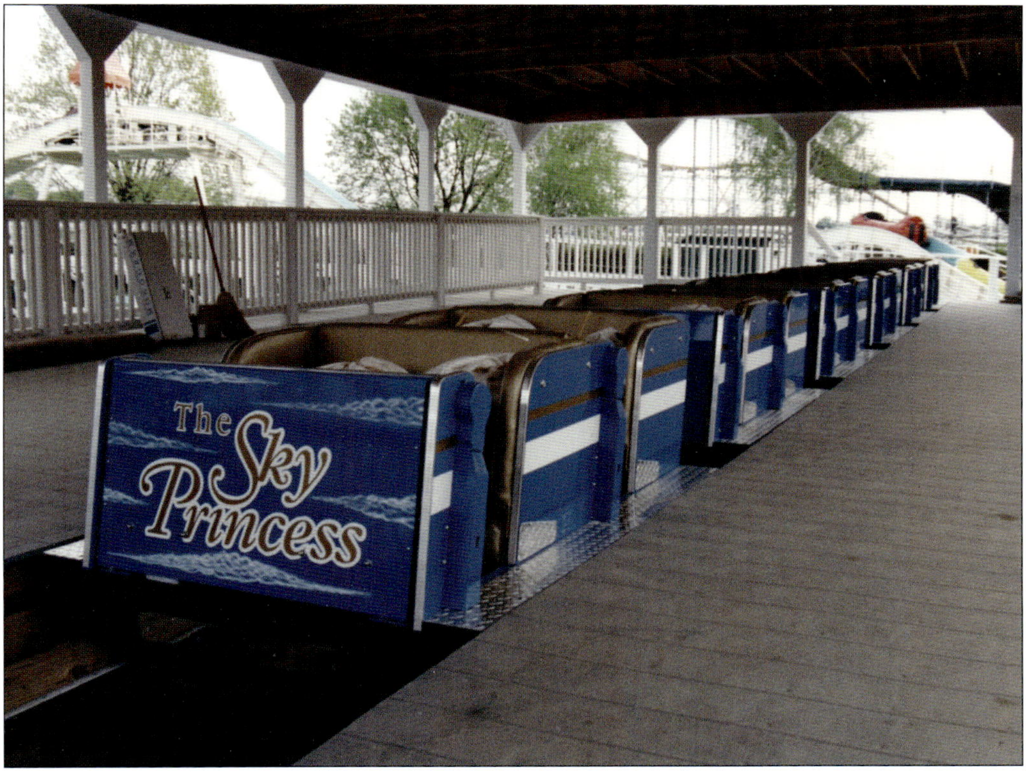

The Sky Princess was the first roller coaster built by Custom Coasters International (CCI). Its success led CCI to build over 30 other roller coasters throughout the world. Its 24-passenger train was manufactured by Philadelphia Toboggan Coasters, Inc. (DW.)

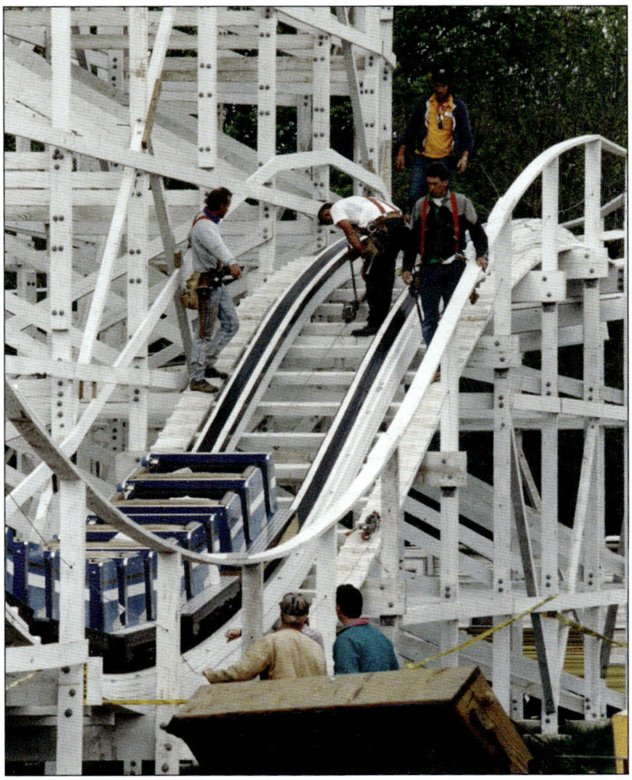

After weeks of successful test runs, the Sky Princess was ready. The park's $1.75 million roller coaster officially opened on Saturday, May 16, 1992, with huge acclaim. Visitors came from all around to experience the new ride. The park was proud of the investment. (DW.)

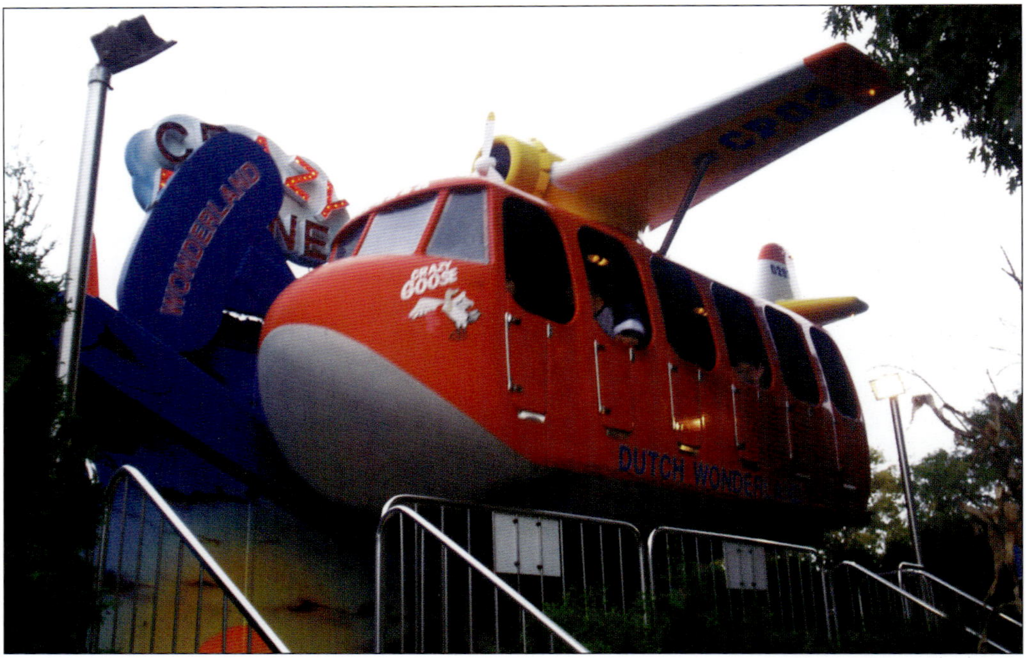

The Crazy Plane prototype was acquired from Zamperla for $190,000 in 1994. The ride reached a height of 25 feet and rotated its 20–25 passengers both clockwise and counterclockwise. After 20 years of service, Crazy Plane was removed to make room for a new Zamperla-manufactured ride, Bon Voyage Balloon Chase, in 2015. (AD.)

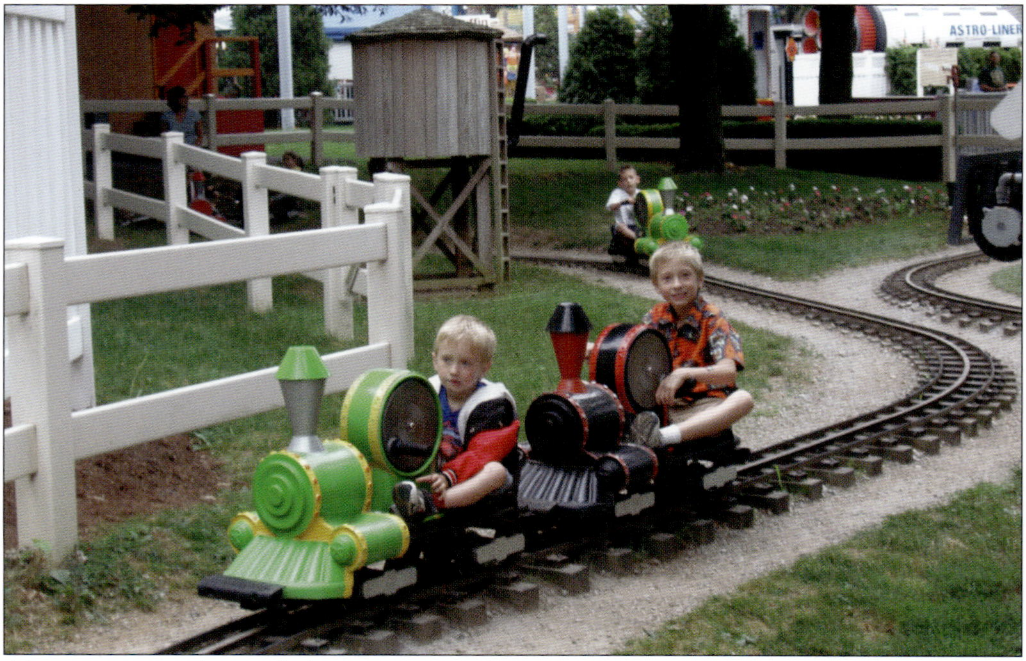

Also in 1994, Dutch Wonderland purchased a handcar ride made by Alter Enterprises of Pompton Plains, New Jersey. Children self-propel miniature train engines along 285 feet of track. The speed of each car depends on how fast the driver can spin the wheel with his or her hands. Dutch Wonderland named the new ride Choo Choo Charlie. (AD.)

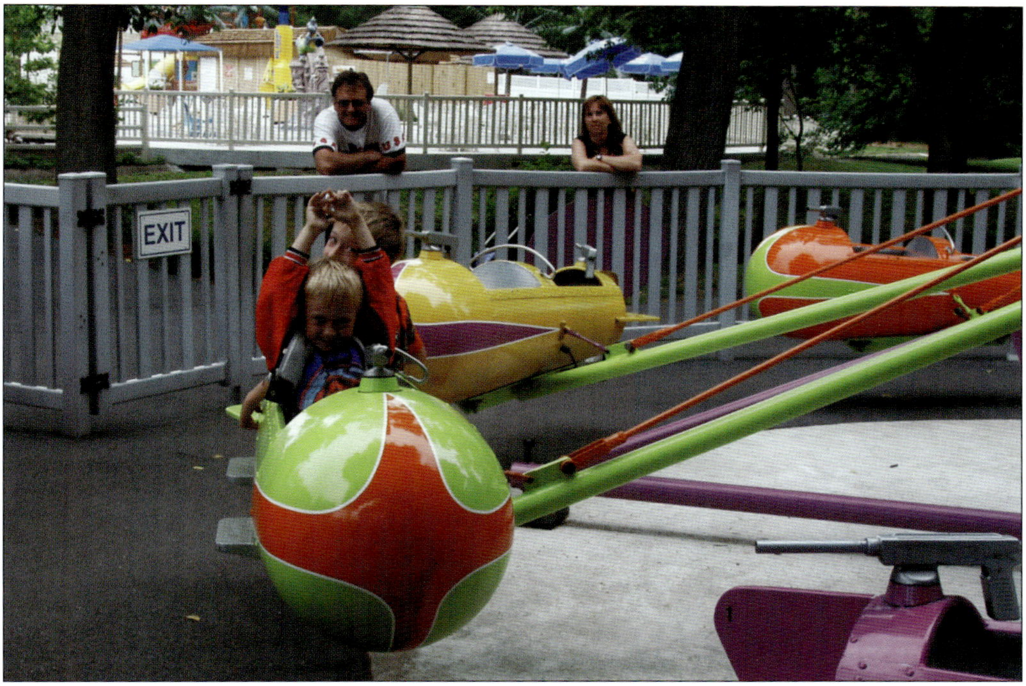

In 1995, Dutch Wonderland launched a space-themed kiddie ride called the Sky Fighter, which was even older than the park. It was manufactured in 1952 by the Allan Herschell Company. Murl Clark bought the ride from Gary Chubb, Dutch Wonderland's new general manager. The Sky Fighter was one of three rides Chubb had owned for his traveling carnival; the other two were a moonwalk and a kiddie fire truck ride. (AD.)

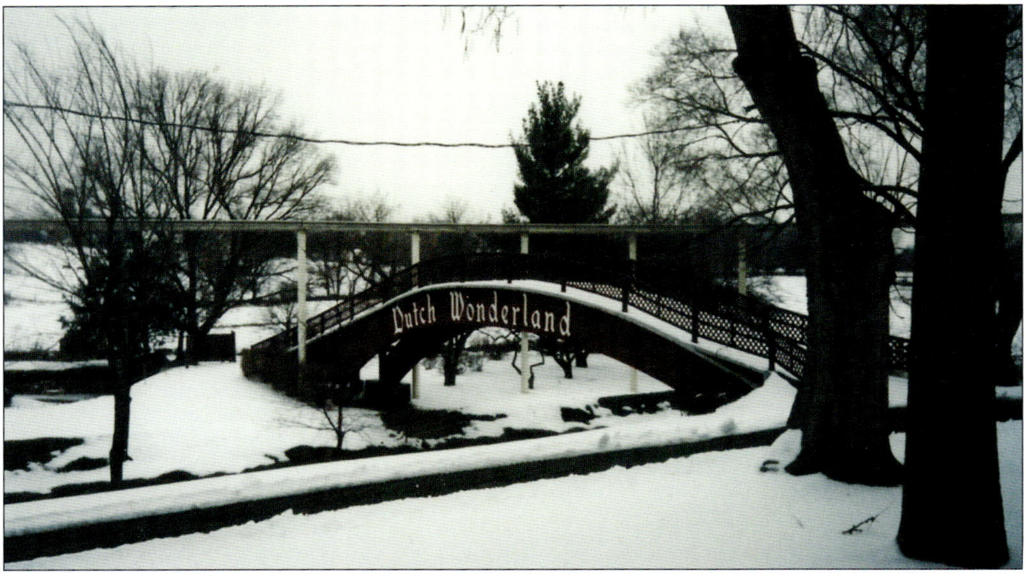

Since Dutch Wonderland is closed for several months following the Dutch Winter Wonderland event in December, the public unfortunately cannot enjoy the beauty of the snow-covered park. Although it may seem quiet in its off-season, the park has a full-time maintenance crew and office staff who are hard at work preparing for the upcoming summer. Many of the rides are brought to the park's repair shop for routine maintenance during this time. (DW.)

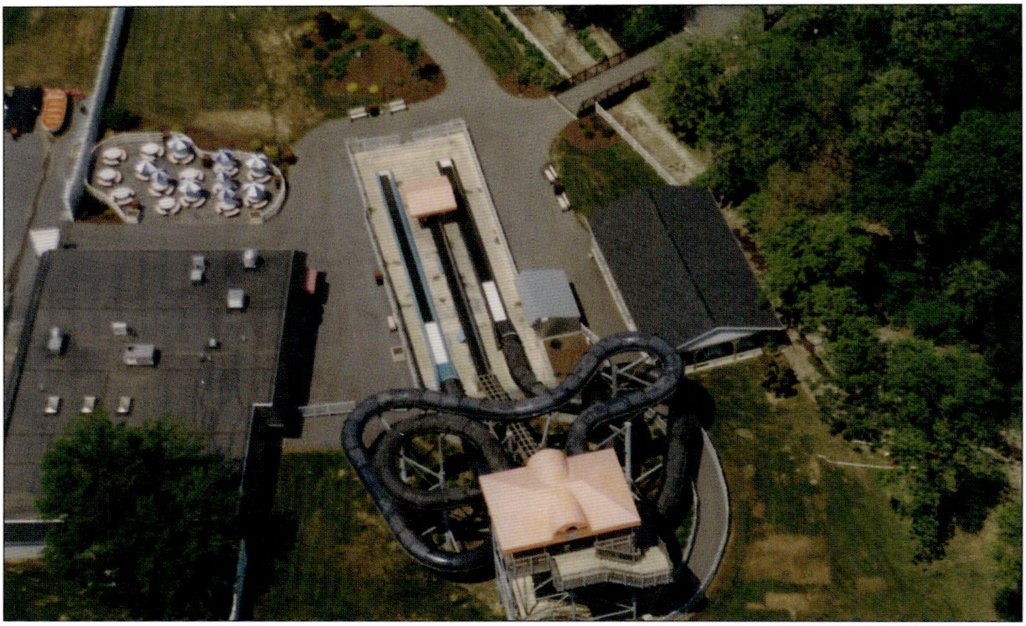

For the 1996 season, Dutch Wonderland created a $900,000 water slide called Pipeline Plunge to compete with those found at other parks. The attraction consists of two winding tube slides. After climbing the steps of the 40-foot tower, riders are given the choice of either slide, both of which are enclosed; one is light blue, providing some light, while the other is completely dark. Depending on the weight in the raft, riders are prone to getting soaked. (Above, DW; below, AD.)

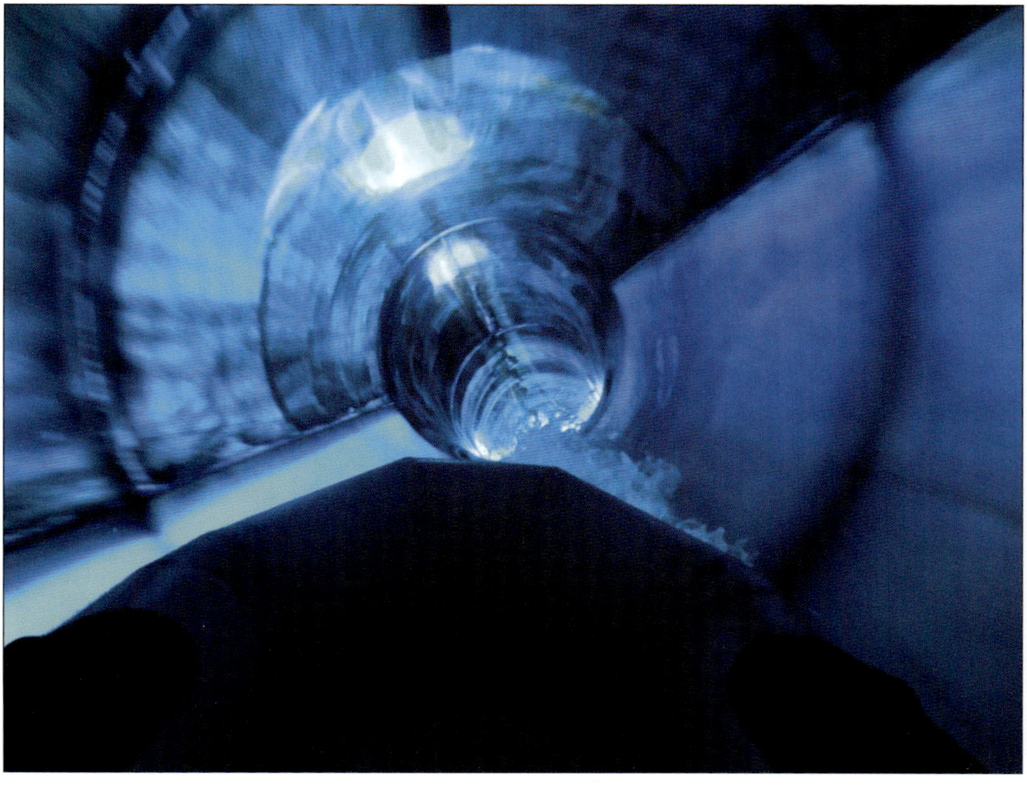

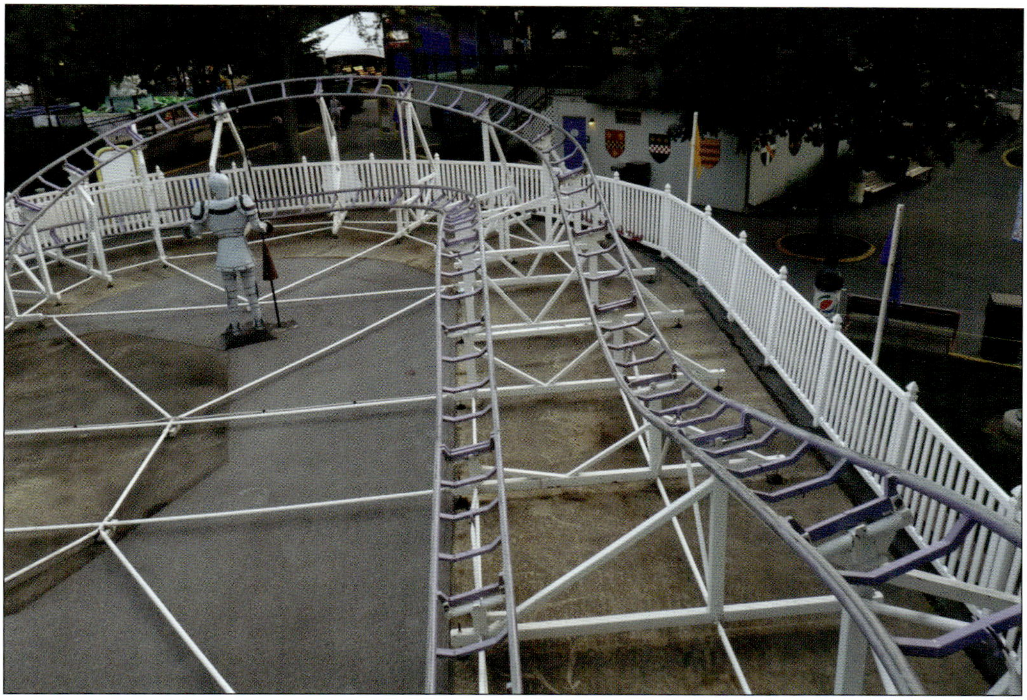

For Dutch Wonderland's 35th anniversary, a second roller coaster, Joust, opened on May 23, 1998. The new coaster, which can hold up to 16 riders per cycle, cost the park $500,000. Joust was the first roller coaster that Chance Rides had built since the Toboggan coasters of the late 1960s and early 1970s. At 17 feet tall with 350 feet of track, Joust is much smaller than the Sky Princess, making it many children's first-ever roller coaster ride. Joust replaced the Flying Trapeze, which was put into storage before being relocated near Pipeline Plunge the following year. (Both, AD.)

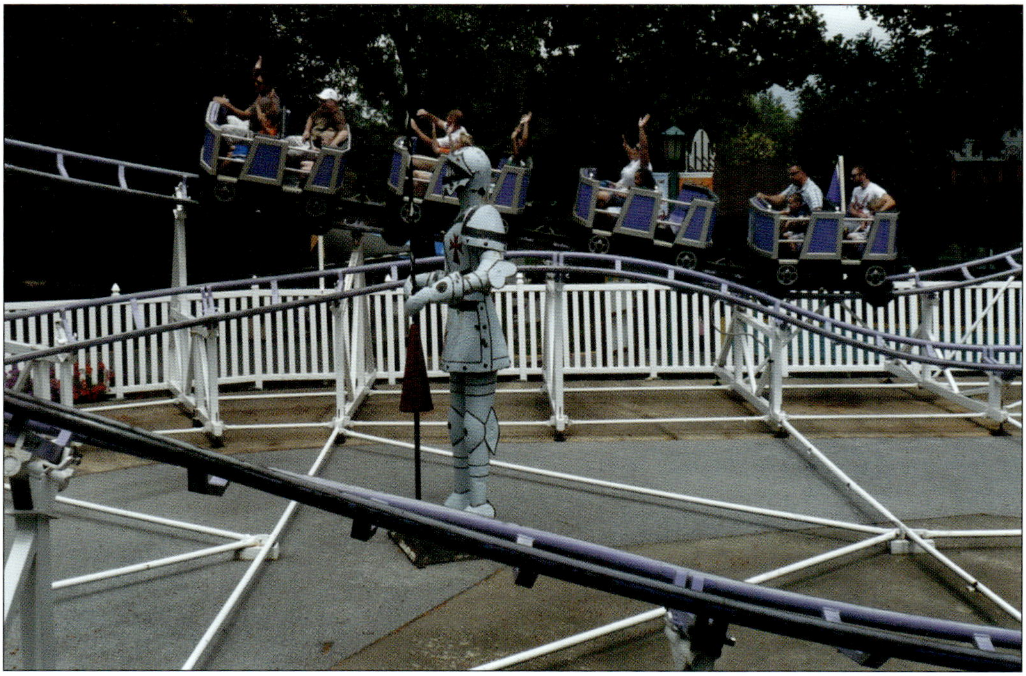

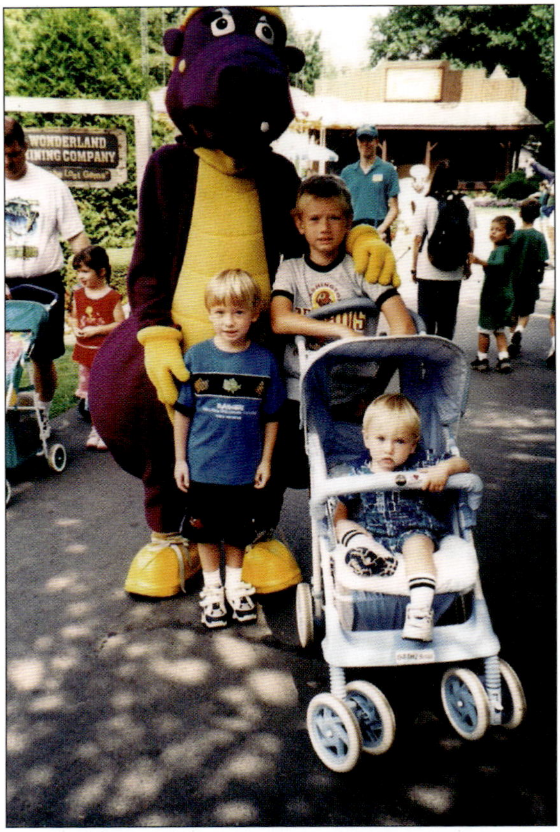

In 1998, Dutch Wonderland introduced a new costumed character and mascot, Duke the Dragon. The friendly purple dragon is perhaps the most loved and well-known mascot the park has ever had. (AD.)

Also in 1998, The Flying Turtle Roller Racers were put back into service after being removed the prior year to make room for the birthday party deck. They were placed next to the Giant Slide, replacing Panda Party, which was relocated near Pipeline Plunge. Both Panda Party and the Roller Racers changed locations several times throughout the next couple of years. The photograph below shows the attraction in its original location next to the Ball Bath building. (Ashley Boquist McDonald.)

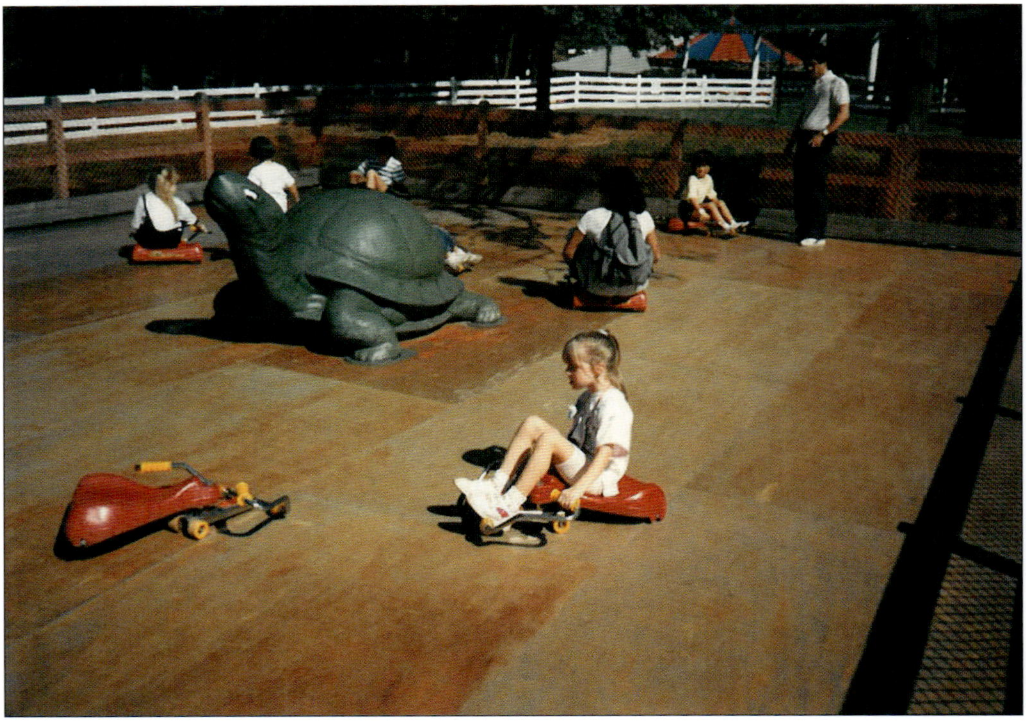

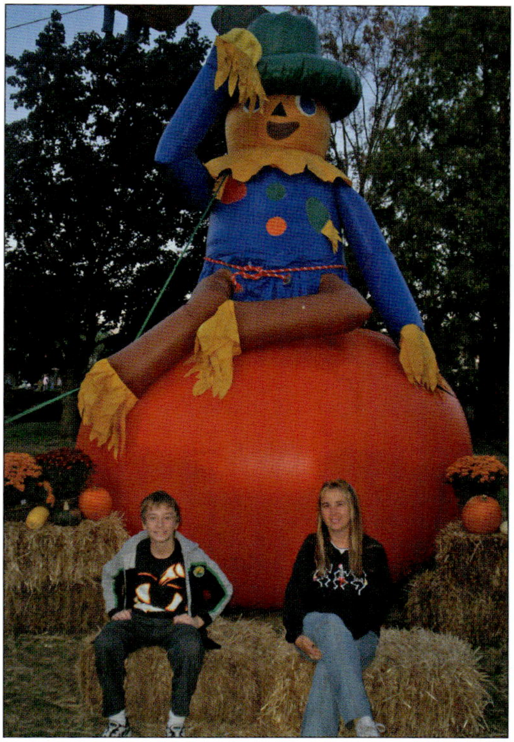

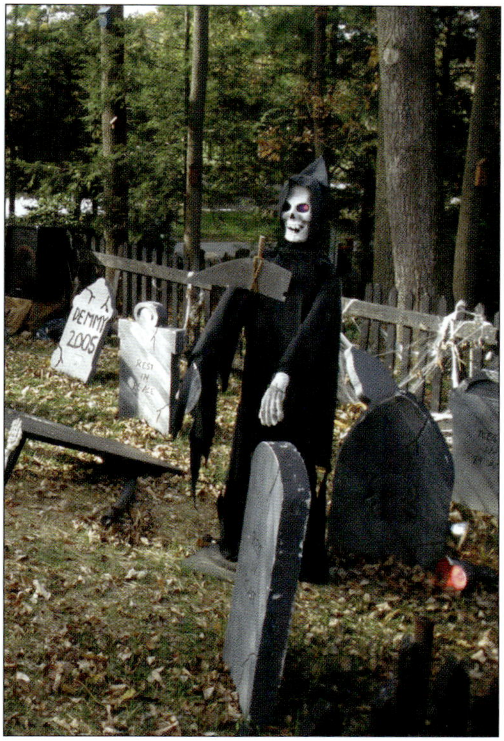

The park extended its operating season to the end of October with the first-annual Happy Hauntings in 1998. The kid-friendly yet spooky event occurs on the last three weekends of October. It includes Halloween decorations and fall-themed activities, such as pumpkin painting. (Both, AD.)

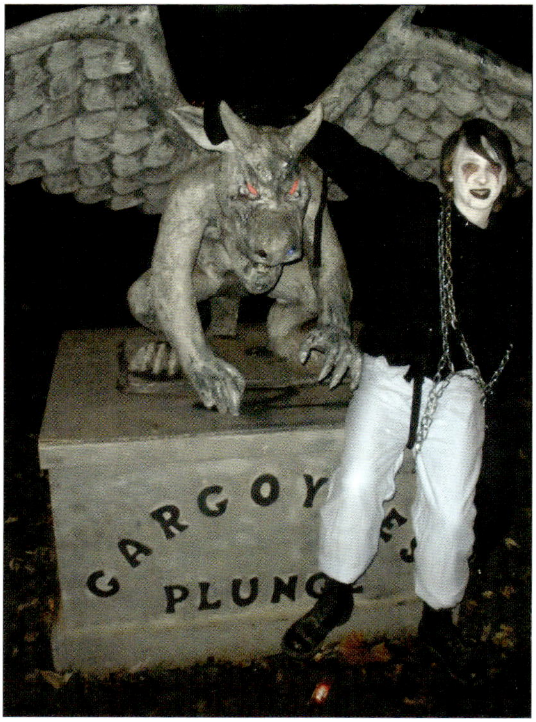

Initially, only select rides were open for Happy Hauntings, and the ones that were had been dubbed with Halloween-themed names. For example, Ripcord was referred to as Gargoyles Plunge, the monorail was Ghost Flight, and the Ball Bath was Frankenstein's Pit of Doom. (AD.)

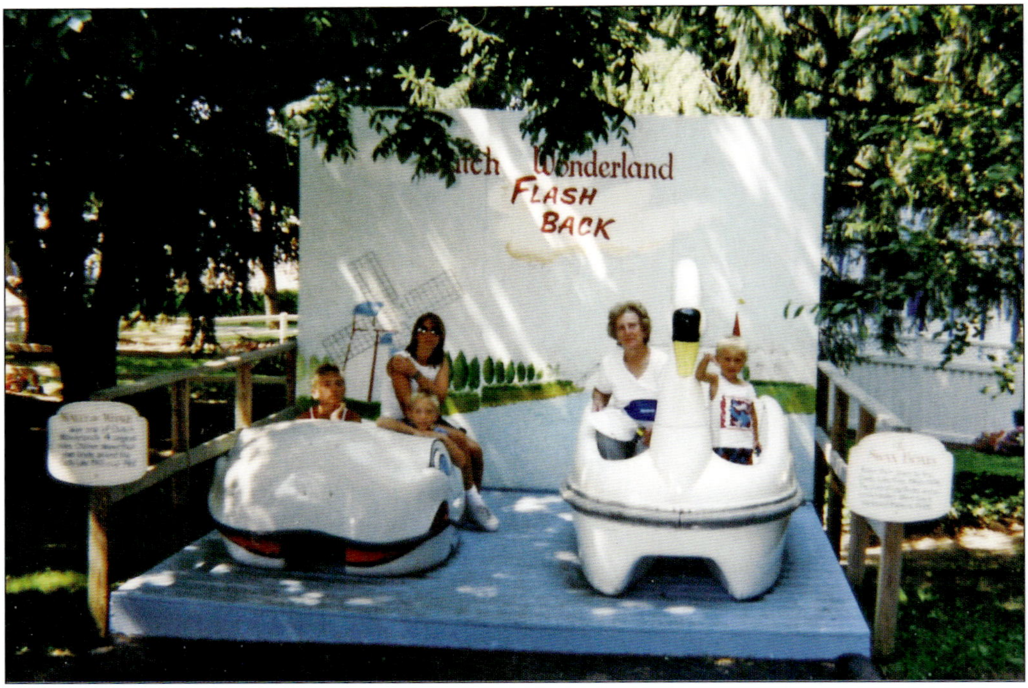

Even though the park is constantly changing, Dutch Wonderland still pays tribute its past with flashbacks to former rides, such as the swan and whale boats pictured here. Visitors can sit in each of the vessels and reflect on the park's history. This setup was moved to the island as part of a new section called Memory Lane, created in 2005. (AD.)

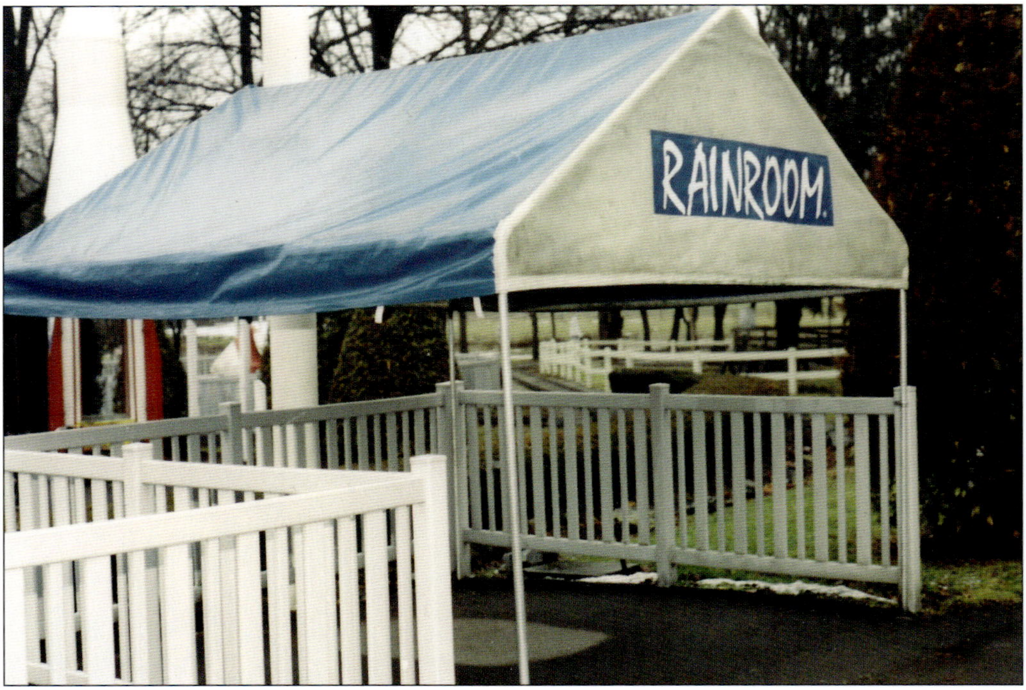

The Rain Room, a small tented structure filled with mist, was used to cool down park guests on hot summer days throughout the 1990s and early 2000s. It was removed after the 2003 season. (DW.)

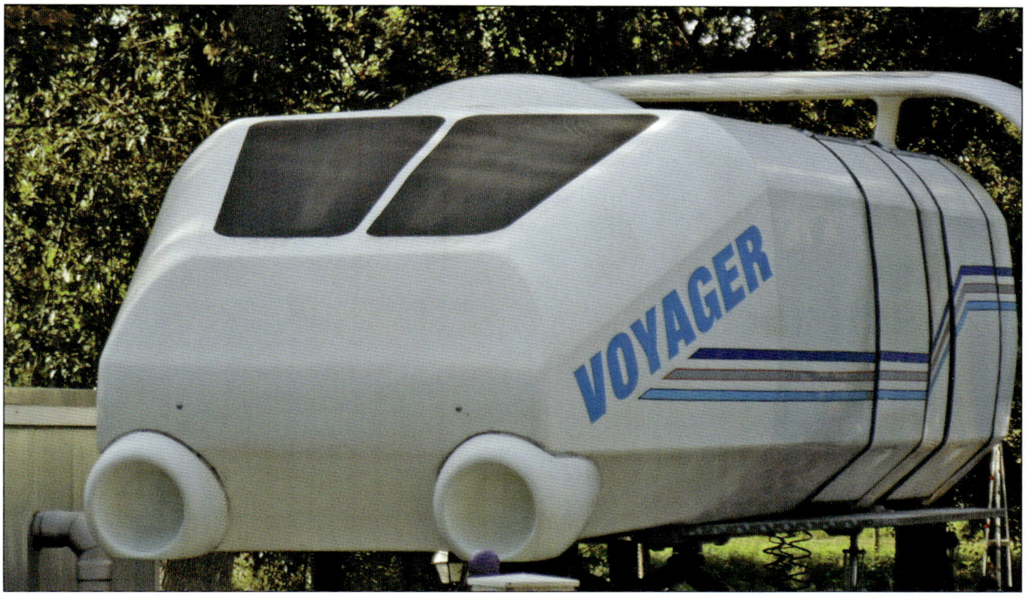

For the new millennium, the park added a $500,000 simulator ride called VR Voyager, manufactured by Flight Avionics of Scarborough, England. The 26-passenger ride has three different movies: *Star Warrior*, *Future City*, and even one about an Egyptian tomb. The park planned to remove Astro-Liner in favor of the updated ride but could not find a buyer, so it was maintained in an effort to show how technology had advanced. (AD.)

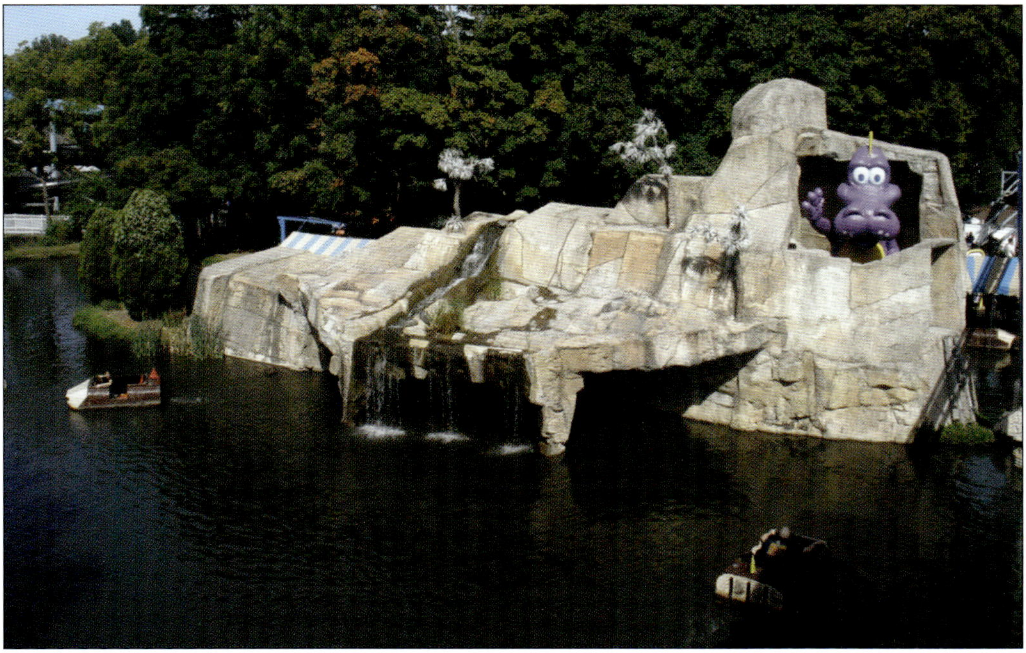

In 2001, the log boat ride received a makeover with the addition of a 30-foot mountain, complete with a 20-foot cascading waterfall. Guarding the mountain from 2001 to 2006 was Duke's father, Sir Scorch. Later, Duke took the throne. In order to make room for the massive footprint of the new 80-foot-by-40-foot mountain, the park had to move the elephant and demolish the windmill that had stood next to the pond since 1963. (AD.)

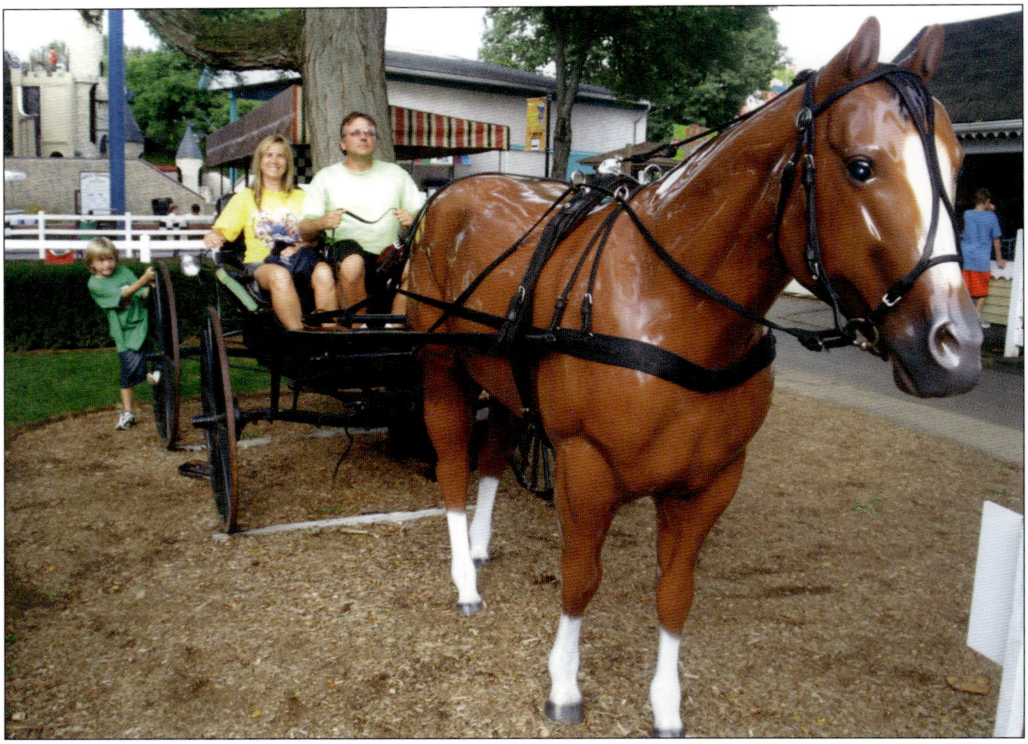

An authentic Amish horse and buggy is located in the Little Dutch Farm area of the park. Guests enjoy climbing into the seat of the buggy to get their picture taken. (AD.)

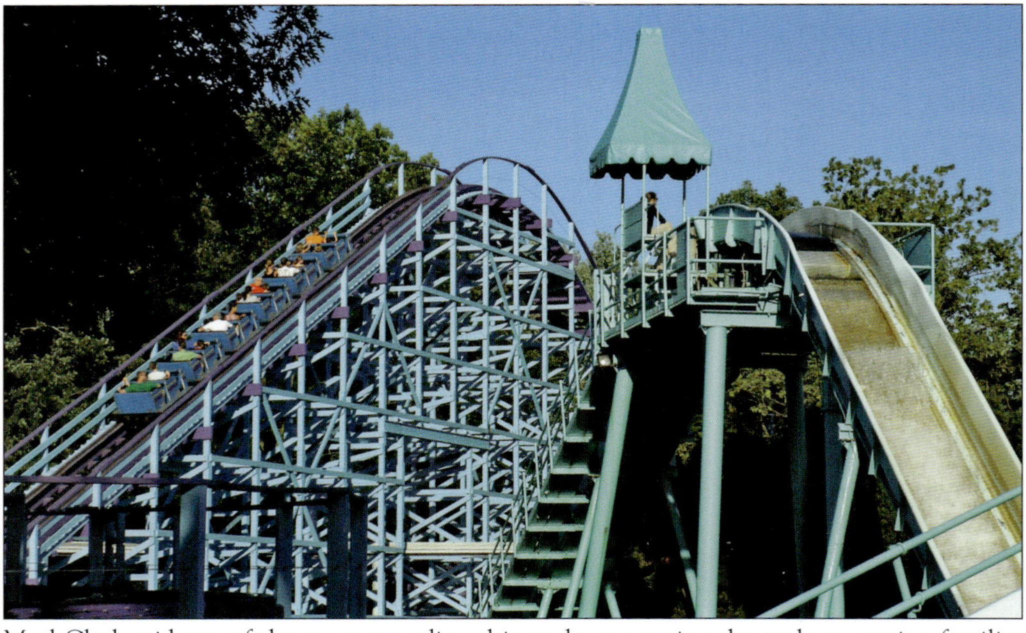

Murl Clark said one of the most rewarding things about running the park was seeing families make memories every day. One of his favorite attractions is the Double Splash Flume, as it was the first ride that he had the opportunity to design. Another is the Sky Princess roller coaster, which he also had a hand in designing. (AD.)

Four

The Hershey Era
2002–2010

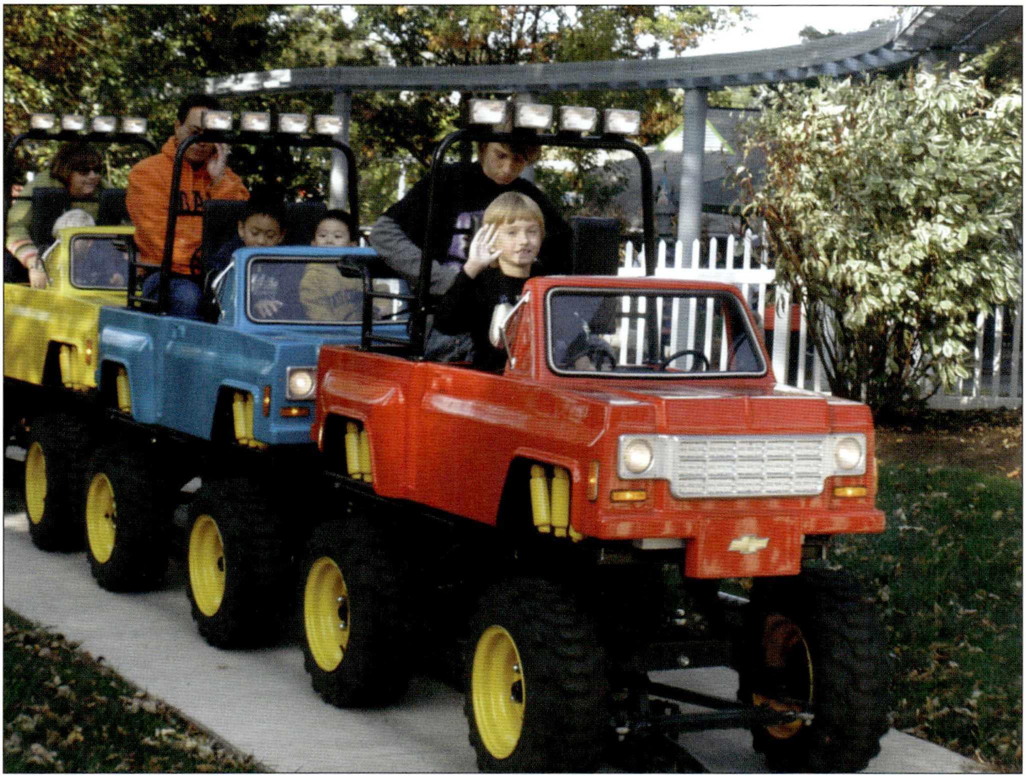

After Hershey Entertainment bought Dutch Wonderland from the Clark family, immediate changes were made to the park. The first of the improvements for 2002 was the addition of two new rides, including the Off-Road Rally. Manufactured by Zamperla, this ride takes passengers around a small track on one of six colorful trucks. (AD.)

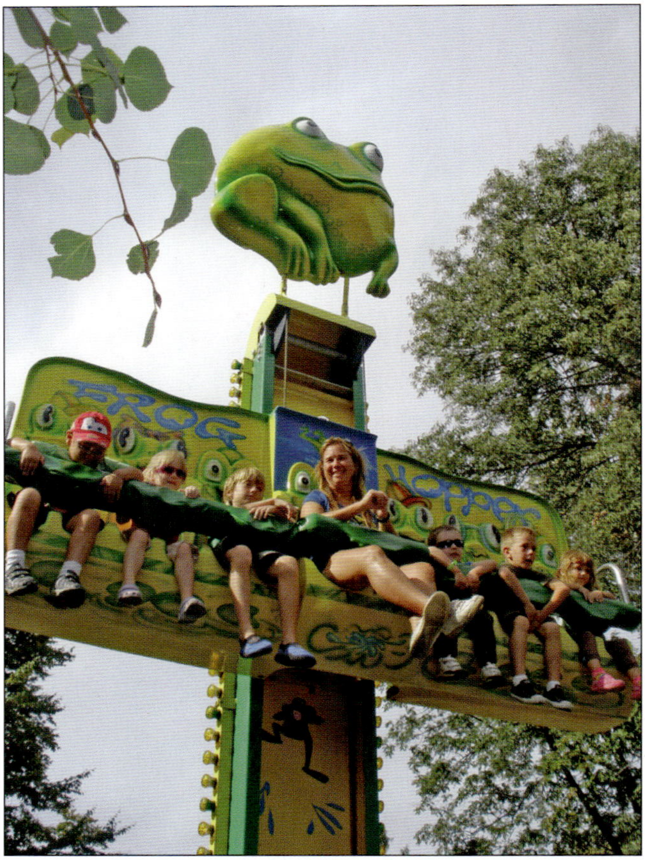

The other new ride for 2002 was the Frog Hopper, manufactured by S&S Worldwide, Inc., of Logan, Utah. The seven-passenger car takes riders up a 20-foot tower and slowly bounces them down. (AD.)

Wonderland Mini Golf was added in 2002. Located in front of the old Wonderland Cinema building, this attraction required a separate admission. The 18-hole miniature golf course presented many unique obstacles for players to avoid, including bridges over water, hills, and a cave. The course was removed at the end of the 2013 season. (AD.)

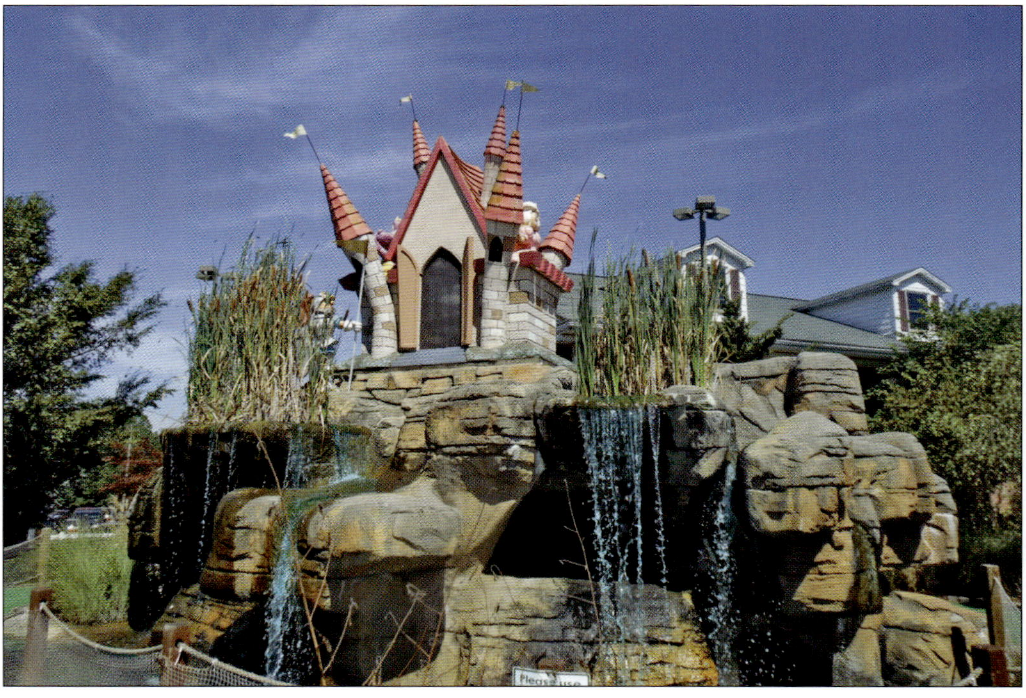

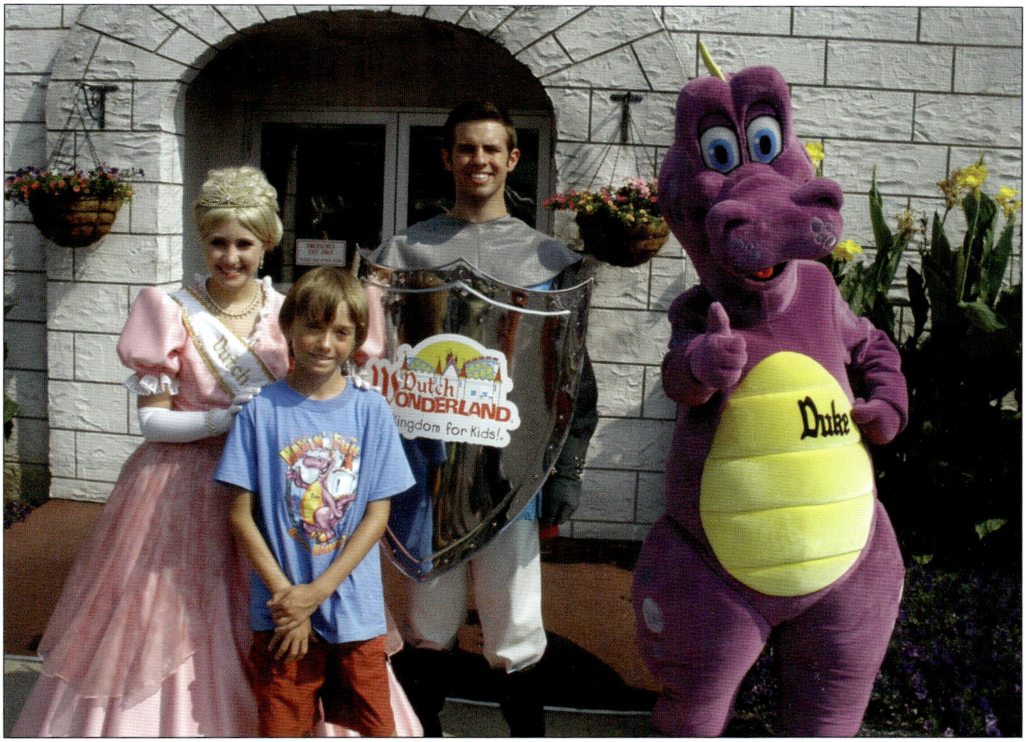

Also in 2002, Dutch Wonderland introduced a new mascot, Princess Brooke, to promote reading among children. A few years later, Sir Brandon, Dutch Wonderland's Knight of Safety, joined the castle crew. Both characters were named after the children of Deb Martin, director of the Lancaster County History Museum. (AD.)

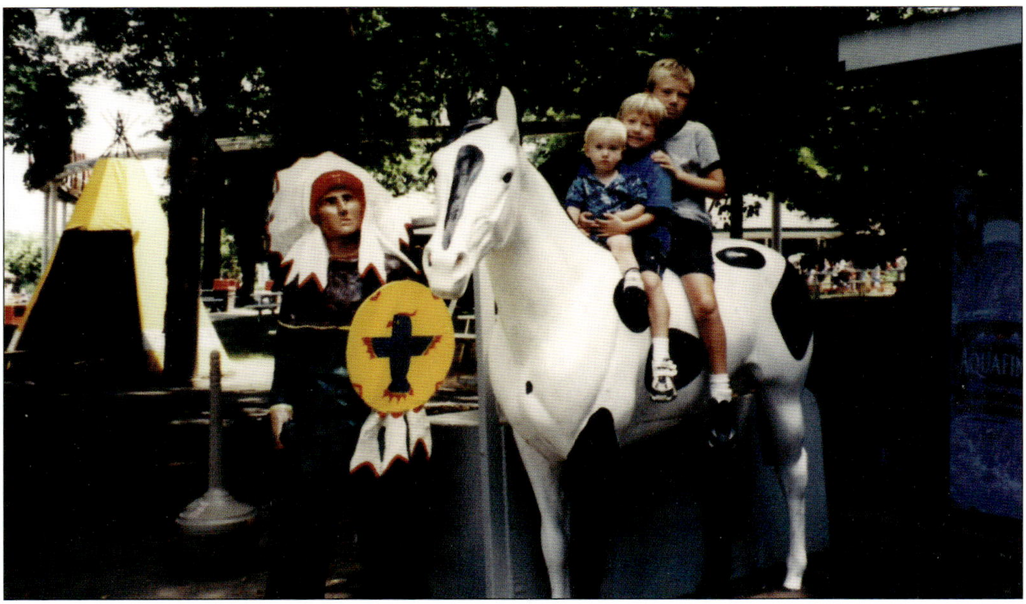

The final year of the Indian Village was 2002. The area would later become home to the Middle Earth Theater, which only lasted a few seasons. Most of the structures from another long-standing attraction, the International Botanical Gardens, were removed after the 2004 season. (AD.)

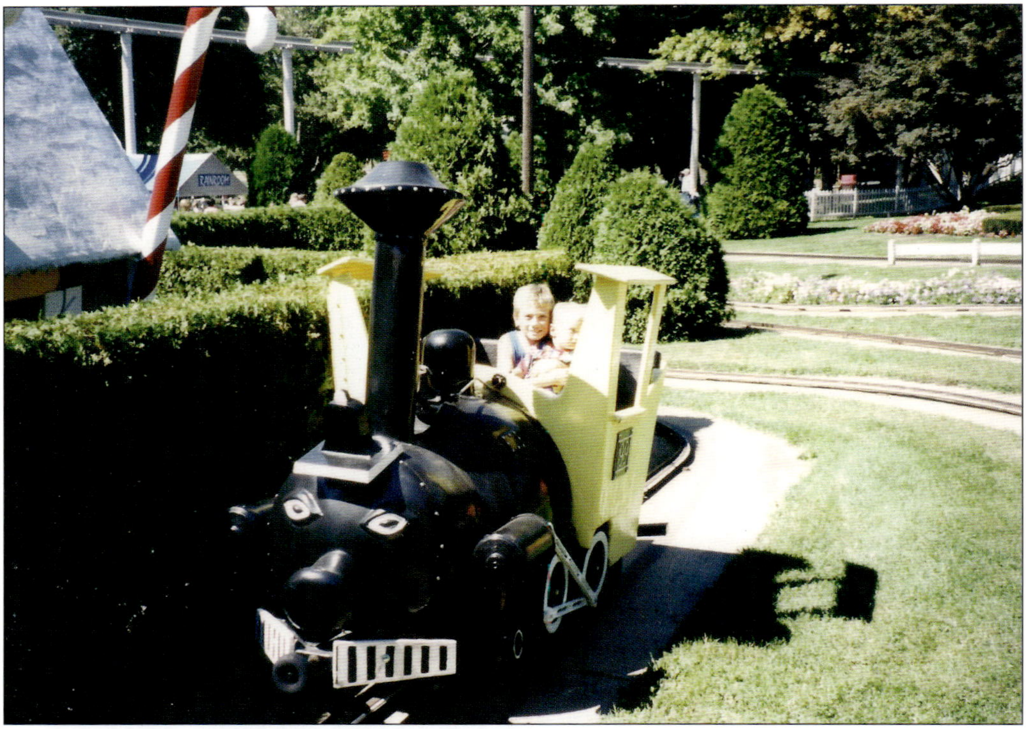

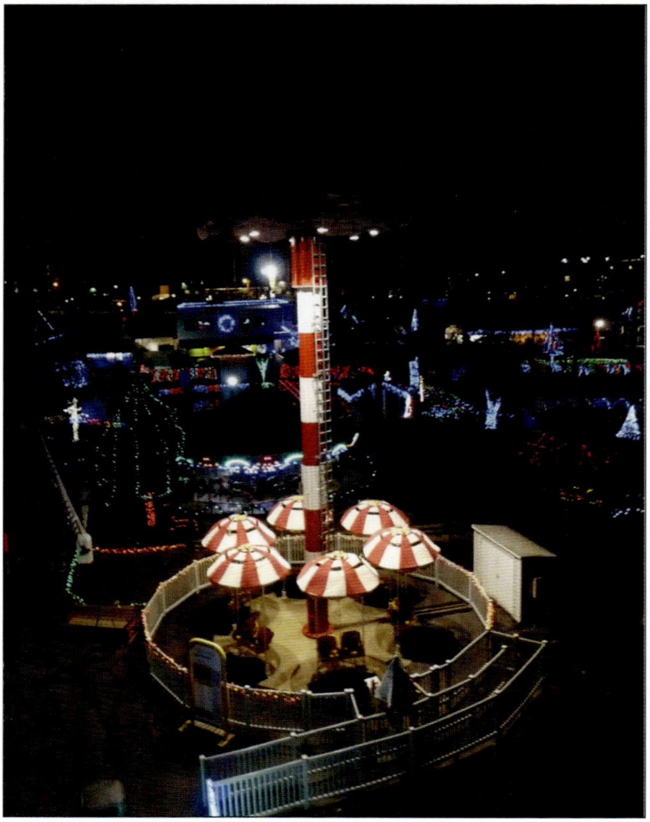

After 28 years of service, the Old 99 ride was removed from the park at the end of the 2002 season. Its last day of operation was October 27, 2002. One of the train engines can now be found in Memory Lane. Its bell still chimes as a new generation enjoys the ride in a different way. The image above was taken during its final year of operation. (AD.)

In November 2002, Dutch Wonderland established a new holiday event called Dutch Winter Wonderland, featuring thousands of Christmas lights throughout the park. Admission to the event was free for its first two seasons. Guests had the option of paying for each ride or buying a wristband that offered unlimited access. (AD.)

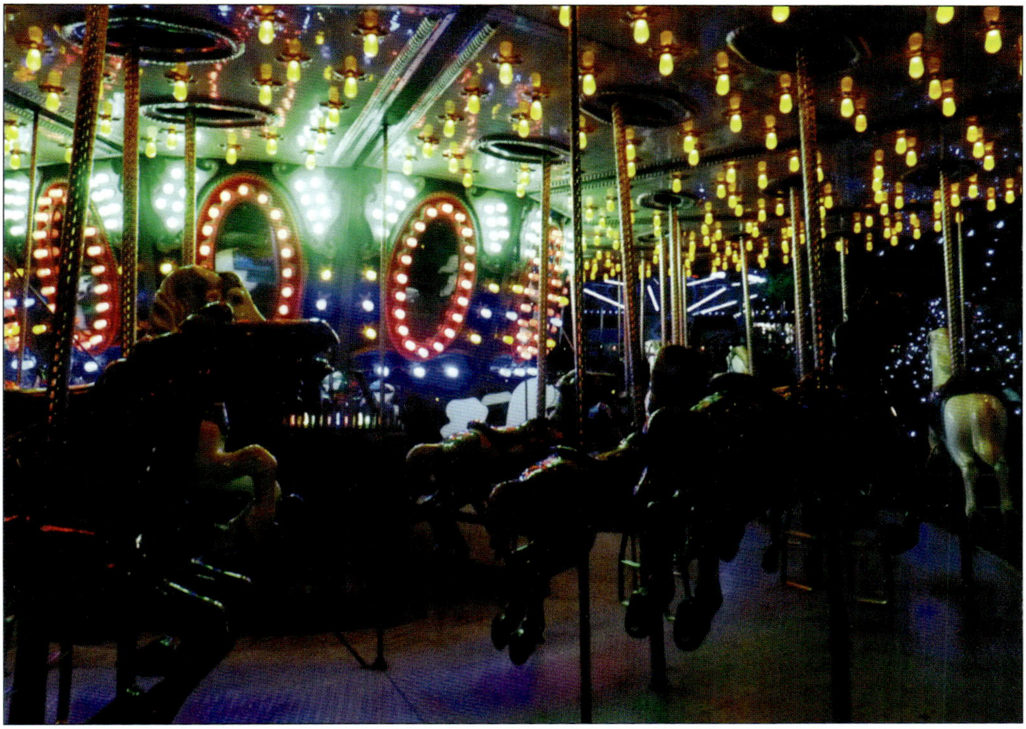

Before the start of the 2003 season, the carousel was moved to the front of the park. General manager Rick Stammel wanted the carousel to be one of the first rides that guests saw upon entering the park. A few years later, its 1,382 lightbulbs were replaced with LED lights. (AD.)

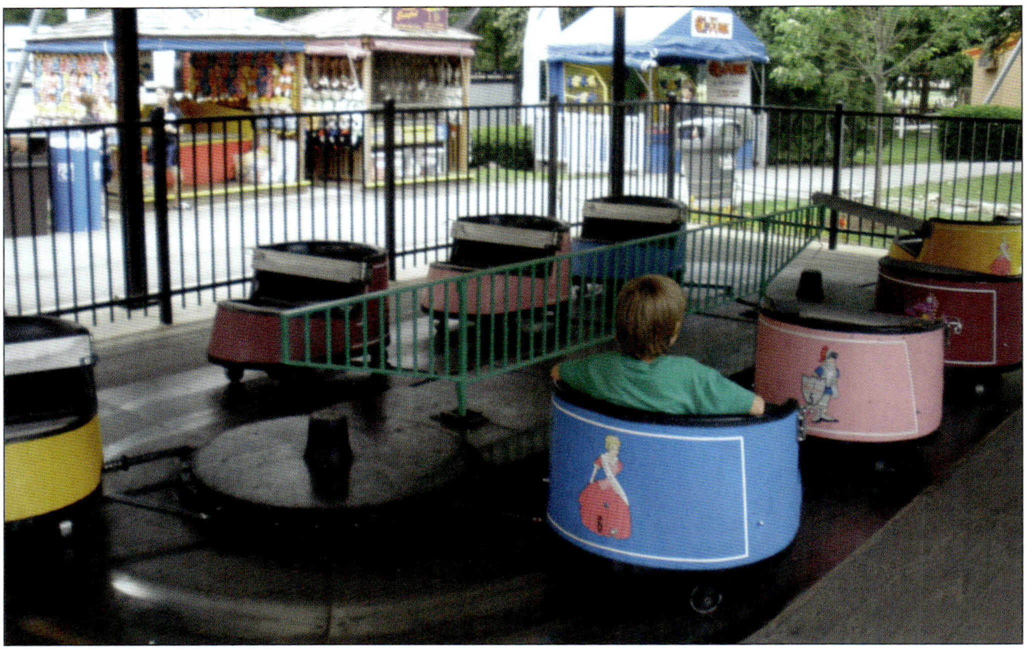

The Wonder Whip was new for the 2003 season. The miniature whip had been transported from Hersheypark, where it was known as Wells Cargo. It originally opened at Hersheypark in 1964. The ride's eight colorful cars can seat up to 16 children per cycle. (AD.)

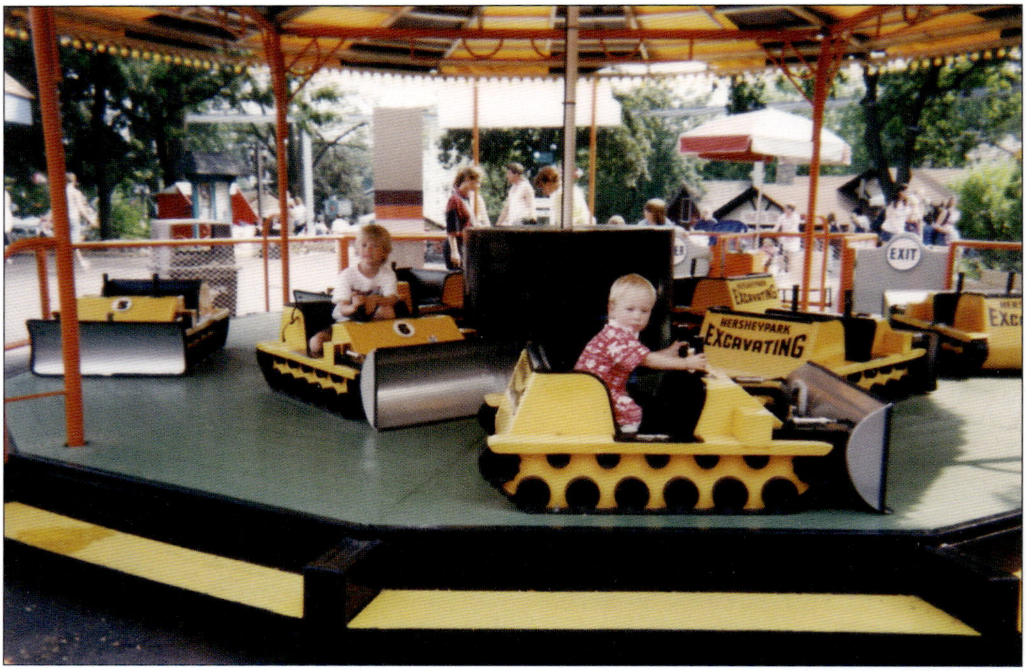

Duke's Dozers were also brought to Dutch Wonderland from Hersheypark in 2003. Allan Herschell introduced this Tiny Tanks ride to the world in 1953. Hersheypark bought the ride used in 1976. At the time, it was based on army tanks. In 1981, Hersheypark completely rebuilt the ride and altered the tanks to bulldozers, making it a one-of-a-kind ride called Earthmovers. Dutch Wonderland changed its name to reflect the park's mascot, Duke the Dragon. Above are the Earthmovers when they were at Hersheypark, and below are Duke's Dozers at Dutch Wonderland. (Both, AD.)

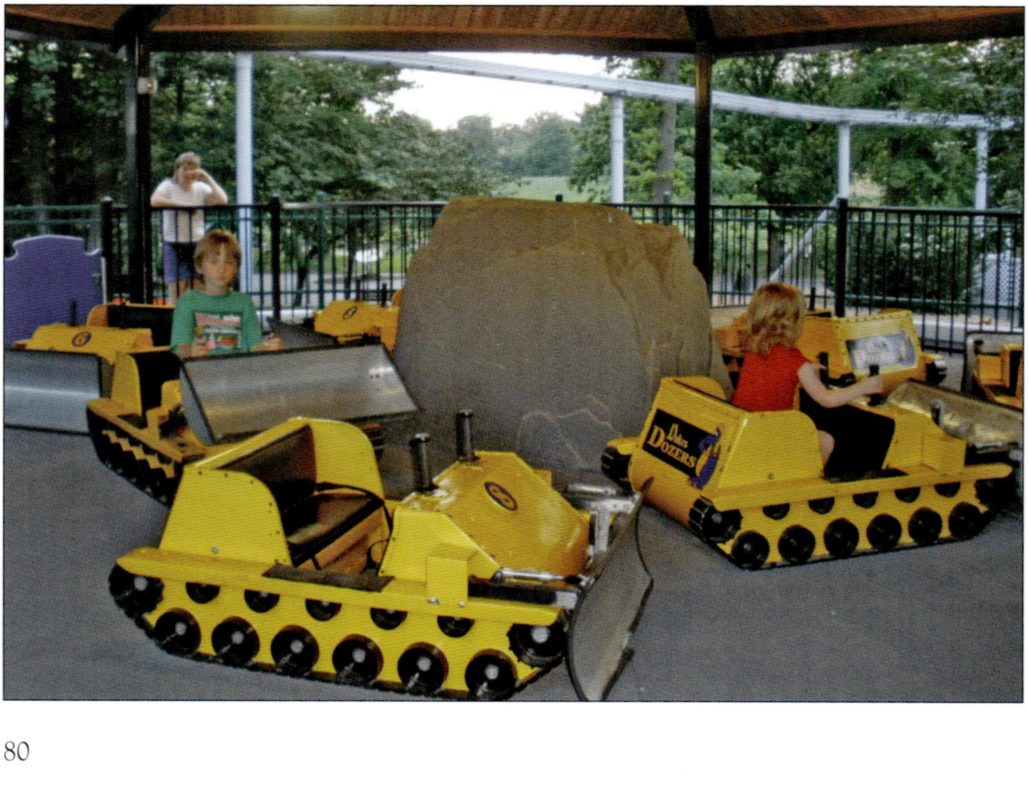

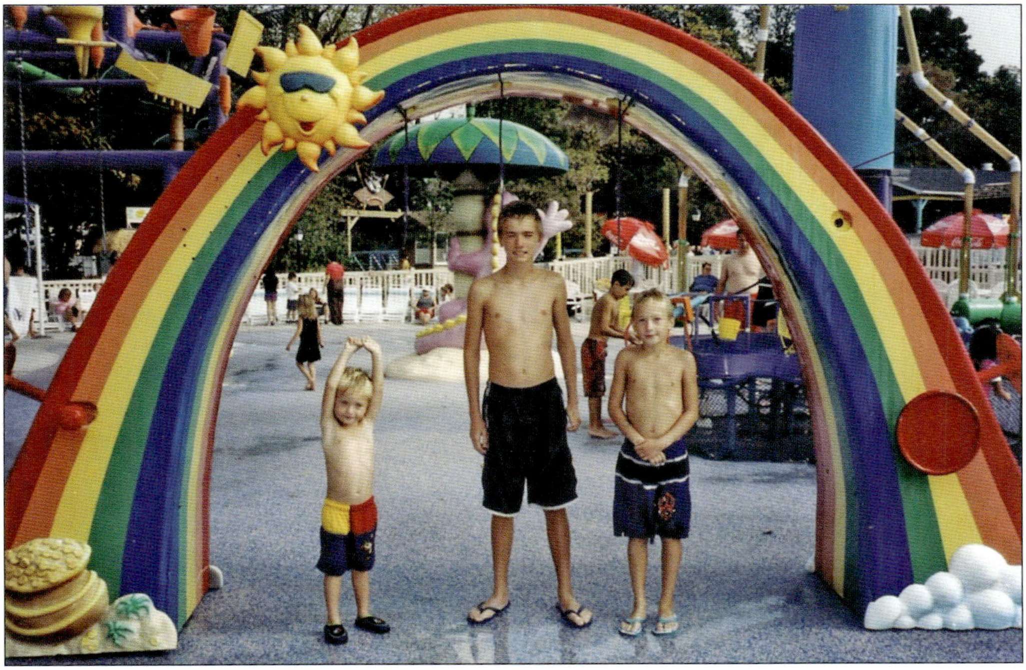

The biggest addition of 2003 was Duke's Lagoon, an interactive water play area. This tropical paradise ensures that everyone who enters gets soaked. Duke's Lagoon was Hershey's largest investment in the park. The new section officially opened on May 24, 2003. (AD.)

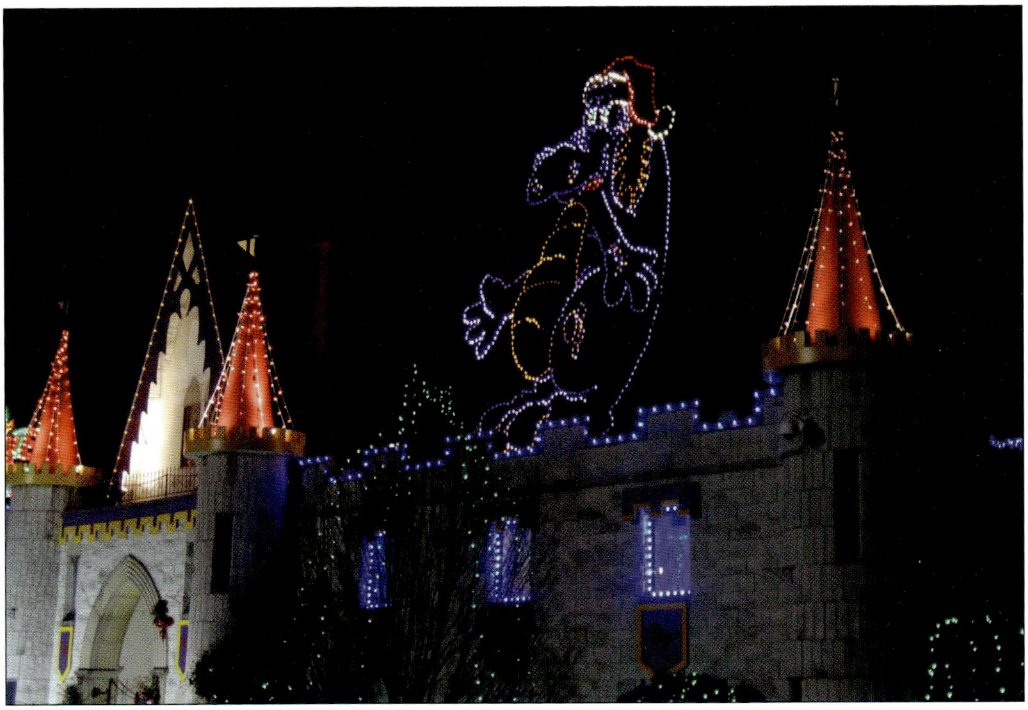

One of the biggest new light displays for Dutch Winter Wonderland's second season in 2003 was a giant Duke the Dragon. During the annual event, the 25-foot holiday display stands on top of the park's castle entrance, welcoming guests to Dutch Winter Wonderland. (AD.)

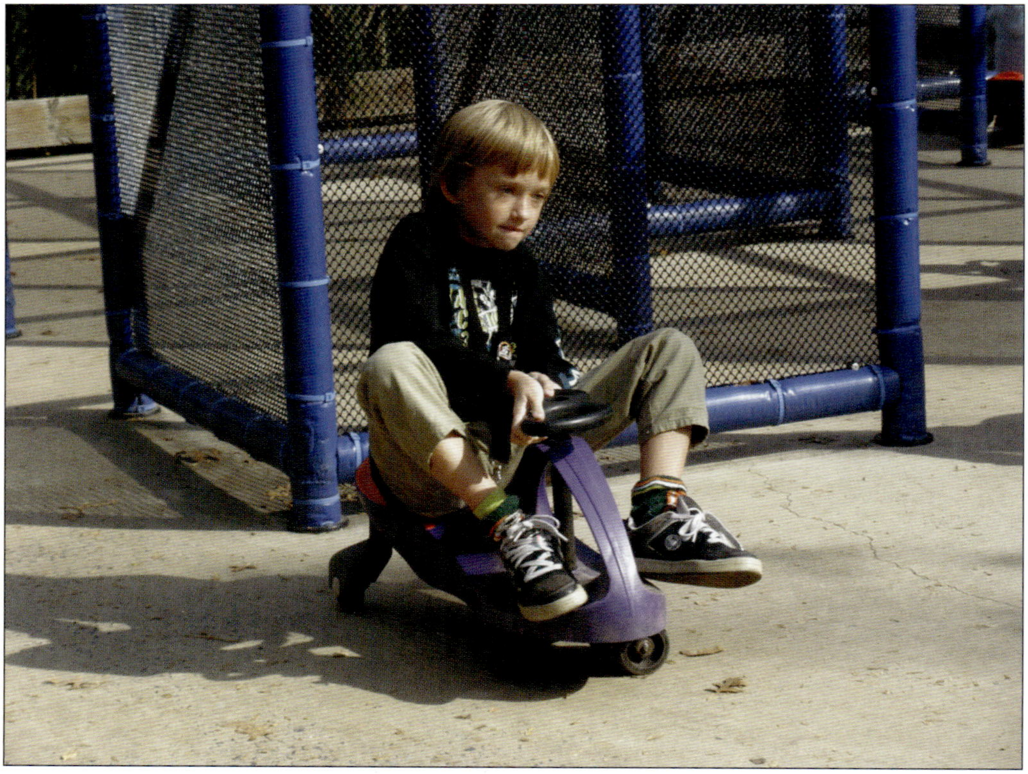

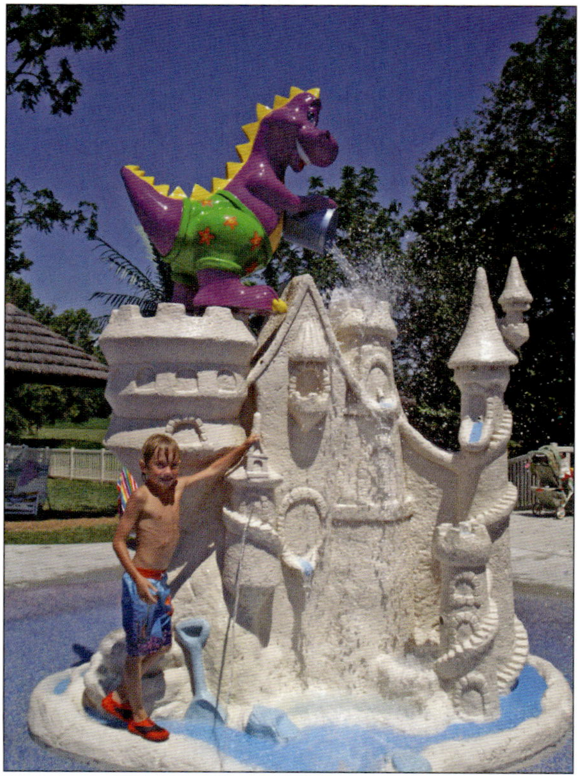

The miniature circus was removed after the 2003 season and was replaced with a miniature train display for the 2004 and 2005 seasons. In 2006, the circus tent was removed completely, and the Flying Turtle Roller Racers were moved to the concrete pad where the tent once stood. The Roller Racers were updated in 2008 with a similar ride called the Wiggle Racers. (AD.)

The popular Duke's Lagoon section was expanded in 2004. The expansion included the addition of a giant sandcastle and a variety of slides for toddlers. The new area opened on May 29, 2004. Due to the expansion, the Flying Trapeze was moved to a third location, near the Choo Choo Charlie ride. (AD.)

In 2004, Dutch Wonderland presented a new diving show called "The Adventures of the Frog Prince" in which divers act out a fairy-tale story. In 2009, a second show appeared at the dive stadium, "A Dragon's Tale," which tells the story of a queen and her pet dragon defending her kingdom. (AD.)

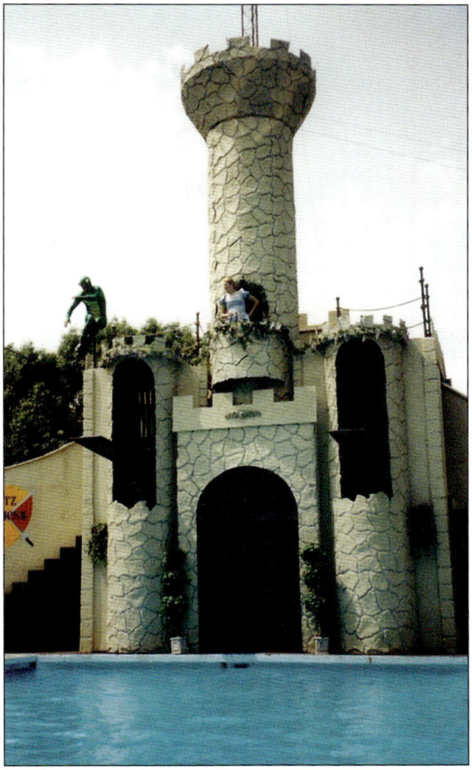

After two successful seasons, Dutch Wonderland opted to charge an admission price for Dutch Winter Wonderland in 2004. All rides, shows, and attractions were included in the $4.95 single-price admission. Throughout the years, the event has been expanded to include more lights, rides, and displays. (AD.)

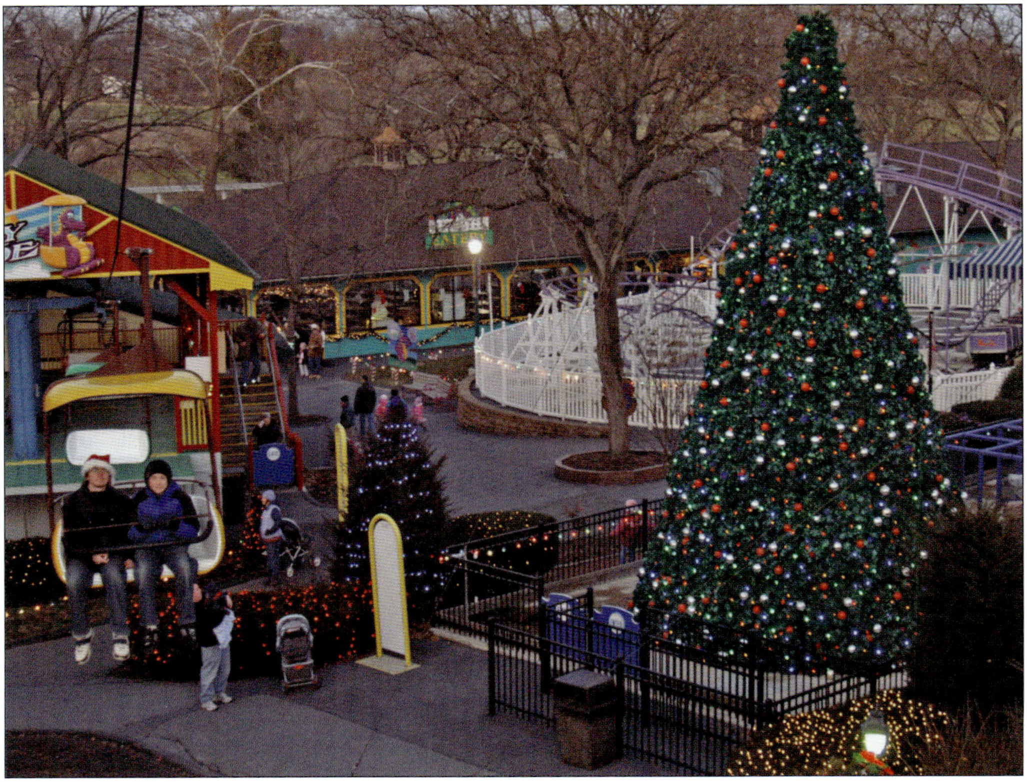

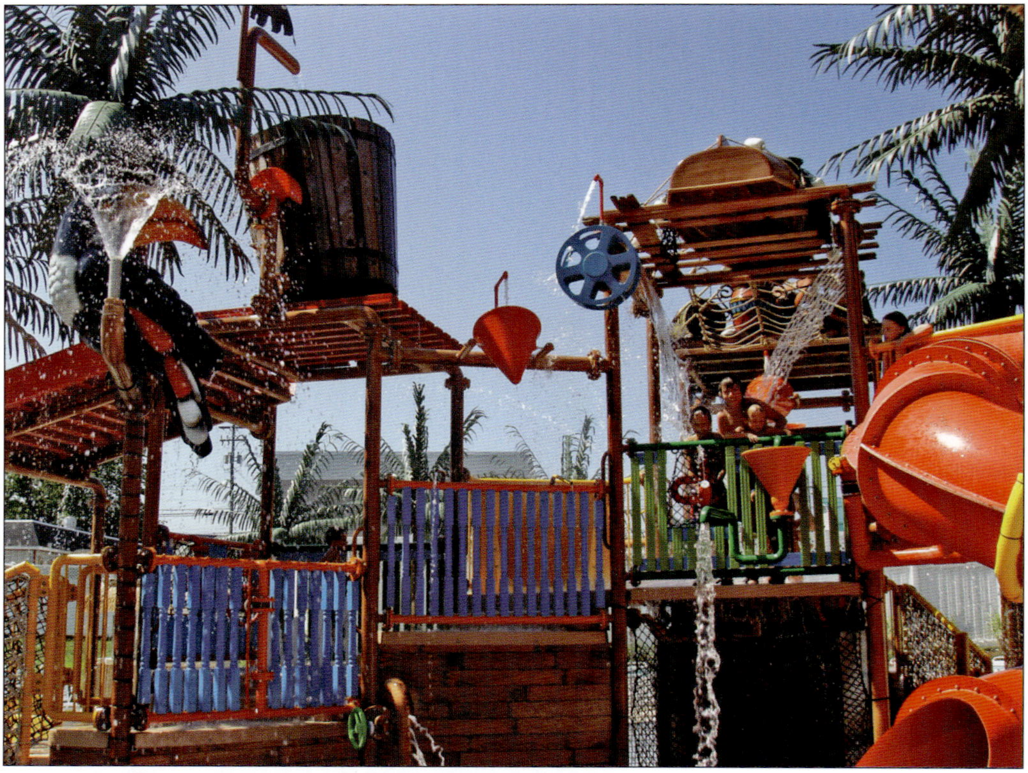

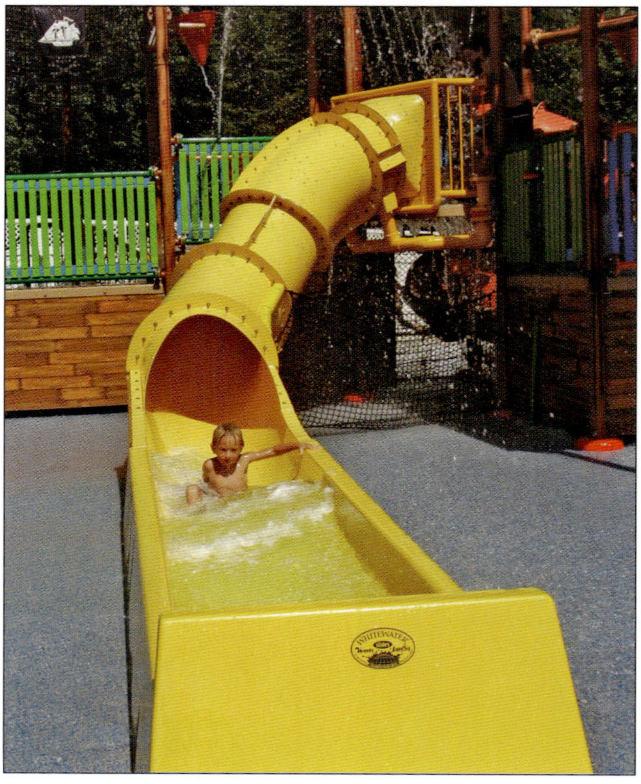

Duke's Lagoon was expanded once again in 2005. Designed and built by WhiteWater West Industries of Richmond, British Columbia, the 6,000-square-foot expansion consists of a multilevel play structure and a lounge area. The play structure features many ways for park guests to get wet and cool off, including three small slides, tipping buckets, spray nozzles, and spinning water wheels. Accounting for 3,400 square feet of the expansion, the lounge area boasts multiple shade structures and artificial palm trees. (Both, AD.)

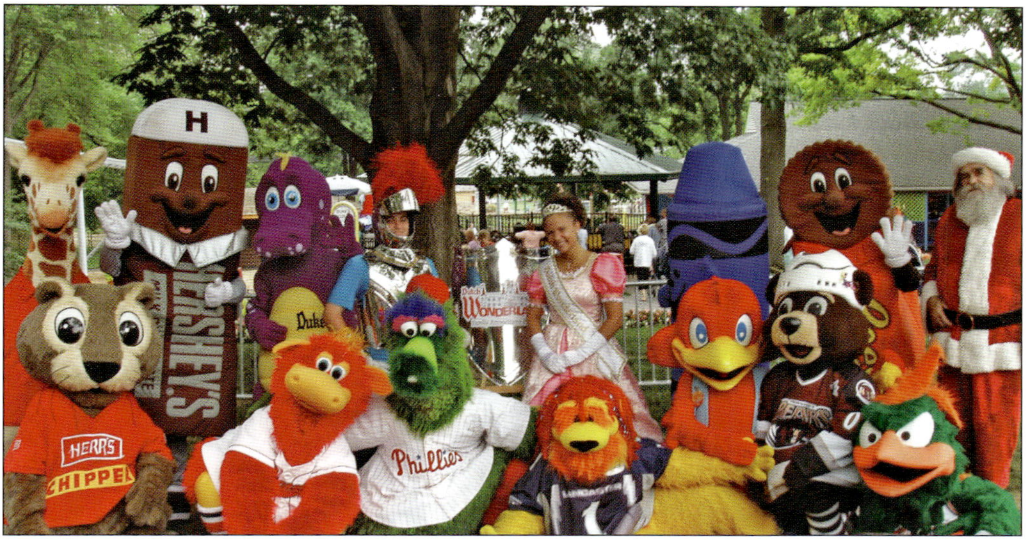

These local mascots are gathered during Character Days of 2005. From left to right are (first row) Chipper, Herr's; Cylo, Lancaster Barnstormers; Phillie Phanatic, Philadelphia Phillies; Boomer, Lancaster Lightning; Red, Red Robin; Coco, Hershey Bears; and Revillee the Rooster, Harrisburg Horizon; (second row) Geoffrey, Toys"R"Us; Hershey Bar, Hersheypark; Duke the Dragon, Sir Brandon, and Princess Brooke, Dutch Wonderland; Tip the Crayon, Crayola; Reese's, Hersheypark; and Santa Claus, National Christmas Center. (AD.)

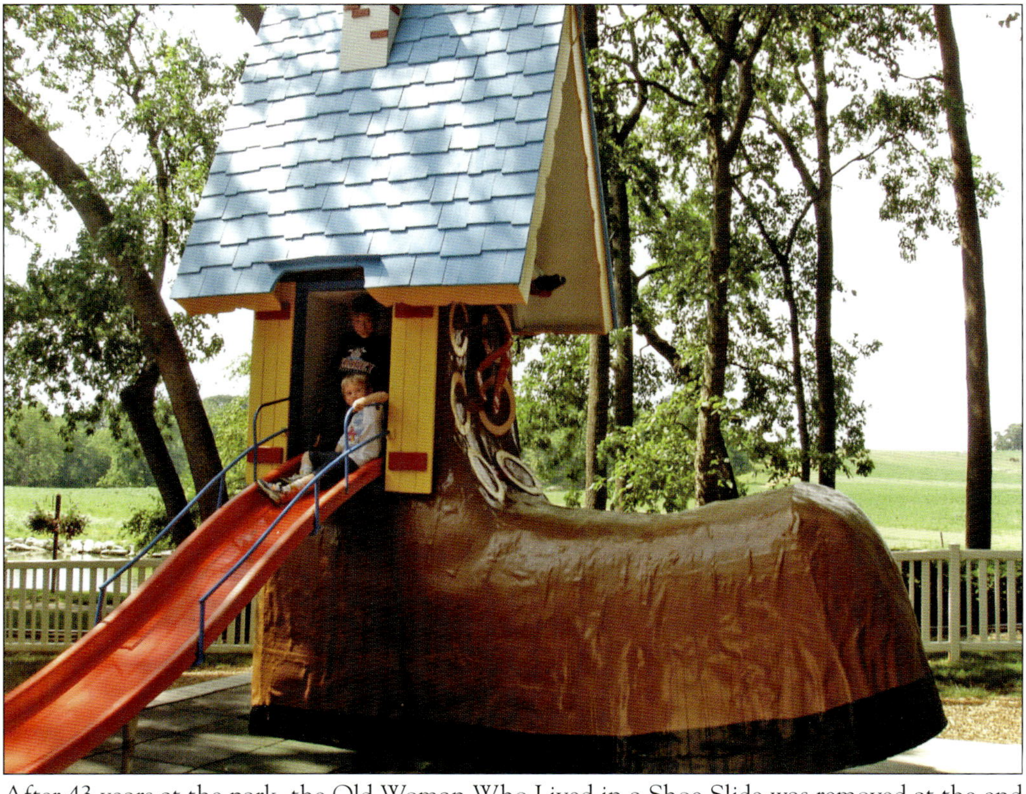

After 43 years at the park, the Old Woman Who Lived in a Shoe Slide was removed at the end of the 2006 season. It was replaced with the Turtle Whirl the following year. (AD.)

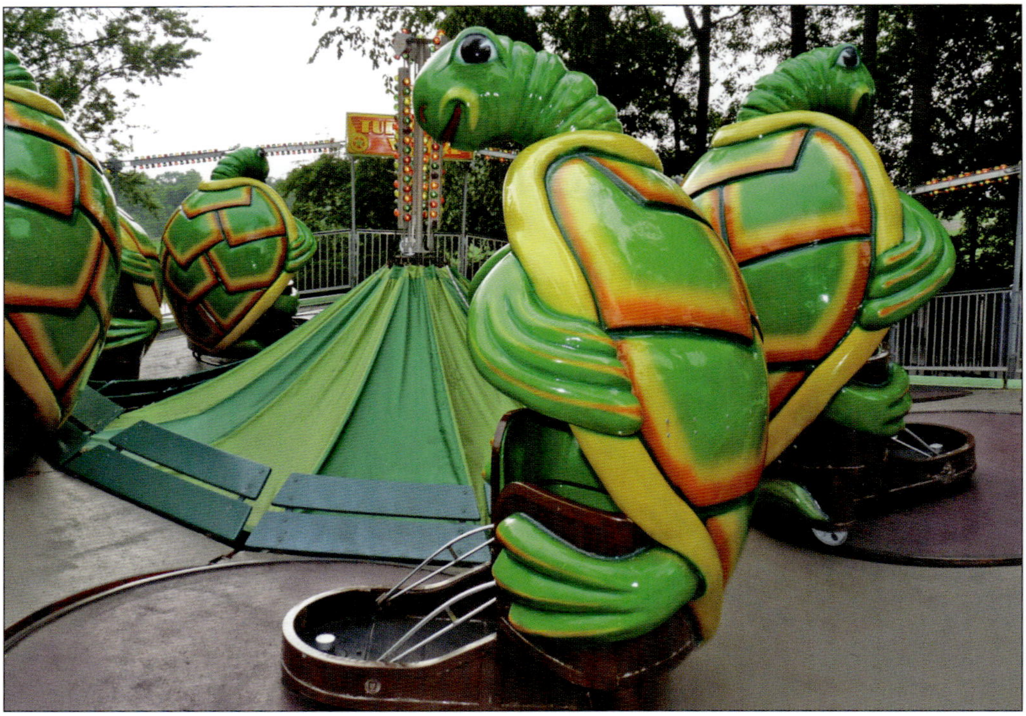

In 2007, Turtle Whirl was purchased from Sellner Manufacturing after its removal from Clementon Park in New Jersey, where the ride had operated since 2002. Its seven giant turtles are a modern take on the classic Tilt-A-Whirl ride. Also in 2007, Treehouse Terrace replaced the Spuds restaurant. When Palace Entertainment bought the park in 2011, the woodlands-themed dining area became the Potato Patch, featuring the recipe for Kennywood Park's famous Potato Patch french fries. (AD.)

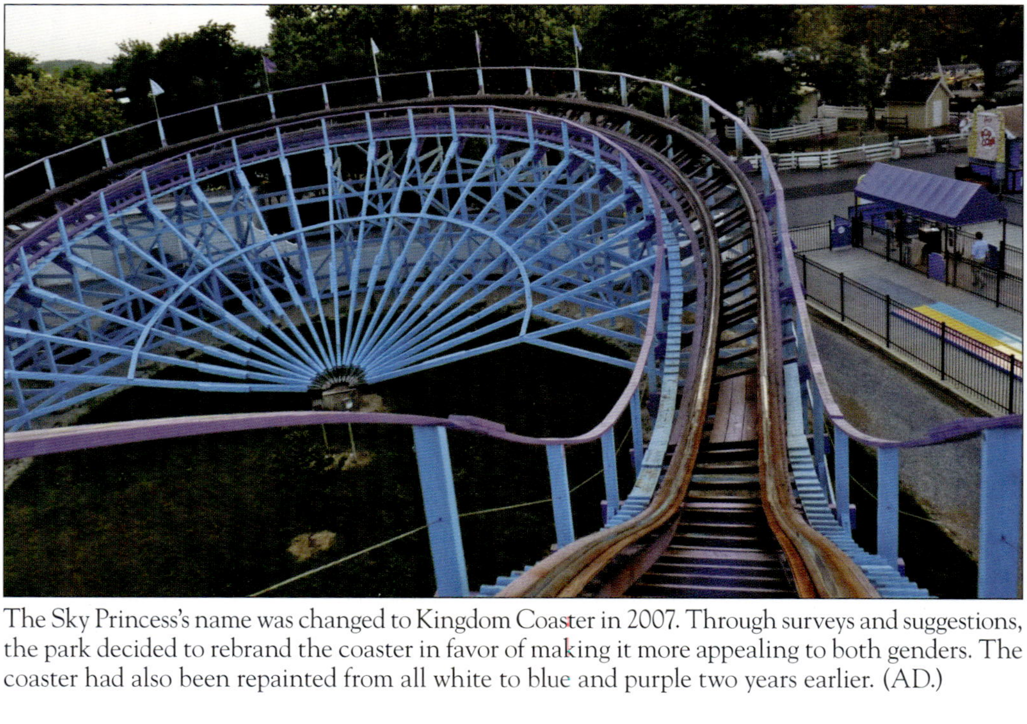

The Sky Princess's name was changed to Kingdom Coaster in 2007. Through surveys and suggestions, the park decided to rebrand the coaster in favor of making it more appealing to both genders. The coaster had also been repainted from all white to blue and purple two years earlier. (AD.)

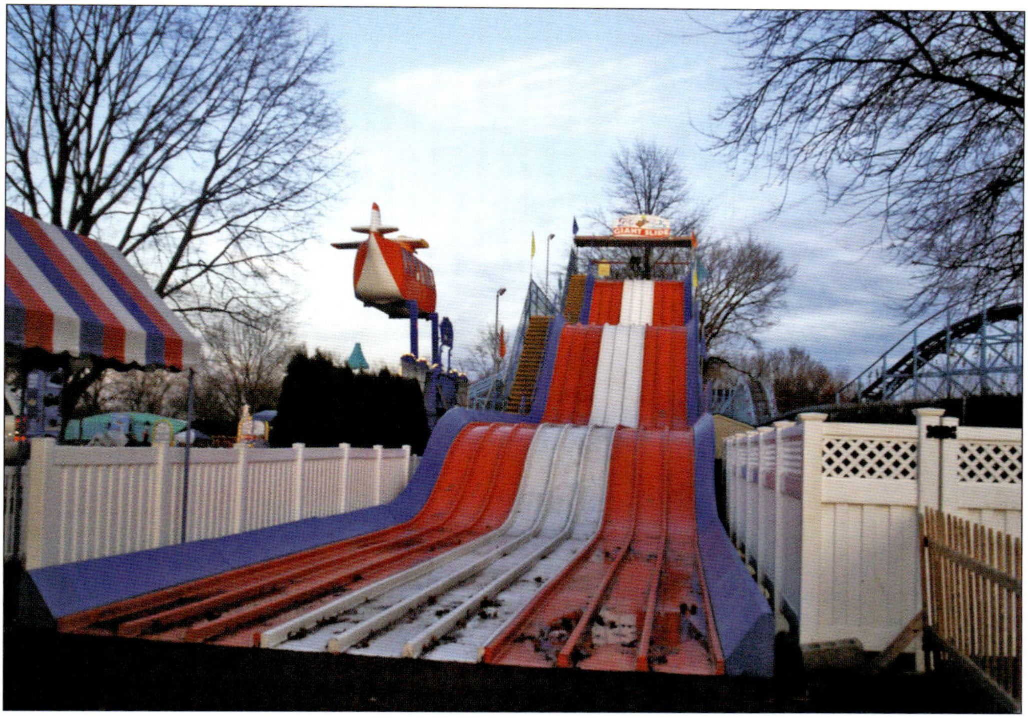

Not long after Hershey Entertainment bought the park, part of the Giant Slide's support structure had to be rebuilt. During the early 1970s, there were over 200 giant slides throughout the country, but in 1987, there were estimated to be less than 30 still in operation. Dutch Wonderland had the last original Giant Slide. Its last day of operation was October 7, 2007. It was removed that winter due to the extensive repairs needed. Two portable slides known as Fun Slides, manufactured by Frederiksen Industries, Inc., now stand in its place. (Both, AD.)

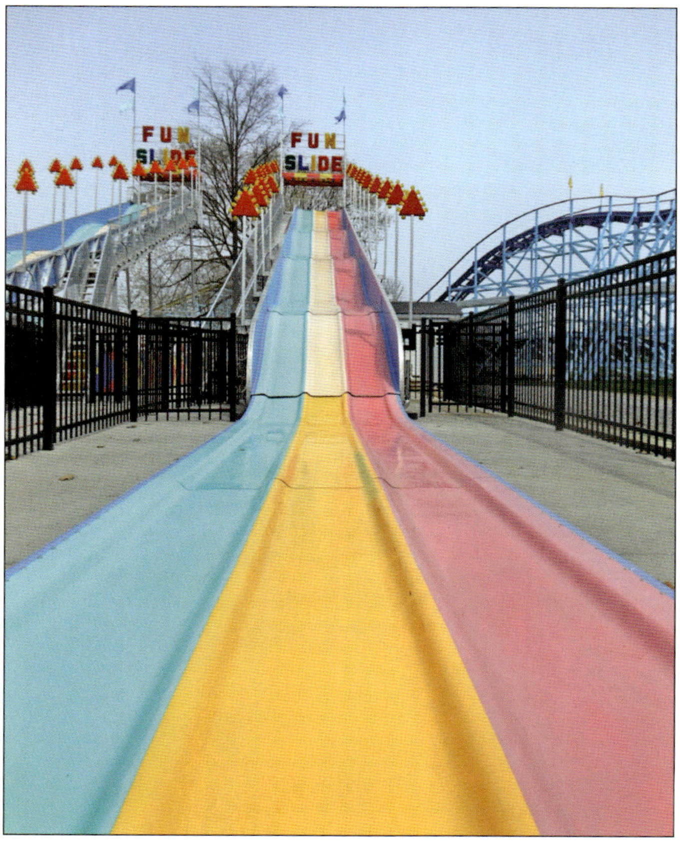

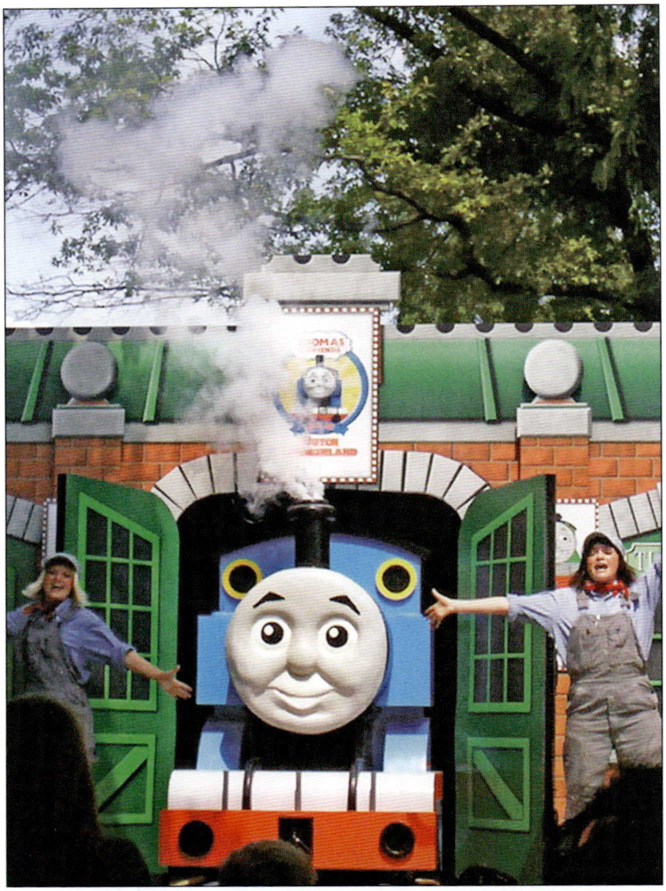

The show "Thomas & Friends Live at Dutch Wonderland" opened in 2008. The musical act was based on the popular television and book character Thomas the Tank Engine, featuring a life-size train character. It was replaced with "Garfield the Great" in 2012. (AD.)

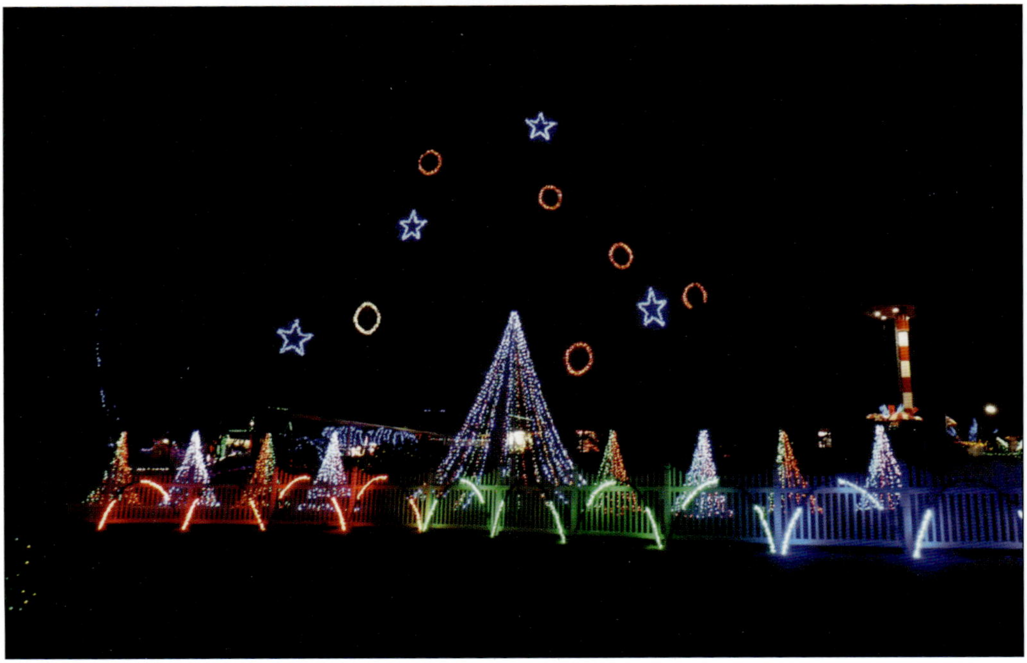

In 2008, the "Royal Light Show" became part of Dutch Winter Wonderland's entertainment lineup. The show presents a spectacular display of over 100,000 LED lights dancing to holiday music, which requires over three miles of wire and 25 park employees to set up. (AD.)

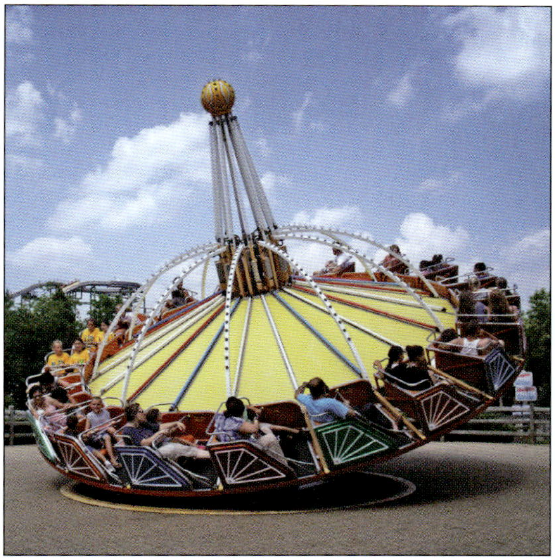

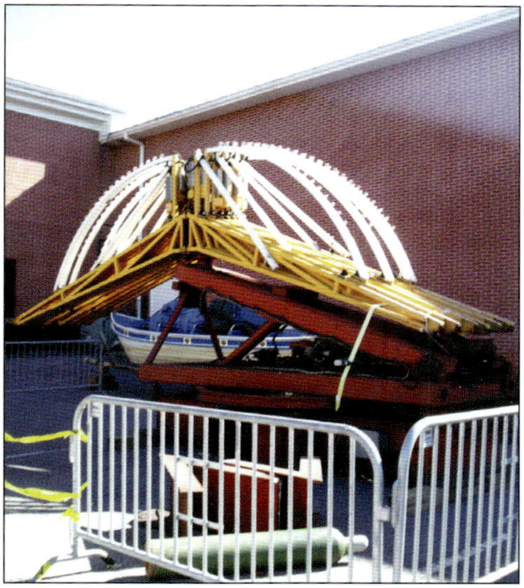

The Twister was originally located at Hersheypark, where it was known as Rodeo. Hersheypark bought the ride new in 1978. In July 2008, Hersheypark announced that the ride would be removed. There were rumors that the Rodeo ride would be moved to Hershey's sister park, Dutch Wonderland. After the ride was removed from Hersheypark in September of that year, pieces of it began to arrive at Dutch Wonderland. Soon those rumors were confirmed when Dutch Wonderland announced that its new ride for the 2009 season was the Twister. Manufactured by Chance Rides as the Trabant, it is one of the company's most manufactured rides. The ride spins horizontally in a wavelike motion with a capacity of 40 passengers per cycle. (All, AD.)

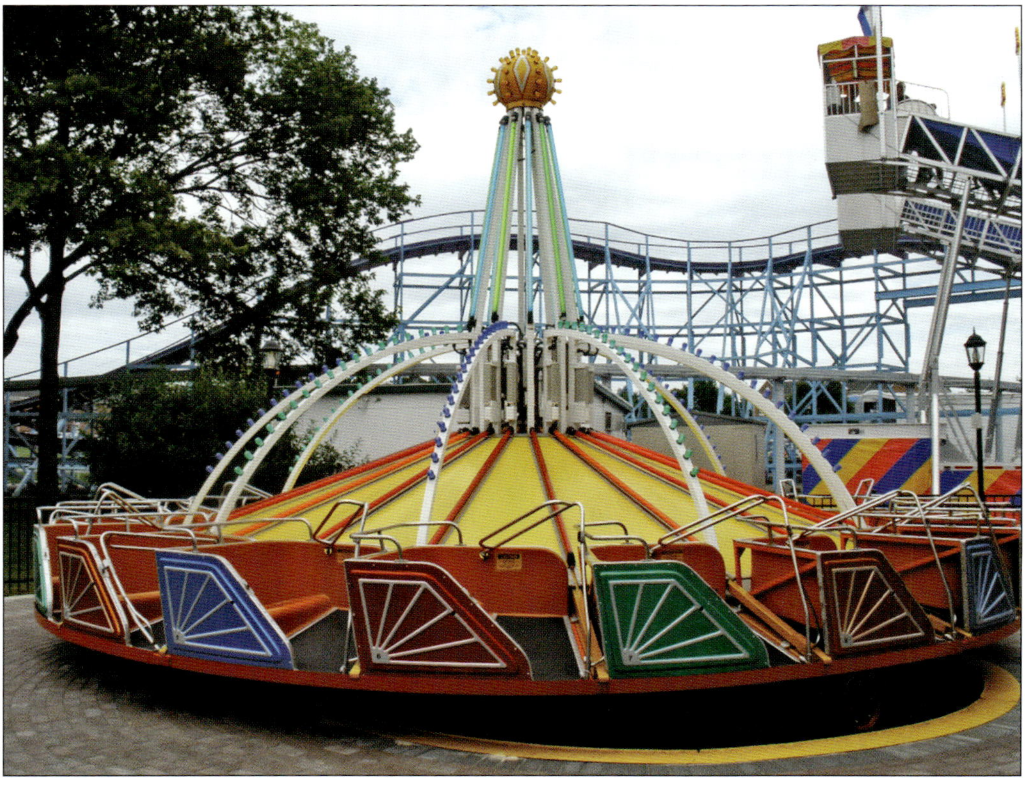

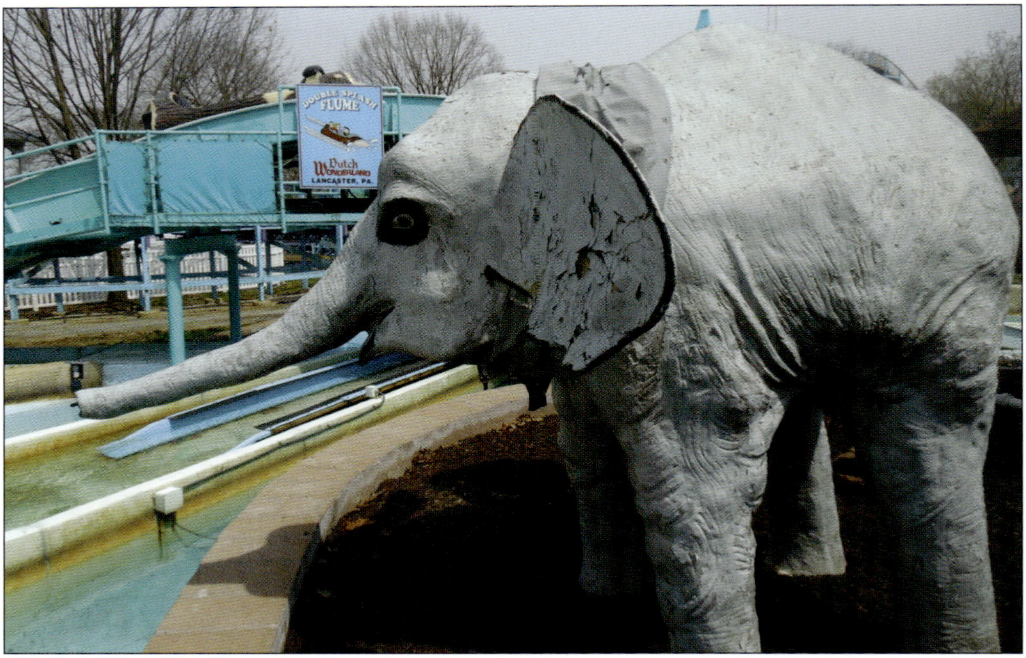

When this elephant was located beside the log boat ride in front of the park, it would shoot water from its trunk into the pond. In 2001, the figure was removed to make room for Duke's Mountain and was later placed next to the Double Splash Fume. The elephant was eventually removed from the park. (AD.)

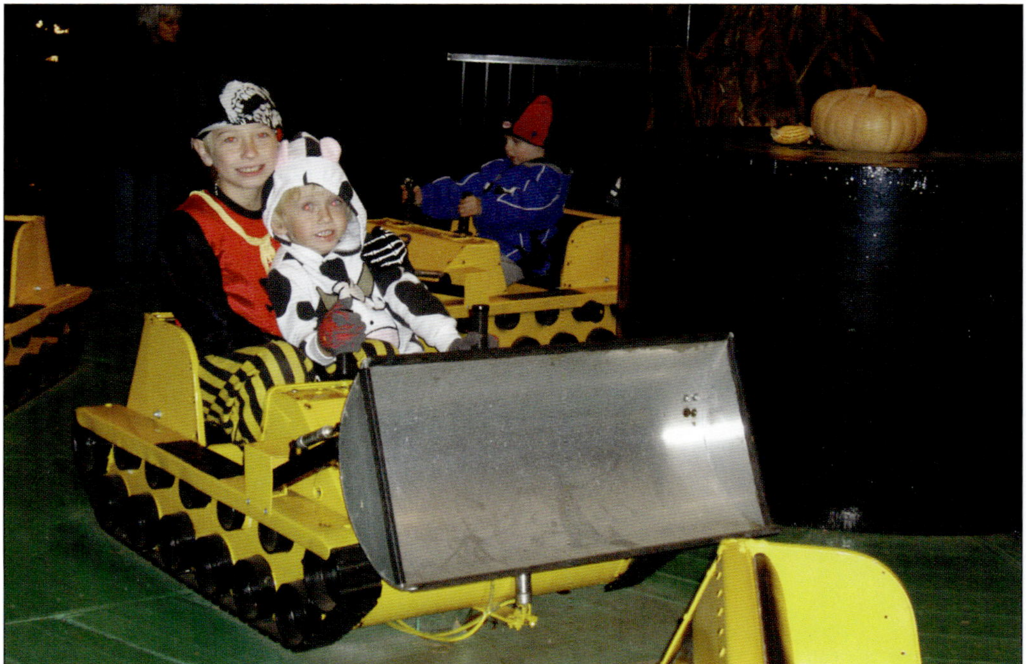

During Happy Hauntings, children are encouraged to dress up in their Halloween costumes to attend the park and compete in a costume contest to win prizes. Having the opportunity to experience their favorite rides while in costume also appeals to young parkgoers. (AD.)

Five

The Palace Era
2011–Present

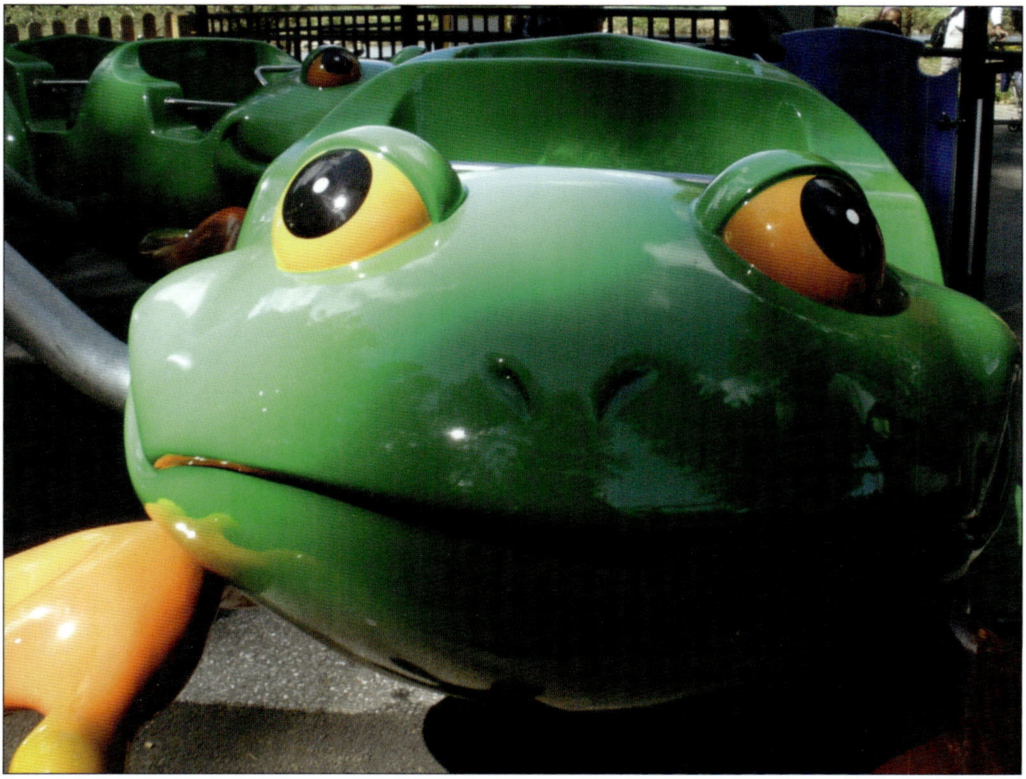

Huck Finn's Leapin' Frogs, a series of bouncing frogs that travel in a circle, was installed near the Mill Stream area of the park in 2011. The ride was purchased directly from Zamperla's US headquarters in New Jersey. In 2014, it switched sites with the Wiggle Racers because of frequent flooding along the creek. (AD.)

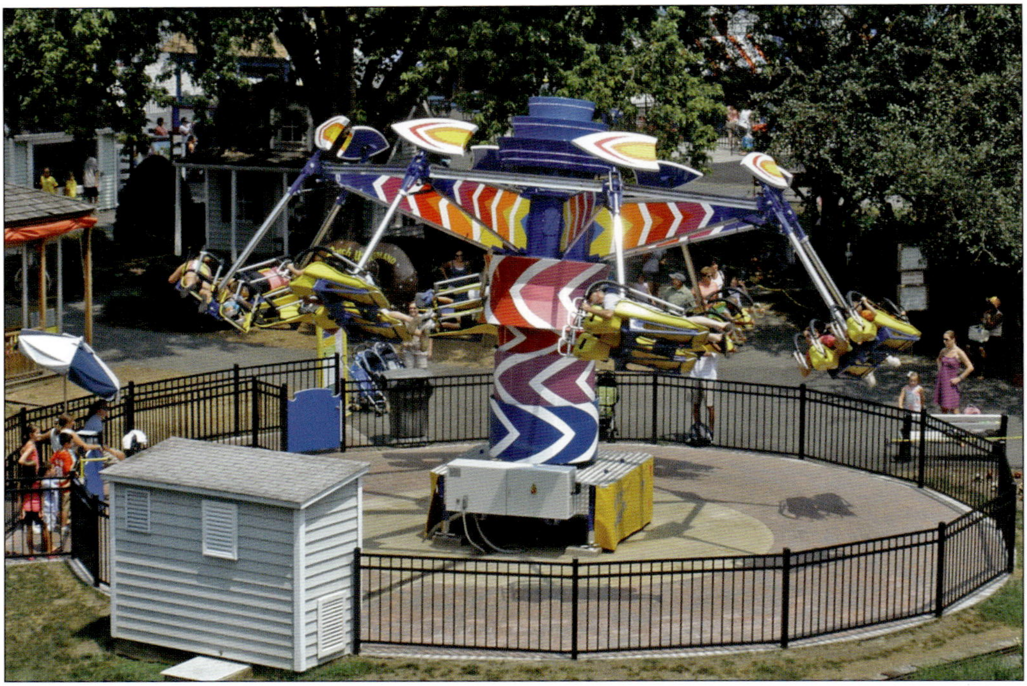

Kite Flight was also purchased from Zamperla in 2011. Unlike other attractions, this ride lifts passengers into a horizontal position to simulate soaring on a hang glider. The ride was a quick replacement for Ripcord, which was removed in early 2011 because of mechanical issues. (AD.)

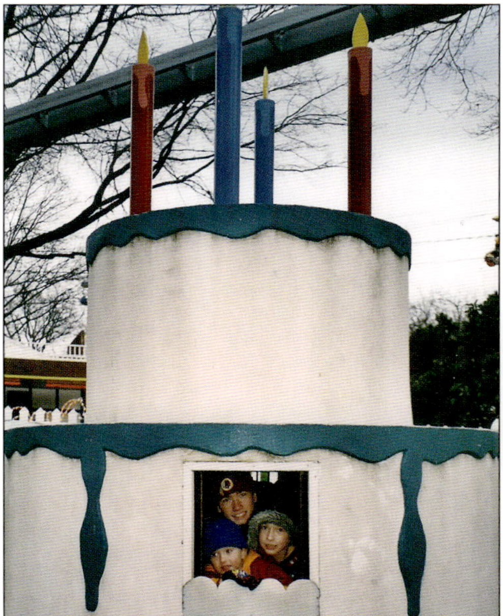

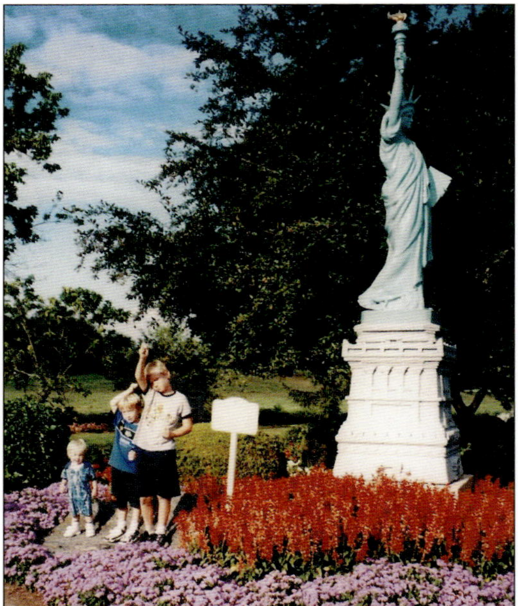

Some of the older decorative structures were eventually removed, along with most of the original fiberglass figures that were scattered throughout the park. The Birthday Cake House (left) was taken away after the 2011 season. The replica Statue of Liberty (right), which became part of the International Botanical Gardens in 1995, was eliminated in 2013. (Both, AD.)

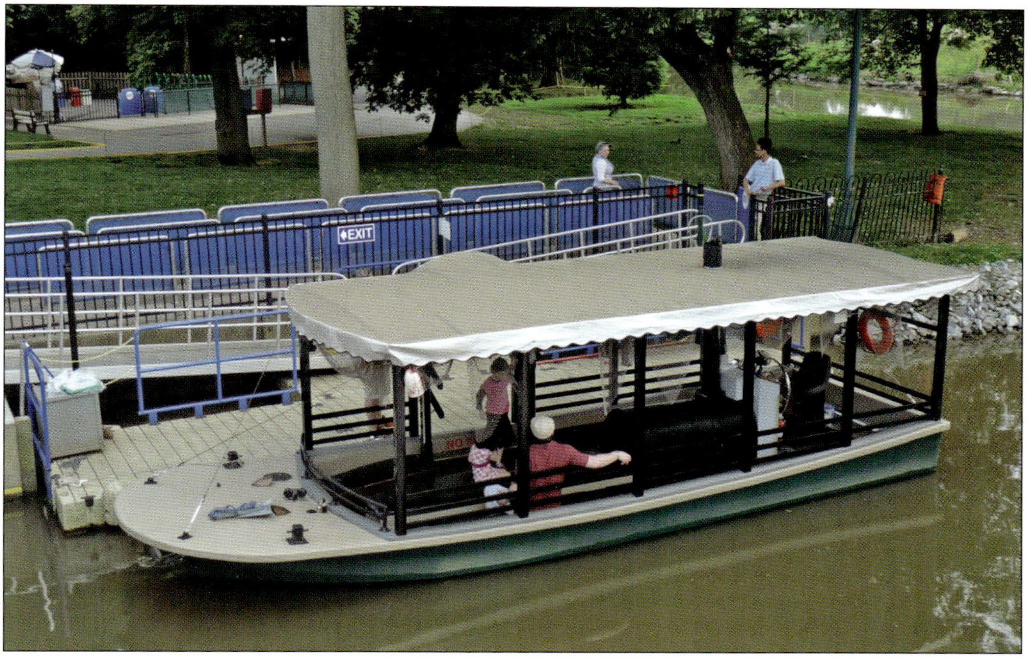

Over time, the Lady Gay River Boat has changed. The paddle wheel was removed, and the roof was replaced. In 2004, the smokestack had to be removed as well to provide clearance under the new bridge to the island. Although the boat has been modified over the years, it is the only one of the first four rides to maintain its original infrastructure. (AD.)

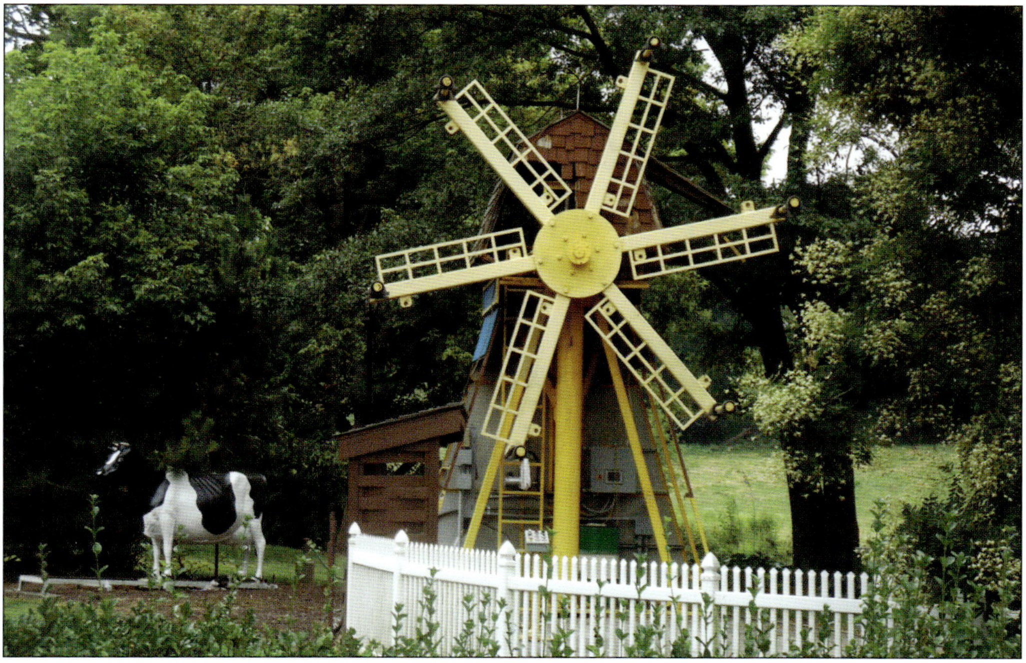

After 30 years of service, the Ferris Windmill ride ceased operation on October 7, 2012. It was dismantled throughout the 2013 season to make way for a new themed area on the island. Construction was done to the ride site, along with the rest of the island, to prepare for the park's premier attraction of 2014. (AD.)

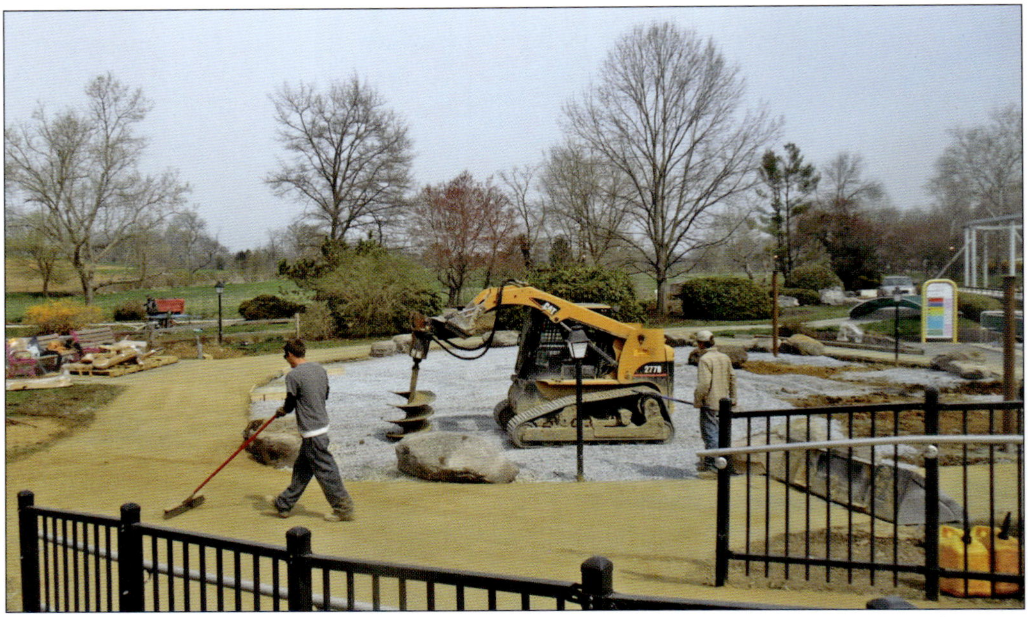

On January 20, 2014, Dutch Wonderland announced its million-dollar project for the 2014 season—Exploration Island. The prehistoric-themed area gives new life to the island. Construction was done during the fall, winter, and spring to ensure a Memorial Day weekend opening. The photograph above shows the Dino Dig while under construction. (AD.)

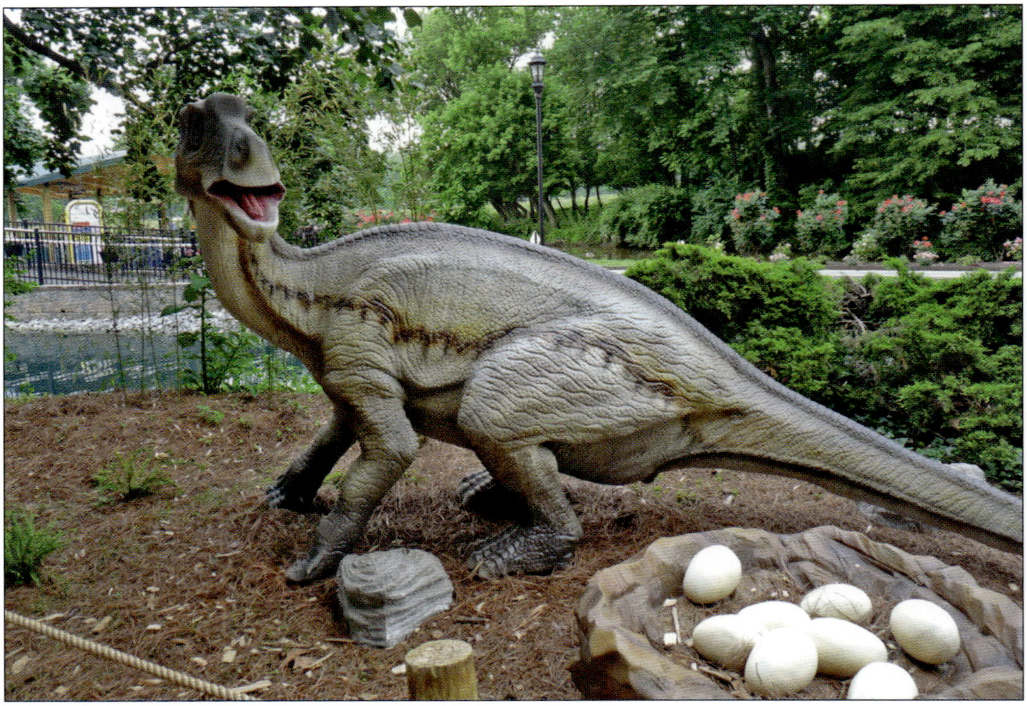

After months of preparation, Exploration Island opened on May 24, 2014. Over 20 new dinosaurs have been unearthed and are now calling Dutch Wonderland home. The dinosaurs on Prehistoric Path range in height from 2 feet to 80 feet. The area also includes Dino Dig, where guests can dig for artificial fossils. (AD.)

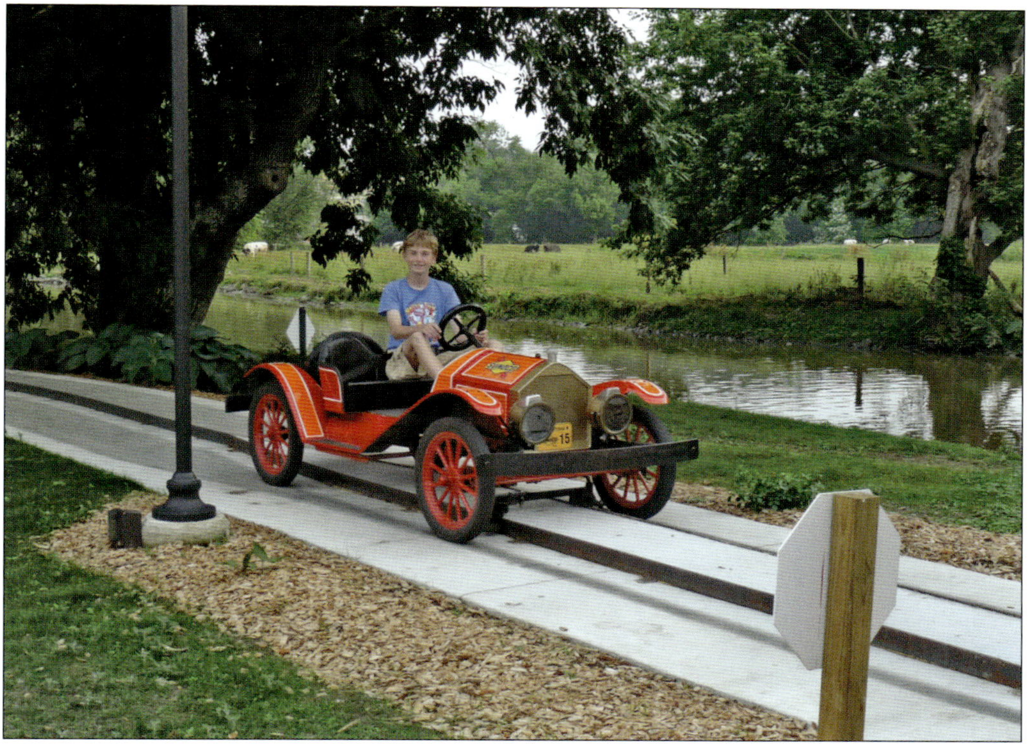

After 50 years at its site in the center of the park, the Turnpike ride was moved to Exploration Island. The ride was not only moved but also doubled in length. At five miles per hour, park guests are now able to motor around the perimeter of the island and view the dinosaurs from a different angle. (AD.)

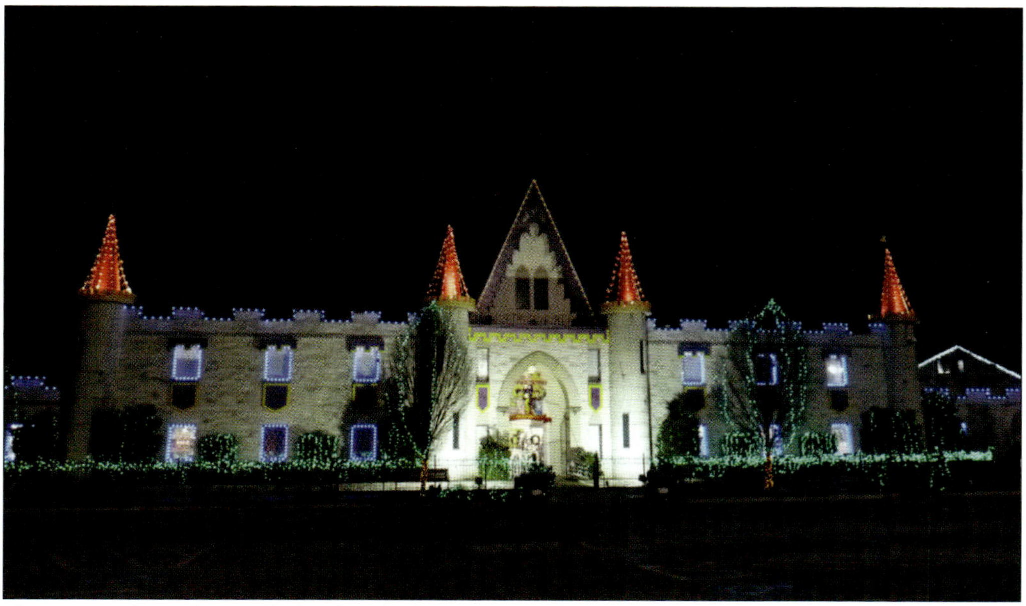

This story of Dutch Wonderland ends the same way everyone ends their day at the park—through the castle. Today, Dutch Wonderland is more popular than ever, with exciting changes every season. Each year, new guests continue to experience the wonderland for the first time. (AD.)